INNOVATION IN THE PUBLIC SECTOR

ADVANCES IN POLITICAL SCIENCE
An International Series

*Published in cooperation with the International
Political Science Association*

Series Editor
Richard L. Merritt
University of Illinois

Editorial Board

Volumes published in this series:

Edited by
Richard L. Merritt
and
Anna J. Merritt

INNOVATION IN THE
PUBLIC SECTOR

*Published in corporation with the International Political
Science Association and the International Institute for
Comparative Social Research, Science Center Berlin*

 SAGE PUBLICATIONS Beverly Hills London New Delhi

For information address:

SAGE Publications, Inc.
275 South Beverly Drive
Beverly Hills, California 90212

SAGE Publications India Pvt. Ltd.
C-236 Defence Colony
New Delhi 110 024, India

SAGE Publications Ltd
28 Banner Street
London EC1Y 8QE, England

Printed in the United States of America

Library of Congress Cataloging in Publication Data

Main entry under title:

Innovation in the public sector.

(Advances in political science ; v. 4)
1. Public administration—Addresses, essays,
lectures. 2. Technological innovations—Addresses,
essays, lectures. I. Merritt, Richard L. II. Merritt,
Anna J. III. Series: Advances in political science ; 4.
JF1411.I56   1984   350.007'8   84-17839
ISBN 0-8039-2395-3

FIRST PRINTING

CONTENTS

FROM THE SERIES EDITOR

Advances in Political Science: An International Series reflects the aims and intellectual traditions of the International Political Science Association: the generation and dissemination of rigorous political inquiry free of any subdisciplinary or other orthodoxy. Along with its quarterly companion publication, the *International Political Science Review*, the series seeks to present the best work being done today (1) on the central and critical controversial themes of politics and/or (2) in new areas of inquiry where political scientists, alone or in conjunction with other scholars, are shaping innovative concepts and methodologies of political analysis.

Political science as an intellectual discipline has burgeoned in recent decades. With the enormous growth in the number of publications and papers, and their increasing sophistication, however, has also come a tendency toward parochialism along national, subdisciplinary, and other lines. It was to counteract these tendencies that political scientists from a handful of countries created IPSA in 1949. Through roundtables organized by its research committees and study groups, at its triennial world congresses (the next of which takes place in July 1985 in Paris), and through its organizational work, IPSA has sought to encourage the creation of both an international-minded science of politics and a body of scholars from many nations (now from more than 40 regional associations) who approach their research and interactions with other scholars from an international perspective.

Innovation in the Public Sector, edited by Richard L. and Anna J. Merritt, is the fourth volume in *Advances in Political Science: An International Series.* Like its predecessors, it comprises original papers which focus in an integrated manner on a single important topic—in this case, how research in various fields about creativity and innovativeness can contribute to our practical and theoretic knowledge of innovative strategies for public agencies.

The volume continues the collaboration between IPSA and the International Institute for Comparative Social Research, Science

Center Berlin (Wissenschaftszentrum Berlin). The conference at which the papers were originally presented was developed and financed by the IICSR. IPSA and the series editor are grateful to the Science Center Berlin and its president, Meinolf Dierkes, for their generous assistance; to Karl W. Deutsch, director of the IICSR, for encouraging the collaboration; and to Konstanze, Prinzessin zu Löwenstein, for facilitating both the conference and the publication.

—*Richard L. Merritt*

INNOVATION IN THE PUBLIC SECTOR
An Introduction

RICHARD L. MERRITT

Many observers feel that the modern Western state is in a crisis of unprecedented proportions. That perception is based on three major concerns. The first is that Western governments are facing a complex of issues at once crucial for their future existence and of a sort for which past solutions are no longer effective. A glance at the major daily newspapers in London, New York, Rome, or any other metropolitan center reveals a deep-seated concern with what is seen as the overweening importance of investors and financial institutions in determining rates of interest and investment, prices, and employment; the power of trade unions to upset industrial planning; massive changes in the clientele and expectations of public education; the rate of use of nonrenewable resources; and the secondary effects of uncontrolled growth, such as environmental pollution and a volatile labor market. The very complexity and gravity of these problems seem to ward off all but the hardiest (or foolhardiest!) politicians from trying to guide a country's destiny.

Second, Western governments are concerned about how they can best respond to ongoing changes within their societies. They know that the failure to do so meaningfully will reduce their capacity for effective governance. Static policies could lead to disaster. Hence, although one or two are seeking to narrow the scope of governmental activity, most aim at improving or expanding the services they offer to their populations, regulating new and potentially harmful practices, and otherwise accepting marginal changes in the parameters within which they operate. Nor do governments cater to those who would overthrow existing values, norms, procedures, or institutions. Officials usually consider it less than helpful to be told that major transformations of the existing system (through, for example, ending private ownership of the means of production, or decentralizing governmental institutions to the point of dissociation) are an appropriate response to current crises. They see their task rather as preserving the main dimensions of the existing system.

Third, governments recognize that they have only a limited capacity to intervene in the social realm. This capacity rests on both the resources, physical and social, available to the government and the ability of governmental personnel to mobilize those resources effectively. A government not on a sound financial footing may find it difficult even to provide for public order. By the same token, a government that taxes the willingness of the politically relevant strata to accept new governmental intrusions into what they consider to be the private sphere may provoke widespread civil disobedience. When the loads on a government outweigh its capacity to deal with them, the overburdened government may break down. In the view of some observers, it is precisely this unwarranted expansion of governmental activity that is at the root of the current crisis of the modern industrialized state.

Whether or not this crisis is unprecedented is, to be sure, a moot point. Perhaps each generation of leaders has felt—or at least adopted the rhetoric expressing the view—that its own problems are unique in the history of mankind and of overriding importance for the world's future. This view is accurate to some extent. Today's West European governments face problems substantially different from those of the early 1930s, when economic depression gripped the world, or of the late 1930s, when Nazism threatened to engulf it. But who is to say which kind of crisis is more, and which less, significant? More to the point is the fact that crises do have something in common. The governments best able to use the experience gained in their own or others' responses to past crises may be those most likely to survive in our troubled times.

The ability of Western governments to surmount the current crisis depends on what might be called their "learning capacity." This is only in part an incremental process of adjusting to whatever new pressures arise or of instituting new procedures to enhance the efficiency of the government's behavior in seeking its goals. It requires in addition a set of more reflective procedures: A government must be able to recognize the existence of a new problem for which past solutions or incremental adjustments are inadequate, develop solutions that can solve the problem without unleashing a plethora of destructive secondary effects, enlist support from relevant groups, and work out a strategy for implementing the proposed solution. Critical to this process of innovation in the public sector is a sensitivity to central social values. Innovation disruptive of the balance among key values may be worse than a failure to respond to new demands in the first place.

Information, germane and accurate, is essential if learning is to take place, whether on an individual or governmental level. Frequently, especially when it comes to governmental decision making, it is not new information that is needed but a comprehension of what is already known. This requires adequate procedures for collecting, storing, and retrieving data, as well as for analyzing these data and synthesizing the findings. The view taken in this volume is that we already know a great deal about processes of innovation and modes of innovative behavior, and that we are learning more all the time. Although more understanding is certainly needed, another major task is to make this current knowledge useful for public policymakers who would innovate.

Approaches to Understanding Innovation

The basic idea underlying this volume is that the systematic, comparative study of innovation can contribute both to policymakers' understanding of innovative decision making and to our theoretic conception of innovation as a process. Throughout, innovation is viewed as the introduction of a new idea, method, or device. In this sense, we are less concerned with its invention as such or its novelty as an invention than with the process by which something new (or something "reinvented") is adopted and diffused. Our concern is more specifically the adoption by governments of new ideas and practices and their diffusion, even internationally; and governmental innovations of the middle range—those important enough to provide some promise of responding to major problems facing a government and yet not sufficiently sweeping that they would transform the government or revolutionize society.

Such an approach has several implications. First of all, it is frankly pragmatic. We assume that the policymaker will be interested in learning what theory in general and which theories in particular could contribute most, rather than an exposition of how any given theory "explains" or "accounts for" relevant phenomena and prescribes appropriate courses of action. Thus, theory-building as such takes a back seat. We asked authors of the more general chapters to direct their analyses at a specific target audience: the policymakers in government who feel that today's problems are of such a kind and magnitude that only creative policies will help solve them, and who want to know what the scholarly community has discovered about the process of innovation that will assist them.

The approach is also oriented toward innovative adaptation rather than system transformation. It assumes that the major Western governments are accepted as legitimate by their populations and exercise their powers to improve the lot of these populations. Accordingly, we are interested in analyzing past innovative behaviors by governments and other social systems that have permitted them to overcome rather than succumb to crises. We are also interested in a government's innovative capacity: (1) the resources that it can reallocate for innovative purposes (including the absolute quantity of resources available to the government, their diversity across social sectors, their fungibility or replaceability, and their liquidity—that is, the excess resources available for immediate reallocation); (2) its information-processing system (including indicators of overall effectiveness, multiplicity and diversity of intake channels, rapidity, and "noise" levels); (3) its procedures for encouraging nonroutine thinking about public policy; (4) the intensity, limits, and rigidity of support for governmental flexibility on the part of relevant population strata; (5) its procedures for evaluating and selecting proposals for tentative adoption; and (6) the development of behavioral patterns to institutionalize innovative policies (see Deutsch, 1975).

Finally, the approach is comparative, in a triple sense of the word. First, the empirically oriented contributions are comparative across nations—especially, to be sure, the Federal Republic of Germany and the United States, but other countries as well. Second, the papers compare innovative strategies in various areas of public life, including education, planning, and agriculture. Third, individual contributions focus on innovation at different levels of behavior—from creativity at the level of single individuals and decision making in small groups, all the way to policy formation at the level of governments, supranational institutions, and other large-scale organizations. The underlying premise of this approach is that the contributions from one country, policy area, or system level can at once inform and be informed by the contributions of others.

Exploring Innovation in the Public Sector

It is thus at the interstices of theory and practice that this volume seeks to make its contribution. The relevance of this focus is made clear in Karl W. Deutsch's chapter, "On Theory and Research in Innovation." Major social and political theories purporting to explain the real world and predict its future course, he points out, have generally foundered on their own inability to allow for innovations that change the very nature of what they seek to describe and predict. He proposes a generative model of innovation that can contribute to mankind's ability to control its own fate—to identify the areas in which innovation in the public sector is needed, the feasibility of various kinds and levels of innovation in these areas, and the means by which governments can encourage the kinds of needed innovation that are becoming increasingly necessary to ensure human survival.

INNOVATION: A CROSS-SYSTEMS PERSPECTIVE

The challenge posed by Deutsch is, in the first instance, to find ways better to understand the process of innovation, wherever it may appear. Innovative behavior occurs at various levels in society, from the individual to world organizations. To some degree, the learning patterns found in creative individuals resemble those characterizing successful decision-making groups and still larger social organizations such as business firms and governments. This is not to say that they are completely identical with each other. Rather, it is that aspects, such as their information-processing procedures, are sufficiently similar that comparisons across these levels of social systems can be productive in investigating the innovation process as such.

The chapters in the first part of the volume focus on creativity or innovative behavior at several levels of society. Dean Keith Simonton, in his chapter on "Individual Creativity and Political Leadership," explores the contribution that historical, quantitative studies of creative individuals have made to this complex topic. Joseph E. McGrath discusses "Groups and the Innovation Process." More specifically, he points to what concepts and findings from social psychology, especially the areas of group and interpersonal processes, tell us about the process of innovation and its consequences. Everett M. Rogers and Joung-Im Kim turn our attention from the group level to the "Diffusion of Innovations in Public Organizations." They argue that a major change in research orientation occurred in the late 1970s, from an emphasis on organizational innovativeness, especially on the individuals responsible for diffusion, toward a concern with the process of innovation.

INNOVATION IN PRACTICE: WEST GERMANY

At its current stage of development, as the more general studies reviewed above make clear, theory building on innovation relies heavily on case studies conducted in various individual and social realms. They at once provide the information on the basis of which general propositions can be drawn and test these more general propositions. The chapters in the second portion of the volume examine various public sectors to explore innovative (and noninnovative) behaviors in the past, as well as conditions that favor innovation.

The first set of empirical studies focuses on innovation in the administrative system of the Federal Republic of Germany. Thomas Ellwein presents a *tour d'horizon* of "Innovation in West Germany's Public Sector" with respect to both structural and process innovation. Herbert König, in his chapter on "Innovation in West Germany: Retrospect and Prospects," asks what it is that must be changed in the FRG's public policymaking procedures to encourage innovations that can improve overall governmental effectiveness. Frieder Naschold reports why the new, socially oriented "Technology Policy in the Federal Republic of Germany," which expanded the government's role in managing corporate investment, did not really change social relationships in the productive process.

INNOVATION IN PRACTICE: COMPARATIVE STUDIES

A second set of empirical chapters examines innovation from a cross-national perspective. Hans N. Weiler raises a number of key questions about innovations in the schools in his chapter on the "Politics of Educational Reform." Noting that the flood of studies in this area have heuristic value as well as both a political and theoretical utility, he continues by arguing that greater attention must be paid to some links between research and practice. The ensuing discussion, with contributions by Dietrich Goldschmidt, Karl W. Deutsch, and Theodor Hanf, as well as Weiler, highlights several problems in both comparative research on and innovation in education policy.

Erhard Blankenburg examines "Legal Culture and the Chances for Legal Innovation" in several Western countries. To what extent, he asks, does a country's legal culture—by which he means its constellation of courts with various competences, the reliance of public and private organizations on precise legal regulations, and the extent to which legal norms permeate society as a whole—affect its ability to respond innovatively to such growing needs as providing the less privileged strata with access to law?

Ronald A. Francisco's comparative focus is at the supranational level, and across social and economic systems: "Large-Scale Policy Innovation in East and West European Agriculture." He looks at how the European Communities in the West and the Council for Mutual Economic Assistance in the East have dealt with issues of agricultural reform, including common agricultural policies.

PROSPECTS FOR INNOVATION IN THE PUBLIC SECTOR

A final pair of papers deals with the question of how the prospects for innovation in the public sector can be improved. Gerhard O. Mensch is concerned with "Trends and Perspectives in Innovation Policies." To this end, he explores the socioeconomic dynamics of entrepreneurial innovation viewed in terms of the theory of economic motion. Manfred Kochen looks at "Social Know-How and Its Role in Invention and Innovation." Paralleling the need for greater technological know-how to meet expectable shortages of nonrenewable resources in the future is the need for social know-how to manage ever more complex societies. How do we plan for new knowledge? Kochen outlines the prospects for "inquiring communities" that can use teleconferencing to seek solutions to important policy problems.

Innovation in the Public Sector: Some General Conclusions

What Kochen is suggesting is a procedure for establishing, on a basis at once permanent and flexible, conferences such as the one held at the Science Center Berlin in December 1979, at which the ideas contained in this volume were first presented. It is both difficult and expensive to bring together for a brief conference experts and public policymakers in various areas, and still more so to keep them subsequently in a communications network that enables them to follow through on some of the more promising ideas discussed at the conference. Teleconferencing may well help to transform such a richness of ideas into innovative policies in the public sector.

Among the points of view expressed and conclusions reached by participants in the conference, several stand out: First of all, even in crises traditional methods of problem-solving are usually applied. The known is viewed as preferable to an uncertain search for truly new ways. The reasons for this are many, but primary among them are pressures of time that require decision makers to focus their energies on the problem immediately at hand and that preclude extensive reflection. What this set of facts suggests is that, if innovative means for either solving problems or searching for solutions are to be applied, they must already be in the consciousness of decision makers *before* they are confronted with crises.

Second, any hope that we shall understand the process by which decision makers introduce innovative policies or searches for solutions requires greater understanding of the motivation of such individuals. Knowing the basic values they hold will provide information about the kinds of innovative strategies that are less or more likely to be accepted. Conflicts of interest among various groups in a society and the relative influence over policymaking enjoyed by these groups also provide clues as to the probable directions of innovativeness. It is not by accident that in the field of medicine there have been greater advances in healing than preventing sickness.

Third, structural conditions also influence the probability that innovative strategies and solutions will be introduced. Pluralistic societies appear to be more capable in this regard than are highly homogeneous societies; and, although states with central planning may be more adept at spreading accepted innovations, they are less likely than others to accept the innovations in the first place. Improving the innovative capacities of agencies in the public sector requires an understanding of the extent to which structural factors facilitate or retard given developments.

Fourth, the more industrialized a state is—and hence the greater the degree of interdependency of economic, political, and social processes within that state—the greater is the need for an innovative capacity to meet both expected and unexpected demands on the system. A failure to respond to changes in the labor market that increases unemployment by even 1 percent can produce self-amplifying effects in other sectors that could very seriously hamper the productivity and growth of such countries as the United States and the Federal Republic of Germany.

Such generalizations, of course, need further exploration, especially through the collection and analysis of relevant data on a cross-national basis. The chapters in this volume offer a step in that direction, both by summarizing and presenting analytically what we know about innovation in various areas and by suggesting directions for future research, as well as ideas about more innovative policymaking in the public sector.

REFERENCE

DEUTSCH, K. W. (1975) "On the learning capacity of large political systems," pp. 61–83 in M. Kochen (ed.) Information for Action: From Knowledge to Wisdom. New York: Academic Press.

CHAPTER 1

ON THEORY AND RESEARCH IN INNOVATION

K A R L   W.   D E U T S C H

To think about theoretical aspects of innovation, we must first ask what is meant by theory. Perhaps theories can be seen as schemes for holding and storing information for its efficient storage and recall, and for the use of items of information in dissociated form so that they can be recombined in new ways. Theory tells us what to remember and what to recall, what to expect through extrapolation and prediction, and, ultimately, what to do given the facts, the capacities, and the values we hold. In this way, theory leads to prediction and action. This chapter focuses on one form of action: innovation.

A Transformation in the Style of Thought

The present-day interest in innovation is the result of a transformation of economic and social thought similar to some of the fundamental transformations that have occurred in other fields of science. Three brief examples may illustrate this change.

The first example is the development of mechanical thinking from Galileo to Newton, and of quantitative chemistry from the Renaissance to the end of the eighteenth century. This style of thought had in common that matter was considered constant and unchanging, and that various material bodies, from planets to corpuscles, were expected to endure. Only at the end of the nineteenth century and into the beginning of the twentieth did scientists learn that matter could decay into energy. The discovery of radioactive decay into energy was an exemplar, to borrow from Kuhn's (1970) phrase, based on exemplary experiments and observations with uranium and radium.

Eventually, these led to the new theory of Einstein, which did not abolish Newton's theory but made it a special case. Something that was a permanent, unchanging unit of the old theory—the atom— was split up, becoming differentiable and changeable. This development made it possible to keep the old theory as a special case but also to open up new areas (Frank, 1950).

The second example, that of Charles Darwin, was associated with the theory of evolution. In the eighteenth century, Linné had assumed that there were relatively fixed species. Darwin proposed that these species were changing very slowly, through the gradual accretion of small chance variations. Approximately forty years later, genetic mutations were discovered by deVries, and mathematically describable gene combinations in hybrids were produced by Mendel. Modern genetics arose, and it turned out that what seemed to be hereditary species were cocktails of genes, composed of dissociative—through the split of the hereditary material—and then recombinable genetic elements. Again, it turned out that what had seemed to be fixed was in fact variable and differentiable, and relatively fixed species became a special case in modern genetics (Huxley, 1942, 1953; Mayr, 1970/ 1977).

The third of these parallel developments occurred in the social sciences. Friedrich Engels compared the work of Karl Marx to the work of Newton and Darwin. Implicitly, both Marx and Engels seem to have had the notion that they had made great discoveries and that, for a good long while, no new ideas would be needed. What was needed now was the diligent propagation and application of the ideas just discovered. For Adam Smith, Karl Marx, and the political economists of the nineteenth century, once again different interest groups, production factors (capital and labor), and social classes were seen as relatively fixed units. Marx wanted to think in terms of dialectics and dynamic change, and he did expect some changes in classes: The big capitalists would become fewer and richer, the lower middle class and the peasants would become proletarians, and the proletariat would grow in numbers and class consciousness. But the basic situation and interest of these classes would remain fixed and unchanging until the proletarians, grown to a vast majority and aware of their interests, would act to abolish the still-unchanged capitalist system. Not only Marx and Engels, but all major nineteenth century social theorists thought in terms of a relatively fixed economic system with relatively fixed units. Their question then was, How would the relationships among these units develop? What conflicts or, according to others, what relations in harmony could be established among them?

It was only around the turn of the century that Schumpeter began to deal with innovation in a fundamental sense (1947, 1949; see also Clemence and Doody, 1950: esp. 36–74; Hicks, 1973a: ch. 10, 1973b, 1974). If production formulas could be split up, the particular relationships and even the structural relationships of modern industrial technology would become differentiable and variable. The older theories could then be treated as special cases; they would still apply wherever innovation was so small or so slow that it could be neglected for the short-term analysis of economic conflicts and interests, profitability, and the business cycle.

Actually, however, if one made the process and effects of innovation explicit, it would, in Schumpeter's view, make a major difference to business cycle theory, and it might make a major difference to the selection of elites and to the decline or growth of classes. The Marxian prediction that small entrepreneurs would disappear, classically expressed in the Communist Manifesto, was counterbalanced by the process of innovation that replaced the disappearing owners of stables, horses, and buggies with gasoline station owners and other attendants of modern technology. Innovations can thus produce new occupations and new reinforcements (or diminutions) of existing social structures.

Innovations and innovation theory have now emerged as major potential modifiers of social and political theory. Their eventual intellectual significance in these fields may be comparable to that of radioactivity in physics and of mutations in biology. Innovation is not just a special marginal subject for a few specialists. It is becoming of central importance in our thought about the social, political, economic, and cultural development of modern industrial society and of the information society that may now be emerging.

The Nature of Innovation

What is innovation? Let us begin with the question of its inner structure. What does it consist of? Viewed at the societal level, innovation is the adoption on a relatively large scale of some invention or discovery. Such inventions and discoveries can be made by one person or by a few. They are related primarily to observations and experiments; they are matters of new knowledge. Innovation, as Schumpeter pointed out, is something different. It is the work of many people and is related to the *adoption* of some new invention or discovery on the level of behavior, of action. Innovation involves new behavior, new habits, new interlocking expectations which we call roles in social theory, and it even involves new interlocking patterns of roles, which we call institutions or practices. To constitute an innovation, any or all of these must occur on a relatively large scale.

This leads to another formulation: Innovation is action and the results of action lead to repeated and widespread action. Innovation must be widespread; it must be repeated. It is collective action, or a set of collective actions. These actions can be parallel or interlocking, or both.

This concept of innovation raises an interesting structural problem: the possibility and limits of innovation in a routinized bureaucracy. Max Weber (1956: ii, 829–845) made routine, repetitiveness, and order the essence of bureaucracy—seemingly the opposite of innovation. Yet Weber knew, and we know, that bureaucracies can innovate and have innovated. There are empirical case studies of such instances of innovation and reform. We may think of what historians had to say about Josephinism in eighteenth-century Austria (Kann, 1960), or about the innovative behavior of the Brandenburg-Prussian monarchy (Fay, 1964). We find the same in studies of the role of General Billy Mitchell in persuading the military bureaucracy of the United States to take aircraft seriously (Hurley, 1975; Burlingame, 1978), and of Admiral Hyman Rickover in persuading the naval bureaucracy of the United States to take nuclear submarines seriously (Clay, 1954; David, 1970; Polmar and Allen, 1982). These are examples of innovation in the bureaucratic sector.

On the individual or internal level, innovation can be called a structural change in memory. It implies, first of all, some change in our memory of facts, of our cognitive map of some part of the world. Thus innovation implies some real change in the combinability of our perceptions and in the probability distribution of their potential combinations.

Second, innovation also implies a structural change in our memory of sequential program instructions and commitments to actions. Such a sequential program instruction to which an active system is already committed can be called the *intention* of the system.[1] Innovation thus requires changes in remembered action programs—that is, changes in intention.

The Environment of Innovation

Where and how does innovation exist, and in what environments does it function? In principle or potential, innovation occurs in all human societies that do not maintain improbable and effective measures to prevent it. In this sense, innovation occurs with radically different frequencies and speeds. These differences among societies are not random. Nor are they random among epochs in the history of what we call the same society, a concept that implies our notion of identity. This notion of innovation and the critical differences in its frequency and speed call for an exploration of both the theoretical and empirical conditions under which innovation is likely to be larger, faster, more widespread as to domain and scope, and fraught with deeper and more far-reaching consequences. Innovation is influenced by social environment, and it can in turn change the environment. In the latter context, we can speak of the power of innovation; its dimensions are parallel to the dimensions of power.[2]

It would be desirable, therefore, to have a wide range of empirical studies of innovation cases and, even better, of innovation curves separated by kinds of innovations, by industries, by countries, by cultures, and by epochs. By an innovation curve, I mean a curve on a Cartesian grid where the vertical dimension is the percent saturation of a particular field of practice and the horizontal dimension represents time. To take an example, Pasteur discovered in the 1860s that milk becomes largely sterilized of many disease-carrying germs when it is heated to a little above $40°$ C. But pasteurized milk became common in Prague, Czechoslovakia, only in the early 1930s. (The progressive Weimar Republic may have got it in the 1920s but probably not much earlier.) The innovation curve would show by decade what percentage of the milk that was drunk, as distinguished from milk worked into cheese and other things, was pasteurized.

Innovation curves can take many shapes. That of the consumption of pasteurized milk would be *concave,* showing that the innovation at first moved very slowly, but then, once it took off, moved very fast, and for a time even faster, right to saturation. Another shape is a *logistic* curve—moving slowly at first, then quickly in the middle range, similar to an exponential curve, and finally flattening out short of saturation, approximating saturation only in an asymptotic manner. The curve could also be *convex.* In this case the innovation curve would be similar to the well-known *search curves,* such as those Morrison and others found in searches for both submarines in the ocean and books in libraries. In many situations, most of the "findable" objects can be found quickly, but the diminishing remnant becomes ever harder to find.

Finally, it could be a *wave* curve going up, then down somewhat, and then up again, like the curves of learning that psychologists have found in laboratory experiments and that Merritt (1966) found in the learning of integrated symbols and habits in the developing American community of colonies and states between 1735 and 1775. In theory, worldwide curves of social learning and innovation could be defined. We need to know whether innovation curves (and which ones) are most similar for one and the same industry in many countries, or for one country or culture for different industries, or for both countries and cultures during the same historical epoch. The epoch could be defined by the calendar, let us say 1950–1960 and 1970–1980, or one could use the definition of Fucks (1978). Fucks defines contemporaneousness as the degree of development, measured by per capita steel consumption. Thus, all countries that consume the same amount of steel per capita are contemporary in terms of this indicator of industrial development.

Who Bears the Costs?

Let us consider five examples of a clearly identifiable innovation spreading in an identifiable universe. One was the case of pasteurized milk. A second is the introduction of electric light (Passer, 1953). A third example is the spread of the linotype machine in the newsprint business. A fourth case is the introduction of photocopying in offices and in commercial copying. Finally, there is the use of computers, and here we can consider both computer use for business bookkeeping and computer use for statistical work.[3]

These examples raise a question about the context of social and economic interests involved in innovations. There are costs and benefits involved, but these costs and benefits are not equally distributed. On whom are the costs imposed, and who reaps the benefits? There are class interests involved, as well as regional and national interests. Typically, particularly in private enterprise economies, innovations occur also, as in investment, by shifting costs to groups weaker in the market or weaker in the political arena. The opposition would then consist of coalition formation or direct action to prevent it (see Naschold, 1978). But to what extent could an effort to safeguard all the various groups against the shifting of innovation costs create secondary costs in terms of slowing down innovation or preventing it? There might be the effort not to let a neighborhood be disturbed by an automobile highway or by a magnetic railroad, or by subway or cinema installations, or by power stations, whether coal burning or nuclear, where the effort to prevent shifts of costs will in turn prevent innovation.

This means that one would also need an analysis of the costs of not having an innovation, delaying an innovation, or preventing one. The costs of not innovating have been very little explored, even though economic and technological history is replete with research and examples. There is at least one city in the United States which in the nineteenth century successfully lobbied against being disturbed by a railroad. City officials succeeded in persuading both the government and the railroad to bypass York, Pennsylvania, by a considerable distance. The result was a slowdown over several decades in York's cultural and economic development. An anthropologist has observed that such a town would offer a splendid opportunity today for field research on possible survivals of midnineteenth-century culture. Anthropologists usually do not take the trouble to estimate economic costs. The city officials did not estimate the costs of *not* accepting an innovation, but with the help of the information available on this and similar places—cities that managed to be bypassed by some innovation in other points—one might see what really happened.

A special advantage in looking at costs and benefits is the opportunity to compare changes in the innovation curves for the public sector with those of the private sector. It is frequently assumed that most innovations are found in the private sector, and in particular within large corporations—which, of course, are bureaucracies, albeit private bureaucracies with feedback from market processes. The other side of this approach would ask, What are the patterns of innovation in the public sector? Are they rising more steeply for an innovation spreading within one and the same bureaucracy, but slowly and less smoothly from one bureaucracy to another? Would computerized bookkeeping be adopted early and quickly within, say, a social security administration but only later and more slowly within, say, the post office, or vice versa? What could account for such differences?

Some highly interesting research could also be done on the interplay of private and public sector innovations. For instance, we could look at how the private sector developed automobiles while the public sector developed new patterns of highway construction, overpasses, and superhighways, so that in the end the private automobile moving on the public highway generated private prosperity, societal change, some societal problems, but also large amounts of societal opportunities.

Finally, one could analyze innovation—still from its existential side—in its function for society. I would propose here a modification of the framework for analysis proposed by Talcott Parsons. We could ask, What have innovations done for the *pattern maintenance* of society? Innovations not only bring about change, but also slow down or prevent change. The creation of the Holy Office of the Catholic Church in the thirteenth century and the innovation of the Inquisition had precisely the latter purpose. Innovations may have an *adaptive* function, such as the shift to the use of mineral coal instead of charcoal in seventeenth- and eighteenth-century England that helped that country adapt to the growing scarcity of its forest resources. Another innovation may promote a society's *goal attainment*. In this manner, the innovations in shipbuilding and navigation, promoted by Prince Henry the Navigator in fifteenth-century Portugal, eventually helped that country, and later other countries, reach its aim of opening direct maritime connections with India and the Spice Islands. Another innovation may increase the *integrative* capacities of a system. Certainly the innovations of all-weather roads, railroads, postal services, general public elementary education, mass literacy, and the press have done much to foster the integration of nations and nation-states in the nineteenth and twentieth centuries.

To these four functions specified by Parsons—pattern maintenance, adaptation, goal attainment, and integration—I would like to add two further ones. First, innovations make it necessary for an organization or society to change its goals. *Goal change* is something different from goal attainment. Indeed, there may be a good deal of tension between the two. The more deeply and completely we are committed to one goal, the harder it is to change it. Second, what contributions can innovations make to *system transformation* to produce a good deal of long-lasting structural change in the system, without completely wiping out the identity of the system? There are many examples of such system transformation in the literature of anthropology, sociology, history, and political science (Balandier, 1970). One is the innovation of representative government, where a delegate acquires the right to bind by his decision those who sent him without having to ask back for their ratification. Representative government of this kind, according to Barker (1913), was invented by the Benedictine monks in the tenth century and later spread to parliamentary and other forms of representative government. A second innovation which has proved system-transforming was the invention of the Elizabethan parliament, which permitted the representative of one constituency to come from another constituency. This strongly influenced the development of the parliamentary system of England (Neale, 1949). A third political innovation was that of federalism, which has changed the governmental system of many countries (see, for example, Wheare, 1964).

The Essence of Innovation

What is the essence of innovation? By essence we mean: To what class of patterns does innovation belong? Plato called such classes of patterns "ideas," taking the notion, according to Jaeger (1965), from the concept of "syndrome" in Hippocratic medicine.[4] On the basis of what characteristics, then, can any event be put into the class of "innovations," and in what larger class does innovation belong?

Innovation on a macrosocial scale is composed of frequent acts of microsocial learning. Accordingly, much of what we know about learning processes should apply to innovation, at least in principle. This should hold for learning on both the individual level and the societal level—in short, to learning on all systems levels. It follows—and this is then a substantive prediction—that innovation must always be related to reinforcement, that it is part of reinforcement learning. Thus the standard models of reinforcement learning proposed by Robert Bush, Frederick Mosteller, James Fitch, the work of B. F. Skinner, and the stochastic learning models of Merrill Flood and others should in principle be applicable to the analysis of innovation processes (see Skinner, 1953: 254–256; 1970; 1971: 27–37). To the best of my knowledge, this connection has not yet been explored in depth, but it is implied in the theoretical approach that is being proposed here.

Innovations rest on an unequal distribution of costs and benefits. Learning processes by reinforcement will, therefore, be in part conflictual and in part countervailing. Groups that mainly receive benefits will learn to accept and foster an innovation which other groups will learn to fear and oppose. This raises a series of questions: What will be the expected and salient reinforcements? What will be the actual reinforcements? What are the mechanisms for the group's perceptions? Here we might wish to distinguish between large and small, prominent and inconspicuous rewards, and between those which arrive early and those which arrive only in the later stages.

Through the notion of reinforcement learning in general, and through a further development in experimentation and theory, we then arrive at Skinner's notion of *probabilistic reinforcement schedules*. A schedule is a sequence that tends to recur in a stable manner. That is, not all sequences are schedules, but all schedules are sequences. Schedules are a subclass of sequences that are stable and recurring. I will accept here Skinner's general finding that probabilistic reinforcement schedules—beginning with frequent reinforcements which become rarer at later stages—are more powerful in teaching new habits than are completely certain ones, but I would be skeptical about Skinner's further philosophical extrapolations (Skinner, 1971).

A third consequence of considering innovations as a part of learning processes is the application of questions of *cognitive consonance and dissonance*. First of all, such questions deal with the consonance and dissonance of perceptions and also of recognition, in accordance with some of the work of Festinger (1957) and Abelson et al. (1968), but eventually they lead us to the consonance and dissonance of reinforcement schedules. Putting Festinger's and Skinner's work together in this manner seems to be theoretically indicated, although no research project has yet done so. There is also the question of the consonance and dissonance of *action schedules*. Can things really be done? This in turn builds a theoretical bridge to the already existing studies and concerns about the cultural acceptability of innovations, something which can be crucial in the transfer of technology and the transfers of administrative practices. At certain times and places, recruitment by the system of bureaucrats, paying officials with money, collecting taxes honestly, and promoting bureaucrats by competence or merit make up a syndrome of interlocking processes which then creates a new "tax-collecting state," as Schumpeter (1918) called it—a state of early modernization that replaces the family system of feudalism. But the new system also requires a suspension of the old ethics of family loyalty, because these loyalties are regarded as corrupt in the merit-oriented bureaucracy.

Finally, the notion of *learning capacity,* which comes from cybernetic thought, also applies to innovation (Deutsch, 1975). Learning capacity is indicated by the amount of recommittable resources—that is, resources that can be shifted from one commitment to another, rapidly and effectively, and by the proportion of such recommittable resources (or operational reserves) to all the resources in a society, and by the kinds of resources. Absolute amounts, proportional weight, and specific kinds of operational reserves in the form of recommittable resources could play a crucial role in success or failure during the initiation at least, but also in the continuation of the innovation.

The essential definition of innovation as a part of learning suggests the notion of *learning to learn,* what Bateson (1972a, 1972b) called *deutero learning,* or second-order and higher-order learning. This notion, applied to innovations, leads to the question: Are there innovations that produce innovations? One example is the innovation of the university that occurred in thirteenth-century Europe (Rashdall, 1958). Earlier, there was the innovation of the Benedictine monastery order, the first order concerned with work instead of only contemplation (Meisel and Del Mastro, 1975; Barker, 1913). A third such higher-order innovation was that of the industrial research laboratory. This was invented by Edison, but it then spread over the whole world and created many new innovations (Clark, 1977; Josephson, 1959; Passer, 1953). There followed the step from the laboratory to the think tank—the social science or administrative centers that produce innovation in its military or civilian forms.

The Genesis of Innovations

How does an innovation come into existence? What do theoretical and empirical investigations of the initiation and early stages of specific innovations tell us? Answering such a question requires several analytic stages: first, research on the evolution of the feasibility of a particular innovation or class of innovations; second, research about the evolution of the perception of expectable reinforcements; third, research to detect the presence of risk factors, or of reassurance against risk.

In combination, these lead to the concept of the *entrepreneurial function*. In the 1940s, Schumpeter, in his seminar at Harvard Business School (Cole, 1949), strongly emphasized the view that the entrepreneurial function resided in highly business-minded, entrepreneurial-minded groups or subcultures, such as Armenians in Turkey, Jains and Marvaris in India, Chinese in southeast Asia, Gallegos in Spain, and Scots in Britain. This viewpoint hypothesized that one could quickly change the development rate of underdeveloped countries by introducing into them large numbers of such entrepreneurial types, so as to infect traditional societies with high degrees of entrepreneurship.

As an alternative to that approach, one could put the entrepreneurial function into the context of a systems function. If we call an entrepreneur a risk-taking decision maker, we would find that in the nineteenth century many owner-managers, as individual businessmen, both made the decisions and took the risks with their own money, but that in the twentieth century—as research by Berle (1932) has shown—modern corporations take their risks with other people's money. Even more often, entrepreneurial work is something performed on a kind of invisible assembly line of societal processes. Just as an automobile is no longer produced by a single craftsman—if it ever was—an entrepreneurial decision need not be produced by a single individual. It is still possible, of course, to find entrepreneurs who as individuals may risk careers and reputations in the bureaucratic context of a large private corporation, or of a competitive market, or of a political arena, or of a bureaucracy in the public sector. But we also may imagine cases where an institutional assembly line produces an innovation. We have, at least from the viewpoint of theory, a larger concept, built both for the one process—the entrepreneurial function that may be performed by a single personality, with or without attendant risks in financial and other values—and also for the performance of the same function by a sequence of discrete operations which nevertheless lead to the same innovative outcome.

Can these approaches lead to our building at least one *generative model* of conditions and processes by which innovations are produced or sustained? It could be that we will end up with a plurality of such models, all equally plausible, until we find (if we ever do) discriminating evidence showing that one model is clearly better than some other one.

This leads to the reverse question: By what processes are innovations prevented or stifled? The invention of gunpowder took place in China and came to the West. The innovation of artillery was then made quickly and thoroughly in the West in the course of several centuries, but not in China. One might look at studies by Needham (1954–76) and others to find what prevented the development of gunpowder as a major military innovation in China, and what limited it there mainly to the more harmless use of firecrackers.

Prospects: The Probability of Innovations

Can innovations be made easier to predict? This would be possible if innovations were seen as large classes of events that occur relatively frequently. Could we see in which country, for instance, or in which particular culture a great many innovations could be expected, or, conversely, in which country or culture or epoch it seems likely that innovations would be few and far between? In what sector of activity are innovations highly expectable, and in which sectors will they be rare and slow?

Both the French and the Russian revolutions, as well as the American revolution, accelerated innovations a great deal in the first twenty to thirty years after they occurred. However, whereas after the French and American revolutions capitalism ensured that a high rate of innovation would continue for a long time, the Soviet Union showed a slowing down of innovation rates after the first twenty to thirty postrevolutionary years. In their place, the communist dictatorships needed to import many more patents and licenses than they could export. One might ask to what extent this is accidental and to what extent it is inherent in collective ownership or bureaucratic political direction, or perhaps some combination of the two. One might also ask in the case of England to what extent there was a rapid introduction of innovations in coal mining and in the public sector for the first ten years after the nationalization of 1947, and what happened in the next twenty years after that. That is, we should like once again to see the innovation curves for various industries and their correlation, if any, with a form of property or a pattern of administration.

So far we have considered general classes, a large class of innovations. Can we repeat this for specific innovations? If so, how far ahead? Can we predict a particular type or kind of innovation and its specific speed of widespread acceptance? There have been successes in this area: H. G. Wells predicted tank warfare and air warfare decades before they took place (1902; 1924–27; 1970; for his more erratic views, 1932, 1936, 1941). But a cheap, light, and powerful electric accumulator was predicted and sought a hundred years ago by Edison, and we still do not have it. Similarly, we do not have a remedy for cancer, although it has been sought and predicted for many years. In short, while there have been predictive successes, there have also been gross failures in predicting innovations, sometimes despite large amounts of money being put into the effort.

A start in improving our predictive capacity is the observation by James Bryant Conant that the probability of large-scale discovery and innovation is inversely related to the degree of empiricism in a field of knowledge. Conant gave examples: Since most elements of the theory of nuclear energy—such as relativity, the neutron, isotopes, and chain reactions—were known by 1939, it was probable that large amounts of money invested would produce nuclear energy, first in the form of bombs and then in power stations. At the same time, said Conant, it was clear in 1941 that even a massive investment of resources in the synthesis of penicillin would have failed, since at that time the formula for penicillin was not yet understood, and therefore no one even knew what was to be synthesized. Only in the 1950s, when the formula of penicillin had become known, did penicillin synthesis become probable and then duly achieved by a suitable investment of resources (Conant, 1951: 310–311). In this manner we might use the degree of theoretical as well as empirical understanding in a field as a predictor for the feasibility of innovation, provided that we also know how many resources can and will be invested and in how sustained a manner.

Such considerations raise the question of policy. What adaptive measures for the consequences of innovation can we undertake? Are there any examples of past successes or failures of adaptation, and what are the conditions for bettering that record?

Innovation and Public Policy

IDENTIFYING THE NEEDS FOR INNOVATION

First of all, what can the political sector do in the search for an identification of needed innovations? To what extent could it at least supplement the market mechanism? Classical economic theory from Adam Smith to Frederick von Hayek pictures the market as an unsurpassed instrument for discovering the desires of people with an adequate amount of money, but not a very good instrument for discovering answers to the needs of people who are poor. The latter, however, are the majority of mankind to this day. To what extent can a public search be developed for the needs, desires, and innovations of those people with inadequate purchasing power? Here we need to find a link between innovation theory and either the concept of basic needs as developed by psychologist Abraham Maslow, or the basic needs theory developed by the Bariloche group in Argentina and the world model based on that basic need concept (Herrera et al., 1976; Kappel et al., 1983).[5]

PROBLEMS OF FEASIBILITY AND DECISIONS

Once basic needs have been identified, together with major gaps in their satisfaction, it may be relevant to ask which innovations might improve the situation. And once such possible innovations have been identified as possible "candidate selections," their feasibility—technical, economic, cultural, and political—must be investigated. Such feasibility studies may decide about the immediate prospects of an innovation; if it is costly enough, it may have to be deferred for the time being.

Questions concerning the cause of a decision by the state to intervene lead us into decision theory. This brings us once again to questions of interests and coalitions of interests, both in private management and in public bureaucracy and policy. Decision theory leads then to decision models, such as the three decision models by Allison (1971) and others.

OPPORTUNITIES FOR PUBLIC POLICY

What can the public sector do to stimulate innovations in general? Ever since the patent legislation of the Tudor monarchs, this has been a relevant question. What about the acceleration of innovations? How can one accelerate their diffusion? Here we encounter a serious problem. That which offers rewards for initiating an innovation through a monopoly or protecting the secret of an innovation may then slow down its diffusion. Here again a structural contradiction is built into most of the past legal reward and support measures for innovation, and no good solutions or alternatives have yet been developed. Whereas the critics of private enterprise argue that it is the greed of private companies that keeps valuable discoveries a secret, it has turned out that the collectivistic dictatorships of Russia and the Soviet bloc in Eastern Europe, and of China, are even more secretive than private enterprise, and therefore offer considerable obstacles to the diffusion of innovations.

Within the general area of policy in the public sector, there are specific questions: Can the public sector provide backing against risks, particularly during the early or pilot-plant stages of an innovation? It is notable that many major private-sector innovations in the United States, and perhaps in other countries, first were based in publicly financed innovations in the military sector. In this way, the automated factory was a development of the automatic fire control systems developed by the U.S. government during World War II. The radar devices that now guide fishing fleets were developed in the military sector, and the development costs were carried there. The miniaturization and the microchips which we now use in a wide variety of ways were to a large extent financed by space navigation and NASA in the 1950s and 1960s. Here once again the public sector provided the seed money for the private sector.

One can argue that it was the labor unions that saved capitalism by preserving enough mass purchasing power to keep the combination of capitalism and modern mass production working. At the same time, it can also be argued that it is the public sector that often has borne the unprofitable burdens of research and development through the final stages and specification in some industrial sectors for innovations which then were very profitably transferred into other industrial sectors by private enterprise. Instead of a quarrel of dogmas between the alleged across-the-board superiority of central planning or market economics, it might be more interesting to ask about the best possible forms of their interplay and the best patterns and proportions for their combination. We could then ask what the public sector can do in regard to guidance and specific actions to assist innovations, and what the public sector can do to control an innovation's unwanted side effects or to compensate for them.

Innovations and System Transformation

What are the large, systematic implications by which single innovations add up to continuations of patterns of innovation and lead eventually to the self-transformation of systems with a continuing identity? During the Industrial Revolution, England was indeed transformed by a string of innovations and yet it remained recognizably England (Reeve, 1971; Ashton, 1948; Clapham, 1930–1938). This process is visible when we look back on history from a distance. But can we discern this process when we live in the middle of it?

During the last eighty years, humanity has passed through what Platt (1980) calls eight evolutionary jumps. He argues that never before in human history have so many revolutionary discoveries and innovations of such importance been made in so many fields within so short a time. Has this led to or been produced by a transformation of our global system? What do innovations do when they add up to the transformation of an entire social and economic system? And what can a changing social system do to innovations? We have been far too busy investigating innovations in isolation. The interplay of innovation and system transformation has been neglected.

A child can ask more questions than ten wise men can answer. Similarly, a theorist can develop more questions than ten or twenty specific experts can answer soon. But many discoveries have started from asking questions, and the asking of such questions may be needed now more than ever before.

NOTES

1. This point is made by Miller et al. (1960) in regard to the plans and structure of action, and by Miller and Chomsky (1963) in their essay on finitary organizations.
2. On the dimensions of power, see Deutsch (1980: 26–28).

3. There is an advantage, of course, in using innovation data surrounding monopolized innovations. The proprietary companies may actually know how the innovation spread, and they may even have projected the expected innovation curve for the purposes of market research.

4. In contrast to the later efforts of Rickert and Windelband to establish a permanent separation between natural and "cultural" sciences (see Collingwood, 1956/1974), Plato took a "natural science" observation of the physicians—the "syndrome," or the frequent association of several symptoms—and applied it to a very abstract philosophic notion and then to political and cultural ideas. From Plato to Kant to Hegel and others, we find a persistent belief in the fundamental unity of science, and the unity of human thought.

5. For critical discussions of basic needs, see also Lederer and Galtung (1980) and, for another view, Kappel et al. (1983).

REFERENCES

ABELSON, R. et al. [eds.] (1968) Theories of Cognitive Consistency: A Sourcebook. Chicago: Rand McNally.

ALLISON, G. T. (1971) Essence of Decision: Explaining the Cuban Missile Crisis. Boston: Little, Brown.

ASHTON, T. S. (1948) The Industrial Revolution, 1760-1830. London: Oxford University Press.

BALANDIER, G. (1970) Sociologie des mutations. Paris: Éditions Anthropos.

BARKER, E. (1913) The Dominican Order and Convocation: A Study of the Growth of Representation during the Thirteenth Century. Oxford, Eng.: Clarendon.

BATESON, G. (1972a) "Social planning and the concept of deutero-learning," pp. 159–176 in G. Bateson, Steps to an Ecology of Mind. New York: Ballantine.

——— (1972b) "The logical categories of learning and communication," pp. 279–306 in G. Bateson, Steps to an Ecology of Mind. New York: Ballantine.

BERLE, A. A., Jr. (1932) The Modern Corporation and Private Property. New York: Commerce Clearing House.

BURLINGAME, R. (1978) General Billy Mitchell: Champion of Air Defense. Westport, CT: Greenwood.

CLAPHAM, J. H. (1930–1938) An Economic History of Modern Britain (3 vols.). Cambridge, Eng.: The University Press.

CLARK, R. W. (1977) Edison: The Man Who Made the Future. New York: Putnam.

CLAY, B. (1954) The Atomic Submarine and Admiral Rickover. New York: Holt, Rinehart & Winston.

CLEMENCE, R. V. and F. S. DOODY (1950) The Schumpeterian System. Cambridge, MA: Addison-Wesley.

COLE, A. H. [ed.] (1949) Change and the Entrepreneur: Postulates and Patterns for Entrepreneurial History. Cambridge, MA: Harvard University Press.

COLLINGWOOD, R. G. (1956/1974) The Idea of History. London: Oxford University Press.

CONANT, J. B. (1951) Science and Common Sense. New Haven, CT: Yale University Press.

DAVID, H. M. (1970) Admiral Rickover and the Nuclear Navy. New York: Putnam.

DEUTSCH, K. W. (1980) Politics and Government. Boston: Houghton Mifflin.

—— (1975) "On the learning capacity of large political systems," pp. 61–83 in M. Kochen (ed.), Information in Action: From Knowledge to Wisdom. New York: Academic.

FAY, S. B. (1964) The Rise of Brandenburg-Prussia to 1786. New York: Holt, Rinehart & Winston.

FESTINGER, L. (1957) A Theory of Cognitive Dissonance. Stanford, CA: Stanford University Press.

FRANK, P. (1950) Relativity, a Richer Truth. Boston, MA: Beacon.

FUCKS, W. (1978) Mächte von Morgen. Stuttgart: Deutsche Verlagsanstalt.

HERRERA, A. O. et al. (1976) Catastrophe or New Society? A Latin American World Model. Ottawa, Canada: International Development Research Centre.

HICKS, J. (1974) "The future of industrialism." International Affairs 50 (April): 211–228.

—— (1973a) Capital and Time: A New-Austrian Theory. Oxford, Eng.: Clarendon.

—— (1973b) "The mainspring of economic growth." Swedish Journal of Economics 75 (December): 336–348.

HURLEY, A. F. (1975) Billy Mitchell: Crusader for Air Power. Bloomington: Indiana University Press.

HUXLEY, J. S. (1953) Evolution in Action. New York: Harper & Row.

—— (1942) Evolution, the Modern Synthesis. New York: Harper & Row.

JAEGER, W. (1965) Paideia: The Ideals of Greek Culture (3 vols.). Oxford, Eng.: Blackwell.

JOSEPHSON, M. (1959) Edison: A Biography. New York: McGraw-Hill.

KANN, R. A. (1960) A Study in Australian Intellectual History: From Late Baroque to Romanticism. New York: Praeger.

KAPPEL, R., M. METZ, and D. WENDT (1983) Technologieentwicklung und Grundbedürfnisse: Eine empirische Studie über Mexico. Saarbrücken: Verlag-Breitenbach.

✓ KUHN, T. S. (1970) The Structure of Scientific Revolutions. Chicago: University of Chicago Press.

LEDERER, K. and J. GALTUNG [eds.] (1980) Human Needs: A Contribution to the Current Debate. Cambridge, MA: Oelgeschlager, Gunn & Hain.

MAYR, E. (1970/1977) Populations, Species, and Evolution. Cambridge, MA: Belknap Press.

MEISEL, A. C. and M. L. DEL MASTRO [tr.] (1975) The Rule of St. Benedict. Garden City, NY: Doubleday.

MERRITT, R. L. (1966) Symbols of American Community, 1735-1775. New Haven, CT: Yale University Press.

MILLER, G. A. and N. CHOMSKY (1963) "Finitary models of language users," pp. 419–491 in R. D. Luce et al. (eds.) Handbook of Mathematical Psychology, vol. 2. New York: John Wiley.

MILLER, G. A., E. GALANTER, and K. H. PRIBRAM (1960) Plans and the Structure of Behavior. New York: Henry Holt.

NASCHOLD, F. (1978) Alternative Raumpolitik. Kronberg/Ts.: Athenäum.

NEALE, J. E. (1949) The Elizabethan House of Commons. London: Cape.

NEEDHAM, J. (1954–1976) Science and Civilization in China (5 vols.). Cambridge, Eng.: Cambridge University Press.

PASSER, H. C. (1953) The Electrical Manufacturers, 1875–1900: A Study in Competition, Entrepreneurship, Technical Change, and Economic Growth. Cambridge, MA: Harvard University Press. (reprinted 1972, New York: Arno Press)

PLATT, J. R. (1980) "Eight major evolutionary jumps today," pp. 149–165 in A. Markovits and K. W. Deutsch (eds.) Fear of Science—Trust in Science: Conditions for Change in the Climate of Opinion. Cambridge, MA: Oelgeschlager, Gunn & Hain.

POLMAR, N. and T. B. ALLEN (1982) Rickover. New York: Simon and Schuster.

RASHDALL, H. (1958) The Universities of Europe in the Middle Ages. London: Oxford University Press.

REEVE, R. M. (1971) The Industrial Revolution, 1750–1850. London: University of London Press.

SCHUMPETER, J. A. (1949) "Economic theory and entrepreneurial history," pp. 63–84 in A. H. Cole (ed.), Change and the Entrepreneur: Postulates and Patterns for Entrepreneurial History. Cambridge, MA: Harvard University Press.

_____ (1947) "Theoretical problems of economic growth." Journal of Economic History, suppl. vii: 1–9.

_____ (1918) Die Krise des Steuerstaats. Graz and Leipzig: Leuschner & Lubensky.

SKINNER, B. F. (1971) Beyond Freedom and Dignity. New York: Knopf.

_____ (1970) "Creating the creative artist," in A. Toynbee et al., On the Future of Art. New York: Viking.

_____ (1953) Science and Human Behavior. New York: Macmillan.

WEBER, M. (1956) Wirtschaft und Gesellschaft: Grundriss der verstehenden Soziologie. Tübingen: Mohr (Siebeck).

WELLS, H. G. (1970) The Complete Short Stories of H. G. Wells. London: Benn.

_____ (1941) All Aboard for Ararat. New York: Alliance.

_____ (1936) The Anatomy of Frustration: A Modern Synthesis. London: Crescent.

_____ (1932) After Democracy: Addresses and Papers on the Present World Situation. London: Watts.

_____ (1924-27) Works. London: Unwin.

_____ (1902) Anticipations of the Reaction of Mechanical and Scientific Progress upon Human Life and Thought. London: Chapman & Hall.

WHEARE, K. C. (1964) Federal Government. London: Oxford University Press.

PART I

Innovation: A Cross-Systems Perspective

CHAPTER 2

INDIVIDUAL CREATIVITY AND POLITICAL LEADERSHIP

DEAN KEITH SIMONTON

The history of human culture and political systems can offer a rich store of data about individual creativity and innovation. The world we live in today is not the same one of yesteryear, precisely because of a long sequence of new ideas and adaptations. Nonetheless, for the historical record to be useful in a scientific sense, we must go beyond the more qualitative efforts of historians and philosophers. If we are interested in empirical findings with the most firm basis, we should rather focus on those studies which utilize *historiometry* (Simonton, 1984). Historiometry is the discipline of quantifying historical data for the purpose of testing scientific hypotheses. In the present review we shall examine those general principles of individual creativity and political leadership which are to be found in historiometric literature. By thus concentrating on the most objective, quantitative, and nomothetic investigations, our understanding of the processes underlying innovation should be more solid.

Lessons of Historiometry

In reviewing the chief substantive findings of historiometric research, we shall center attention on three main topics. We begin with an examination of developmental influences on leadership and creativity, and then turn to personality or individual differences. Finally, we close with an overview of significant cultural, social, and political processes.

DEVELOPMENTAL INFLUENCES

Our review of age-related findings looks at (a) the impact of early personal experiences on the emergence of eminent leaders and creators, (b) the sociocultural context of creative development, and (c) the relationship between age and achievement in positions of creativity and leadership.

Early Personal Experiences of the Eminent

In a book entitled *Cradles of Eminence,* Goertzel and Goertzel (1962) attempted to detect the childhood environment most likely to generate eminent individuals in all fields of human endeavor. They carefully studied the lives of over 400 twentieth-century creators and leaders. The Goertzels found, among other things, that the eminent are not likely to come from large metropolitan centers. Their homes feature a patent love for learning, even though the eminent do not seem to like schools and schoolteachers. Curiously, a common background connects dictators, military men, and poets; these three groups all have the highest percentages of overpossessive or dominating mothers.

Many years later the Goertzels expanded their efforts by studying a new sample of over 300 personalities who had attained eminence since the 1962 investigation (Goertzel et al., 1978). They included many new variables, such as birth order and adult sexual preferences. Furthermore, they attempted to see if the requisite childhood background varied from one field of endeavor to another. For instance, although only children and first-born children tended to be overrepresented among the eminent, political figures departed from this norm: In-between children frequently became political figures, whereas only children rarely did. Politicians also differed in their more favorable attitude toward school, their more conventional life style, and their greater stability (with politicians having lower rates of divorce and suicide). In stark contrast, literary figures looked much more like the stereotypical creative genius. Their homes were much less happy or stable, their dislike of school most pronounced, their unconventionality quite conspicuous, and their tendency to suicide and divorce appreciably stronger.

While the Goertzels looked at many variables all at once, other historiometricians have focused on a smaller number of variables that fit within a specified theoretical framework. Let two examples suffice. First, Eisenstadt (1978) proposed a psychodynamic theory which predicts a relationship between eminence and the early loss of one or both parents. To test the theory, he applied an objective measure of orphanhood to a sample of 699 eminent persons. These persons represented a wide range of fields, from politics to music. Eisenstadt found that these eminent individuals had rates of orphanhood exceeding almost any other comparison group.

The second illustration is the theory of Matossian and Schafer (1977) concerning the relationship among family tensions, fertility rates, and political violence. They hypothesized that the population growth accelerated by high fertility rates tends to increase tensions within the family. The increase of negative emotional interactions within the family then raises the probability of political violence, especially insofar as father-son conflicts provide the paradigm for larger-scale revolutions and rebellions. To test their theory, Matossian and Schafer not only obtained data on political violence and population growth in Europe and the United States, but also gathered a sample of eminent writers (literary figures tend to write a lot about their family lives). Using these autobiographical data, Matossian and Schafer developed a complex coding scheme for quantifying the quality and intensity of interpersonal relationships within the family. For the most part, the data seemed to support the basic predictions. Matossian and Schafer may thus have given the social forecaster a predictive potential. If their theory survives further historiometric scrutiny, the study of family conflicts may provide indicators for predicting future political turmoil.

Sociocultural Context of Creative Development

Though personal experiences during childhood no doubt play a major part in the emergence of innovators, the larger and more impersonal sociocultural milieu must prove influential as well. Indeed, the rise and fall of creativity during the course of civilization are often attributed to underlying fluctuations in political, economic, or social conditions. A pioneer historiometric examination of this possibility was made in a pilot study by Naroll and his students (Naroll et al., 1971). Using the lists of creative individuals recorded by Kroeber (1944), Naroll et al. measured the influence of wealth, geographical expansion, democratic government, and external challenge. They found that there was a positive correlation between the amount of creative activity and the degree of political fragmentation. That is, those centuries when a civilization area was broken into a large number of independent states tended to produce a larger number of eminent creators in the arts and sciences. What makes this finding particularly impressive is that it was found to hold over two millennia of history and across four civilizations (China, India, the Middle East, and Europe). Hence, the probability is very high that increases in political unification are paid for by a decline in artistic and scientific innovation.

The main difficulty with the study by Naroll et al. is that its temporal unit of analysis—the century—is far too large to determine the precise way in which the sociocultural system influences the individual creator. There are two major possibilities: On the one hand, political and social events may affect the developmental period of a creator's life, raising or lowering the growth of a creative potential in the individual's personality. On the other hand, sociocultural events may influence the productive period of a creator's life, either retarding or enhancing the active expression of creative impulses in adulthood. Clearly, this distinction is critical. If a certain political event only affects the adult productivity of a creator, its effect will be direct and immediately obvious. Yet if a political event operates only during the childhood and adolescence of a potential innovator, the aid or damage done may not be evident until many years later—after it is far too late to rectify the situation.

"Generational analysis" nonetheless permits an assessment of whether or not a given sociocultural event is more likely to influence youthful creative development or creative productivity in adulthood (Simonton, 1975b). Rather than employ centuries as the temporal unit of analysis, this design utilizes twenty-year periods to which eminent individuals are assigned according to an estimated peak productive age of forty years. Generational analysis applied to a wide range of variables finds a provocative result: The vast majority of sociocultural events function as developmental influences (Simonton, 1978a). Accordingly, the full repercussions of a historical event, whether for good or ill, may not emerge for a couple of decades. The following four sociocultural conditions appear to have a particularly significant impact on creative development:

(1) Naroll et al. (1971), as already indicated, showed that major creative activity is most likely to occur when a civilization is broken into a large number of sovereign political units. Simonton (1975b), in a study of over 5,000 eminent creators in Western civilization, demonstrated that political fragmentation affects youthful creative development more than mature creative productivity. The reason for this lagged effect evidently is that the development of a young person's creative potential may require exposure to cultural diversity. Yet

political unification of a civilization normally cannot proceed without first achieving some degree of cultural homogenization, especially in terms of language, religion, and customs.

(2) Such civil disturbances as popular revolts and revolutions nurture creative development, particularly if these violent mass movements are directed against large empire states (Simonton, 1975b). In other words, if an individual must grow up in a large imperial political system, his or her chances of becoming creative are enhanced if that empire is shaken by political turmoil among the masses (for example, suppressed national minorities). This finding is consistent with Kroeber's (1944) linkage of creativity with nationalism, and with Toynbee's (1946) connection of a stable empire with creative decline. The result also dovetails well with the previous finding concerning political fragmentation. If it is true that creative development requires an environment of cultural diversity, and that political unification tends to undermine cultural diversity, then mass revolts, revolutions, and rebellions may ameliorate the detrimental effect of the homogeneous empire by intensifying the degree of diversity. Nationalistic revolts of minority groups would have this advantageous influence, as would the ideological conflicts usually attending popular revolutions.

(3) Sometimes political turmoil does not engage the masses, but rather solely involves a few select individuals who already occupy powerful civil or military positions. Such internecine struggles among those in power may entail military coups d'état, dynastic conflicts among rival claimants to the throne, or palace coups. Unlike civil disturbances, such political instability has a deleterious effect on creative development in virtually all areas of creativity (Simonton, 1975b, 1976e). Perhaps for most creative endeavors to proceed, the individual must develop an appropriate belief that personal effort can have some impact on the world. Such a belief presupposes that human society is at least partially rational and predictable, an attitude that would be seriously weakened in any youth exposed to capricious political instability.

(4) A young potential innovator can draw encouragement from mature innovators actively producing during the youth's developmental period. Put differently, potential creators in one generation can use actual creators in the previous generation as role models. Hence it comes as no surprise that role-model availability has a significant impact on the emergence of creative individuals (Simonton, 1975b). The number of creators in a given generation is in fact a positive function of the number of creators in the preceding *two* generations. This fact is important, for it implies that any factor that

directly influences creativity in one generation will indirectly affect creativity in the next two generations. For example, by depressing the amount of creativity in one generation, political instability will indirectly harm innovation in the following two generations. Since political instability itself operates only after a time lag of one generation, this result means that the detrimental aftermath of coups d'état will carry over for three generations—a time span of over a half century.

Age and Achievement

So far we have looked at the role of early developmental experiences, whether personal or impersonal in nature. Historiometric techniques have also been applied to the study of the adult careers of eminent individuals. Biographical and historical information can thus be quantified to investigate how such factors as warfare, revolution, physical illness, biographical stress, and social reinforcement affect the productivity of innovators (Simonton, 1977a). Yet the most obvious question is how productivity, influence, or power varies according to the age of the eminent creator or leader. Is there a peak age for producing creative masterpieces or for making shrewd political decisions? The classic attempt to address this issue is Lehman's *Age and Achievement* (1958). For a large number of activities, Lehman plotted the relationship between a historical figure's age and his or her creativity and leadership. In the case of creative endeavors, he discovered that the peak productive age tended to fall in the late thirties, even though the precise optimum varied from one discipline to another.

When Lehman turned to leadership, several interesting results emerged. In the first place, the peak age for political influence lags twenty years behind the peak age for creative productivity; most leaders attain their highest influence in their late fifties rather than their later thirties. This result holds for such leadership areas as American presidents, the presidents of various world republics, members of British cabinets, chief ministers of England, American ambassadors, naval commanders, and justices of the U.S. Supreme Court. As in the instance of creativity, however, some exceptions do appear. Thus, military leaders in land battles tend to be in their late forties. In the case of religion, a very dramatic contrast appears: The leaders of most established religious institutions, such as the Roman Catholic Church, are in their eighties, whereas founders of religions or religious sects tend to be in their late thirties. In a sense, those leaders who formulate new religious doctrines are more similar to creators than to other leaders as far as the optimum age of influence is concerned. The same is true in politics. Older leaders are most prominent when a group is "long established, firmly entrenched, and relatively complacent or satisfied with the status quo" (Lehman, 1958: 282). Nevertheless, when a group is in its formative period, or when substantial unrest disrupts a well established group, the younger leaders are much more conspicuous.

Lehman's conclusions find support in more recent research (for example, Simonton, 1977a). As an example, the youthful age peak for poets has been shown to be valid over the past two thousand years for all the world's literary traditions (Simonton, 1975a). Many of Lehman's conclusions are also consistent with a number of related findings. A recent historiometric test of "Planck's principle" may serve as an illustration (Hull et al., 1978). The founder of quantum physics, Max Planck, argued that new scientific ideas do not win acceptance by converting older scientists, but rather by recruiting younger scientists who still have a creative receptiveness to new ideas. A detailed examination of the reception of Darwin's evolutionary theory reveals that Planck's principle has some merit. Those scientists who had accepted Darwin's theory within ten years or less averaged around forty years of age, whereas those who still rejected evolutionary theory after ten years were over fifty years old. Hence, not only is forty a peak age for innovation, but it is also a peak age for the acceptance of innovation. The two processes of innovation and innovation acceptance are thus somewhat complementary.

INDIVIDUAL DIFFERENCES

One of the key aims of historiometric research is to determine exactly how individual-level differences affect sociocultural change. Here we shall focus on four broad personality dimensions: intelligence, productivity, motives and values, and cognitive complexity.

Intelligence and Achieved Eminence

Many historiometricians have focused on attempts to discern the relationship between intelligence and achieved eminence as a creator or leader. This research can be said to have begun with Galton's (1870) classic, *Hereditary Genius*. Galton tried to show that achieved eminence runs in families, and hence that superior ability is inherited. He was not altogether successful in his goal. Although achieved eminence can be inherited in some areas (for example, politics, law, and music), other activities seem to be largely devoid of heritability (for example, warfare, science, and poetry) (Galton, 1870). Moreover, Galton did not adequately address the problem of environmental influences and personal contacts, factors that may explain far more than inherited intellect.

A more convincing case may be found in Woods's *Heredity in Royalty* (1906). Woods first gathered extensive genealogies for the principal royal houses of Europe and then estimated both the intellectual ability and the moral character of all members, whether male or female, monarch or princeling. Besides showing that a positive association existed between intelligence and morality (see also Thorndike, 1936), Woods demonstrated that both traits tended to be inherited. Indeed, the precise manner in which heredity operated seemed consistent with the predictions of genetic theory. Woods also attempted to show that environmental influences play a relatively minor part. Even though Woods did not draw such a conclusion, the implication is clear that monarchy has some advantages as a political system. As long as the ruling house has "good genes," the principle of hereditary succession promises competence in the head of state.

Both Galton and Woods were more concerned with showing that intelligence is inherited than with showing that intelligence actually influences achieved eminence. The study that Cox made of *The Early Mental Traits of Three Hundred Geniuses* (1926) stands out as a truly remarkable contribution in this regard. Unlike her predecessors, Cox undertook the stupendous task of measuring the "intelligence quotient" (IQ) of 301 of the most eminent figures of modern Western history. All major fields of leadership and creativity were represented, and the sample ranged in time from Leonardo da Vinci to President Ulysses S. Grant. Biographical information about these 301 geniuses was meticulously gathered and coded. The outcome was an estimated IQ score for each historical figure, a datum intrinsically intriguing by itself. Among leaders, Robespierre had an IQ of 170, Admiral Nelson 150, Luther 170, and Disraeli 165. Among creators, Newton had an IQ of 190, Descartes 180, Cervantes 155, Michelangelo 180, and Mozart 165. Yet Cox went far beyond the mere calculation of IQs, for she also attempted to demonstrate that these IQ estimates correlated with the achieved eminence of each genius.

Unfortunately, at the time Cox did her study, sophisticated multivariate techniques were not available to tease out the full implications of the data. Recently, Simonton (1976a) returned to Cox's 301 geniuses. Employing advanced statistical controls, he was able to show that even though the 301 geniuses were in fact very bright, with an average IQ of 164, there is no correlation between IQ and achieved eminence. The problem is that the sample is probably far too selected for such a correlation to be evident. Several other relationships were nonetheless identified. For one thing, whether or not an individual attends college or even finishes high school has a strong impact on achieved eminence, but the effect differs between leaders and creators. In the latter instance, achieved eminence increases with formal education up to a certain optimum point (around two years of college); thereafter, additional formal education is associated with a decline in achieved eminence. Evidently, creators need enough formal education to render their intellect capable of productive thought, but excessive training induces an overcommitment to traditional views and techniques. For leaders, the effect is more dramatic. There is a strictly negative relationship between formal education and achieved eminence as a leader.[1] Although leaders tend to like school more than creators do, the truly eminent leaders are not very likely to have doctorates.

Another finding concerns the effect of intellectual versatility. The more versatile the leader, the greater the achieved eminence. Leaders like Franklin, Jefferson, and Disraeli earn extra points for their ventures outside politics, whether into science or the arts. We might style this the "John F. Kennedy effect," for the fame that accrued to that president may have been partly the result of the unusual range of his accomplishments, from military heroism to prize-winning authorship.

The thought of John F. Kennedy brings us to another finding: To formal education and versatility must also be added life span (Simonton, 1976a). There may be a "patriarch effect" which gives those leaders or creators who manage to live to a ripe old age a few extra points, perhaps due to the increased number of generations under their influence. At the same time, creators or leaders who die very young may produce a "tragedy effect." That is, lamentations over the individual's unrealized promise or potential may take the place of actual accomplishments, and the brevity of life may truncate the opportunity for accumulating failures. Thus, the reputation of a creator like Pascal or a leader like Robespierre may actually have benefited from an early death. The data show that both effects operate; the most famous leaders and creators tend to be those who either died unusually young or who survived and became living monuments to their own past.

Returning to intellectual characteristics, one further result should be mentioned: Leaders are less intelligent than creators (Simonton,

1976a). Apparently, a leader cannot afford to be too intelligent, since a leader who talks over the heads of his or her followers will shortly be without followers. Creators are in quite another position. An artistic or scientific genius has the option of creating for a select few, and even for posterity alone. In contrast to a leader, a creator does not have to be understood in his or her own time.

Productivity

One of the hallmarks of eminent creativity is exceptional productivity. Albert Einstein had some 248 publications to his credit, for example. Part of this immense productivity is a result of the fact that creative genius tends to be very precocious, with productivity beginning at a phenomenally early age (Dennis, 1954a, 1954b; Simonton, 1977b). The classic case is Mozart, who composed his first work at the age of six. Another factor is the productive longevity of creative individuals. A genius not only begins early but ends very late in life, usually after about a half-century of effort (Albert, 1975; Simonton, 1977b). Pablo Picasso, for instance, devoted over three-quarters of a century to painting. It would nonetheless be wrong to infer that the exceptional lifetime productivity of innovators is simply due to uncommon career length. The rate of productivity per year is also characteristically high. For example, Nobel laureates in science publish over two times as much per year as their colleagues who are almost as distinguished but are nonlaureates (Zuckerman, 1977). Hence, creative individuals produce earlier, end productivity later, and have higher rates of output. Finally, this quantity does ultimately relate to perceived quality. Though it is no doubt true that there exist prolific nonentities and procrastinating major minds, by and large the relationship between quality and quantity is very high. In science, the total number of publications is thus a good predictor of whether or not a given scientist will be honored with an entry in a standard reference work (Dennis, 1954a; see also Simonton, 1977b).

This contrast between a prolific and a nonprolific innovator is dramatic. Creative productivity is not distributed according to the normal bell-shaped curve, as is the case of intellectual or physical abilities. The distribution is highly skewed. In fact, an inductive statement, Lotka's Law, asserts that the number of people who produce n publications is inversely proportional to n^2 (Price, 1963: ch. 2). Hence, the number of creators who publish only once is huge, whereas the number who publish as much as Einstein is quite tiny. A small percentage of creators account for a large percentage of all innovations in any given field. As a rough summary, the most productive 10 percent of the individuals in any field account for almost 50 percent of all publications, while the bottom half of the individuals in a field account for only around 15 percent or less (Dennis, 1955). Stated in terms of another principle known as Price's Law, half of all contributions are produced by the square root of the total number of contributors to a field (Price, 1963: ch. 2). If there are 100 researchers in a given area, for example, then half of all the advances in that area can be attributed to about 10 individuals. The upshot of this imbalance in individual productivity is that creativity is more elitist than many would like. This elitism is probably the combined outcome of competition for the very restricted resources and publication outlets (Simon, 1955; Price, 1976), and of an underlying distribution of intellectual abilities (Allison and Stewart, 1974).

Curiously, to date no effort seems to have been made to show whether or not equivalents of Lotka's or Price's Law apply to leadership as well. The only possible exception is Pareto's Law of income distribution, which does fit the broad elitist scheme (Price, 1963: ch. 2). Yet it seems that the same principles would apply to the influence of political leaders, too.

Motives and Values

Some historiometricians have attempted to measure individual differences in underlying motives or values to determine what their effect is on the sociocultural system. The most impressive research program in this vein is described in McClelland's *The Achieving Society* (1961). McClelland and his colleagues attempted to show that a strong relationship exists between the need for achievement and economic prosperity in any society. To make their case, cross-cultural and laboratory research was complemented with a large number of transhistorical studies. Such inquiries included ancient Greece, Spain between the thirteenth and twentieth centuries, and England in the three centuries leading to the Industrial Revolution (McClelland, 1961: ch. 4). Achievement motives were usually measured by applying content analysis to such primary sources as imaginative literature and visual art. Economic prosperity was gauged by such indicators as shipping and coal imports. McClelland concluded that the rise and fall of a nation can be partly explained in terms of the ups and downs in the populace's need to achieve.

Since personal motives or values may also influence the course of political events, some investigators have focused on the beliefs and drives of political leaders, such as American presidents. An example is an exploratory study of American inaugural addresses by Donley and Winter (1972). Drawing upon the same research tradition found in McClelland's (1961) work, a coding scheme was created for measuring the amount of need for achievement and need for power (see also Winter, 1973). Donley and Winter then examined whether or not needs for achievement and power could be used to predict the course of a president's administration. One finding was that those presidents who have the strongest need for power are more likely to engage the United States in war, to have many cabinet changes, and to be the object of assassination attempts (Winter, 1973: ch. 7). Although there is still a long way to go before we can effectively predict the political future of American presidents, this approach represents an initial quantitative effort in that direction (see also Simonton, 1981a; Wendt and Light, 1976).

A more recent study by Etheredge (1978) further exemplifies the potential benefits of this type of research. Etheredge was interested in how personality variables affect American foreign policy. He examined a large number of intra-administration debates from 1898 to 1968 to ascertain whether or not the position advocated by a given policymaker fit with that person's own disposition in interpersonal relationships. A quantitative examination of American presidents, cabinet secretaries, and advisers gave support to the hypothesis: Highly dominant policymakers are more likely to advocate the use of coercion and threat in foreign policy, and personal extroversion is strongly associated with the advocacy of a more conciliatory policy toward the Soviet Union and the Soviet bloc. Personality does indeed influence political decision making—sometimes in ways that do not best serve the national interest.

Cognitive Complexity

Suedfeld has launched a research program on the role of personal conceptual or integrative complexity in political events. The personality variable of cognitive complexity has often been associated with creativity on both theoretical and empirical grounds, but Suedfeld's research is the first significant attempt to discern the repercussions of cognitive complexity in the crucial decision making of historical political leaders. The value of this historiometric extension can be readily appreciated in two of his papers.

Suedfeld's work first investigated how changes in conceptual complexity might be necessary for the long-term success of revolutionary leaders (Suedfeld and Rank, 1976). To carry off a successful revolution, Suedfeld hypothesized, the leader must exhibit a low degree of conceptual complexity. In other words, during the period of revolutionary strife, it is highly advantageous for the leader to be dogmatically single-minded in outlook. But once the revolutionary movement achieves its goal of seizing power, this same dogmatism proves detrimental to the maintenance of newly acquired power. The complexities of running a government demand more flexible, refined, and integrated perspectives on domestic and foreign affairs. Hence, the revolutionaries who stay in power must display a shift toward greater conceptual complexity. To test this predicted shift, Suedfeld calculated from archival materials conceptual complexity scores for nineteen leaders in five successful revolutions. The results confirmed the hypothesis.

A second study concentrated on the integrative complexity of official communications during international crises (Suedfeld and Tetlock, 1977). Integrative complexity as a dimension similar to conceptual complexity is "characterized at one pole by simple responses, gross distinctions, rigidity, and restricted information usage, and at the other by complexity, fine distinctions, flexibility, and extensive information search and usage" (1977: 169). The study hypothesized that information crises ending in war would feature diplomatic messages with very low integrative complexity. By comparison, a high degree of integrative complexity in diplomatic communications would raise the chance for a peaceful resolution of the conflict. To verify this prediction, Suedfeld calculated complexity scores for messages during two crises that ended in war (1914 and 1950) and three crises that were resolved peacefully (1911, 1948, 1962). The outcome supported the hypothesis: Those crises resulting in war were characterized by the significantly lower complexity of the diplomatic messages issued by governmental leaders.

SOCIOCULTURAL PROCESSES

The previous two sections have concentrated on the individual within the context of the greater sociocultural system. We reverse this perspective now to look at more massive cultural, social, and political movements. We first investigate the issue of the relative significance of genius versus Zeitgeist. Afterwards we can examine research on cyclical movements and political violence.

Genius versus Zeitgeist

Almost any given historical event can be interpreted from two contrasting viewpoints. On the one hand, history can be seen as the product of a few exceptional leaders or creators. This theory of history is frequently associated with Thomas Carlyle, whose essay, *On Heroes*, contains the extreme claim that general history "is at bottom the History of the Great Men who have worked here" (1841: 1). On the other hand, different observers of human affairs see the individual as more epiphenomenal, a mere symptom of far more massive social forces. According to this view, both the creator and the leader are creatures of the prevailing Zeitgeist, or the "spirit of the times." A classic defense of this position is the Epilogue of Leo Tolstoy's *War and Peace* (1865–69/1952). But which perspective is more justified by the facts?

Sociocultural conditions undoubtedly influence the ultimate impact of thinkers on intellectual history. One study examined over 2,000 Western philosophers from the time of ancient Greece until the early twentieth century (Simonton, 1976e). The specific goal of the investigation was to determine why some thinkers are much more eminent than others (that is, why some philosophers have a more massive influence on the thought of subsequent generations). It was found that certain sociocultural environments are most conducive to the emergence of truly notable thinkers. For example, major minds are most prone to develop in an intellectual vacuum; that is, during periods in which there is a conspicuous dearth of active philosophical discussion. Such a finding shows that the philosopher is partly made by the prevailing ideological Zeitgeist. Evidence nonetheless emerged for a genius position as well. In the first place, the belief structure that a given philosopher advocates has critical consequences for the eventual judgment of posterity. Unlike their more obscure or esoteric colleagues, the great thinkers of history tend to deal with a wide range of philosophical issues, advance extremist positions, and combine beliefs in unusual and what may seem at first glance inconsistent ways. In short, the major intellect tends to be a manifest risk-taker.

This picture is further supported by an examination of the relationship between a thinker's beliefs and the dominant ideological Zeitgeist. Contrary to what is often maintained, intellectuals do not attain eminence by epitomizing the most popular philosophical views of their generation. Rather than representing the current Zeitgeist, major thinkers offer minority and often unpopular beliefs. This independence from contemporaries is not some form of precursiveness.

The most famous philosophers are not ahead of their times, but rather behind their times; their dedication seems to be toward integrating or synthesizing the vast intellectual heritage of preceding generations rather than exploring preliminary orientations for the future. In any event, even though there can be no doubt that the sociocultural milieu affects the attainment of posterity's applause, the philosophical genius has some volitional latitude too.

Another phenomenon relevant to the Zeitgeist-genius question is the occurrence of "multiples" in science and technology. To offer some of the most famous examples: The calculus was independently created by Newton and Leibniz, oxygen was independently and almost simultaneously generated by Scheele and Priestley, Neptune was simultaneously but independently predicted by Leverrier and Adams, and the theory of evolution by natural selection was independently put forward by Darwin and Wallace. Since such multiple discoveries and inventions have occurred frequently, many behavioral scientists have concluded that this phenomenon bolsters a Zeitgeist view of historical events (Merton, 1961). Once science and technology reach a certain point, the emergence of any given contribution becomes highly probable, and hence the individual scientist is largely irrelevant to technoscientific progress (Ogburn and Thomas, 1922).

Two historiometric investigations challenge this traditional interpretation (Simonton, 1978b, 1979a). The appearance of such multiples seems to be largely a matter of pure chance or coincidence. Their frequency distribution is almost perfectly predicted by a Poisson probability model, a model that applies to rare concurrences of events. Moreover, those scientists or inventors who are most productive also tend to participate in the most multiples (as would be expected on the basis of chance alone). Despite this and other evidence for a predominantly random model, we might conclude that Zeitgeist and genius both exert some modest influence on the emergence of independent discovery and invention. For instance, because the more eminent scientists are probably more in tune with the technoscientific Zeitgeist, they participate in more multiples, even if we control for their exceptional creative productivity.

Historiometric research on political leadership also has implications for the debate on Zeitgeist versus genius. The potential impact of political leadership is revealed by an investigation of absolute monarchs. The institution of the absolute monarch offers a unique opportunity for assessing the effect a single individual can exert on an entire nation. Only twentieth-century totalitarian dictators have ever enjoyed as much or more power than such rulers as Louis XIV,

Frederick the Great, or Peter the Great. Yet unlike modern dictatorships, which tend to be rather ephemeral, absolute monarchies
have lasted in several nations long enough to provide ideal test cases.

Woods measured two variables in *The Influence of Monarchs* (1913).
One was the personal strength of hundreds of kings and queens in
the major European hereditary monarchies. The other was the cultural, economic, military, and political power of the state under each
reign. After calculating the correlation between personal and national
strength, Woods concluded that "strong, mediocre, and weak monarchs are associated with strong, mediocre, and weak periods respectively" (1913: 246).

Sorokin (1926) also published some findings on monarchs as well
as other rulers, such as Roman emperors, prime ministers, presidents,
and popes. One interesting discovery was that those rulers who exert
the greatest influence on the course of human events tend to have
the longest reigns. But Sorokin also discovered a more tragic aspect
of being a political ruler: Not only are rulers highly likely to suffer
death by violence, but even those who die of natural causes have
shorter life expectancies, possibly due to the severe stress of decision
making. Indeed, Sorokin found that the younger the monarch upon
ascension to the throne, the shorter his or her expected life span.

Perhaps the genius-Zeitgeist question is nowhere more dramatically raised than on the field of battle. Although the credit for victory
is more frequently assigned to the commanding general, the Zeitgeist
could conceivably play a much larger part. Tolstoy's *War and Peace*
(1865–69/1952: 448) contains a detailed analysis of the epic battle of
Borodino in which he attempts to show that the ultimate military
decision "was not decided by Napoleon's will but occurred independently of him, in accord with the will of hundreds of thousands of
people who took part in the common action." One historiometric
study focused on Napoleon to determine the relative adequacy of
genius and Zeitgeist explanations of military success (Simonton,
1979b). As one might expect from a genius perspective, Napoleon
had a much higher success rate than did his French military colleagues
during the French Revolutionary and Napoleonic wars (85 versus 47
percent). Yet, in a manner quite fitting with the Zeitgeist standpoint,
Napoleon's success rate for any given year in his career correlated
highly with the success rates of other French generals. In other words,
although Napoleon was more successful than his colleagues, the ups
and downs in his career closely followed the ebb and flow of French
military might on the national level.

A second historiometric study of 326 land battles suggests a broader
degree of generality for this basic conclusion (Simonton, 1980a). It

strove to predict two crucial military variables—namely, which side would win the battle and which side would inflict the larger "kill-ratio" on its opponent. Both criteria of success were hypothesized to be a function of individual and situational factors. The study showed that tactical victory on the battlefield went to the side with more years of experience, longer winning streaks, greater willingness to take the offensive, and more equal-status commanders. Thus, victory is determined more by individual variables than by situational variables. In contrast, a kill-ratio advantage went to the side with a larger army and a divided command, and whose general had the most cumulative victories. Hence, superiority in the infliction of battle casualties is more influenced by situations than by individual variables. Translated into broader terms, military genius plays a critical role in victory or defeat, but the sociocultural context has greater repercussions for the question of which side leaves a larger proportion of casualties on the battlefield.

It is clear from the above historiometric research that the genius-versus-Zeitgeist issue cannot be dispatched with a facile either-or answer. Not only do both individual and situational factors participate in historical change, but chance may have a significant part as well.

Cyclical Movements

In a manner quite consistent with a Zeitgeist theory, the temporal fluctuations in historical events seem to be governed by large trends over which a single individual can exert no effective control. The most intriguing are the possible cyclical fluctuations in political and cultural events. In the general cultural domain, Kroeber (1944) attempted to show that creativity in the arts and sciences rises and falls to form specific aperiodic configurations in a given civilization. Sorokin (1937–41) tried to demonstrate that the prevailing ideological Zeitgeist for all creative activities fluctuates in grand alternating cycles of sensate and ideational personalities and sociocultural systems (see Simonton, 1976c). Other researchers have concentrated on more specialized creative activities rather than on massive systemic cycles. Some have studied cycles in the content of literary creativity (Martindale, 1975), others the ups and downs of changes in fashion (Richardson and Kroeber, 1940; Robinson, 1976, Simonton, 1978c), and still others cyclical patterns in scientific discovery (Rainoff, 1929).

Why do such cyclical movements appear in history? There are two principal schools of thought. Some behavioral scientists attribute cycles to extrinsic or environmental influences—that is, to cycles in causal antecedents. Thus, Gray (1958, 1966) has proposed that the configurations observed by Kroeber (1944) in cultural creativity are but the effect of underlying political, economic, and social cycles (see also Simonton, 1976c, 1977c). Similarly, aperiodic movements in political violence have been explained in terms of population pressures (Lee cited in Sorokin, 1937–41, vol. 3). The chief difficulty with accepting the extrinsic perspective is that the explanation of cyclical phenomena is only transferred to some other cyclical phenomena. The other approach explicates cyclical fluctuations in terms of intrinsic or dialectic factors. Sorokin (1937–41) maintained that the shift from a sensate to an ideational Zeitgeist (or the reverse) was propelled by progressive dissatisfaction with the limitations imposed by a given ideological mentality. Kroeber (1944) explained the rise and fall of creative activity in terms of the development and exhaustion of an initial esthetic or scientific paradigm.

Sociocultural cycles may well be a function of both extrinsic and intrinsic causes (Simonton, 1981b). Simonton (1975b) has shown this to be the case for cultural creativity. The aperiodic cycles in the number of eminent creators per generation are determined partly by the intrinsic intergenerational effect of the availability of role models, and partly by the extrinsic impact of cycles in political instability. Cyclical changes in the philosophical Zeitgeist also result from both dialectic and environmental causes. On the one hand, such philosophical beliefs as empiricism, skepticism, materialism, evolutionism, nominalism, individualism, and hedonism rise and fall with the slow cyclical shift in political fragmentation (Simonton, 1976e). On the other hand, fluctuations in empiricism are partially responsible for the cyclical changes in materialism and individualism (Simonton, 1978c). Hence, the ups and downs in the number of materialists and individualists are caused both by an external reaction to the number of sovereign states and by an internal response to the number of empiricists.

War and Revolution

One of the central topics for historiometric investigation may be political violence, whether international or intranational. Many political leaders read history to learn how to avoid war. Most historiometric studies treat either the causes or the effects of political violence. For example, Winter (1973: 190–196) has indicated a relationship between a nation's tendency to go to war and the appearance of power imagery in its national literature. Another study revealed that when skeptical and materialistic philosophies emerge, there is an increase in warfare around two decades later (Simonton,

1976e). Taken together, these investigations suggest that a cynical or Machiavellian Zeitgeist may favor the use of war to achieve policy ends.

For our current purposes, the most interesting question is how political violence, whether foreign or domestic, affects the creation and diffusion of new ideas. One recent study demonstrated that balance-of-power and defensive wars inhibit scientific discovery and technological inventions (Simonton, 1980b; also see Simonton, 1976b, 1976d). International and intranational political violence can even directly shape the course of women's dress fashions (Simonton, 1977c). At other times the consequences of warfare are more indirect and delayed. Nowhere is this more apparent than in the ways that violent political conflict affects the ideological Zeitgeist (Simonton, 1976e).

As pointed out earlier, generational analyses have shown that political events can operate as potent influences on the developmental phase of an individual's life. In particular, certain events may affect the ideological content of the individual's thinking, but it may require a couple of decades for this effect to materialize. Thus, twenty years after an international war, there appears to be a marked decrease in the number of thinkers who advocate empiricism, nominalism, singularism (individualism), temporalism (evolutionism), and hedonistic ethics. Since some of these beliefs are essential to the growth of science and technology, the implication is that warfare may harm technoscientific advance after a lag of two decades. Civil war has an even more fascinating effect; the occurrence of political violence within a nation tends to polarize beliefs on almost every major philosophical issue. Twenty years after civil disturbances, more advocates appear of both empiricism and rationalism-mysticism, materialism and idealism, eternalism and temporalism, nominalism and realism, singularism and universalism, determinism and indeterminism, principled ethics and hedonistic ethics—all polar opposites. It is as if the political conflicts of one generation reappear as the ideological conflicts of the next generation. Such shifts in ideological diversity may in turn alter the receptiveness of society to new ideas in general.

Conclusion

Judging from the foregoing review, we can quite meaningfully speak of a "creative society"—that is, a society that is exceptionally prone to originate new ideas and techniques, thereby being susceptible to innovation and sociocultural change. The creative society is the product of both intrinsic and extrinsic causes. In the case of extrinsic or external influences, we have seen that political conditions play a significant role in establishing the appropriate milieu for potential innovation. Warfare, for example, was shown to have a concurrent detrimental impact on scientific discovery and technological invention. Thus, to a certain extent, a creative society is at the mercy of the world's leaders. Moreover, the failings of political leadership can have consequences far into the future. As repeatedly pointed out, political events sometimes affect the creative development of the younger generation far more than they do the creative productivity of the older generation exposed to such events as adults. If a political system disintegrates into an unpredictable anarchy of coup d'état, countercoup, political assassination, and pervasive internecine conflict among members of the power elite, the negative repercussions may not be witnessed for a score or more years. A whole generation of potential creators will be missing.

Creative societies are subject to their own intrinsic growth patterns as well. The reality of an internal developmental logic is most apparent in the quasicyclic nature of many cultural phenomena. Although aperiodic fluctuations in discovery, invention, or imagination can be partly attributed to underlying movements in such external forces as the political context, such fluctuations partially result from the inner workings of role-model availability. Because the number of creative individuals in any given generation is a positive function of the number of creative individuals in the previous two generations, the ups and downs in social creativity have a built-in enertia. A creative society is therefore incapable of being either established or destroyed overnight. If an intellectually or esthetically stagnant society wishes to build its capacity for innovation, favorable measures (such as stabilizing the political system) may take far more than half a century to be fully realized. By the same token, if a nation's leaders make choices that discourage creative development, the children, grandchildren, and even great-grandchildren may all be punished for the sins of their progenitors.

The creative society consists of creative individuals. Indeed, we have noticed that a small percentage of persons account for an overwhelming majority of the contributions to any given field of creative activity. This productive elite is also characterized by a definite set of biographical experiences and personality traits. Even individual age has been seen to affect both the original conception of new ideas and the final acceptance of those ideas. The Zeitgeist is not potent enough to make even technoscientific progress inevitable without the participation of genius. Yet the manner in which individuals shape the course of innovation and sociocultural change can be quite complex. Political decisions of leaders, as we have seen, can have both an immediate and a delayed impact on creative development and productivity. Such decision making is affected by a leader's interpersonal style and conceptual complexity, and the scope of the leader's intentions is confined by situational variables. At the same time, creative individuals can provide the technological and ideological foundations of a political system. The prevailing philosophical Zeitgeist, for example, is not irrelevant to the incidence of war. Thus the creative society is the outcome of many intricate interactions of creators and leaders.

What makes these leader-creator interactions especially subtle is the fact that the consequences may take decades to materialize fully. Suppose we accept the suggestion that technological innovations ultimately cause accelerated population growth (Taagepera, 1979). On the individual level, this increase in effective fertility means larger families, with the concomitant increase of antagonistic father-son relationships (Matossian and Schafer, 1977). A couple of decades after the population spurt, there appears an increase in revolt and rebellion. A score of years after these popular disturbances, a new generation may emerge which is highly polarized on major ideological questions and far more creative (Simonton, 1978). Since this creativity includes science and technology as a subset, we have come full circle. Not only may the causal time lags be greatly due to the importance of developmental influences, but in addition the causal sequence may eventually reset itself back to the beginning in the formation of a large-scale feedback loop. Perhaps the most significant lesson of historiometry is that the creator-leader interactions that determine innovation tend to occur with such causal complexity and with such immense unfolding times.

NOTE

1. A more recent inquiry into American presidents found that there may be more similarity between leaders and creators than first meets the eye (Simonton, 1981a). The most idealistic and inflexible presidents tend to have either the least or the most formal education; moderate amounts of education are associated with far less dogmatism. The curve is virtually a mirror-image of that observed for creativity, a finding consistent with the idea that dogmatism and creativity are negatively related. Somewhere in the last couple of years of undergraduate training, students begin to become

less creative and more dogmatic. If some of these students become leaders, continued education will therefore affect their ability to be innovative.

REFERENCES

ALBERT, R. (1975) "Toward a behavioral definition of genius." American Psychologist 30 (February): 140–151.

ALLISON, P. D. and J. A. STEWART (1974) "Productivity differences among scientists: evidence for accumulative advantage." American Sociological Review 39 (August): 596–606.

CARLYLE, T. (1841) On Heroes, Hero-worship and the Heroic. London: Fraser.

COX, C. (1926) The Early Mental Traits of Three Hundred Geniuses. Stanford, CA: Stanford University Press.

DENNIS, W. (1955) "Variations in productivity among creative workers." Scientific Monthly 80 (April): 277–278.

——— (1954a) "Bibliographies of eminent scientists." Scientific Monthly 79 (September): 180–183.

——— (1954b) "Predicting scientific productivity in later decades from records of earlier decades." Journal of Gerontology 9 (October): 465–467.

DONLEY, R. W. and D. G. WINTER (1972) "Measuring the motives of public officials at a distance: an exploratory study of American presidents." Behavioral Science 15: 227–236.

EISENSTADT, J. M. (1978) "Parental loss and genius." American Psychologist 33 (March): 211–223.

ETHEREDGE, L. S. (1978) "Personality effects on American foreign policy, 1898–1968: a test of interpersonal generalization theory." American Political Science Review 78 (June): 434–451.

GALTON, F. (1870) Hereditary Genius. New York: Appleton.

GOERTZEL, V. and M. G. GOERTZEL (1962) Cradles of Eminence. Boston: Little, Brown.

GOERTZEL, M. G., V. GOERTZEL, and T. G. GOERTZEL (1978) Three Hundred Eminent Personalities. San Francisco: Jossey-Bass.

GRAY, C. E. (1966) "A measurement of creativity in Western civilization." American Anthropologist 68 (December): 1384–1417.

——— (1958) "An analysis of Graeco-Roman development: the epicyclical evolution of Graeco-Roman civilization." American Anthropologist 60: 13–31.

HULL, D. L., P. D. TESSNER, and A. M. DIAMOND (1978) "Planck's principle: Do younger scientists accept new scientific ideas with greater alacrity than older scientists?" Science 202 (November 17): 717–723.

KROEBER, A. (1944) Configurations of Culture Growth. Berkeley: University of California Press.

LEHMAN, H. C. (1958) Age and Achievement. Princeton, NJ: Princeton University Press.

MARTINDALE, C. (1975) Romantic Progression. Washington, DC: Hemisphere.

MATOSSIAN, M. K. and W. D. SCHAFER (1977) "Family, fertility, and political violence, 1700-1900." Journal of Social History 11 (2): 137-178.

MERTON, R. K. (1961) "Singletons and multiples in scientific discovery: a chapter in the sociology of science." Proceedings of the American Philosophical Society 105: 470-486.

NAROLL, R., E. C. BENJAMIN, F. K. FOHL, M. J. FRIED, R. E. HILDRETH, and J. M. SCHAFER (1971) "Creativity: a cross-historical pilot survey." Journal of Cross-Cultural Psychology 2 (June): 181–188.

OGBURN, W. R. and D. THOMAS (1922) "Are inventions inevitable?" Political Science Quarterly 37 (March): 83–93.

PRICE, D. (1976) "A general theory of bibliometric and other cumulative advantage processes." Journal of the American Society for Information Science 27 (September-October): 292-306.

_____ (1963) Little Science, Big Science. New York: Columbia University Press.

RAINOFF, T. J. (1929) "Wave-like fluctuations of creative productivity in the development of West-European physics in the eighteenth and nineteenth centuries." Isis 12 (2): 287–319.

RICHARDSON, J. and A. L. KROEBER (1940) "Three centuries of women's dress fashions: a quantitative analysis." Anthropological Records 5 (October): 111–150.

ROBINSON, D. E. (1976) "Fashions in shaving and trimming of the beard: the men of the Illustrated London News, 1842–1972." American Journal of Sociology 81 (March): 1133–1141.

SIMON, H. A. (1955) "On a class of skew distribution functions." Biometrika 42 (December): 425–440.

SIMONTON, D. K. (1984) Genius, Creativity, and Leadership. Cambridge, MA: Harvard University Press.

_____ (1981a) "Presidential greatness and performance: can we predict leadership in the White House?" Journal of Personality 49 (September): 307–320.

_____ (1981b) "Creativity in Western civilization: intrinsic and extrinsic causes." American Anthropologist 83 (September): 628–630.

_____ (1980a) "Land battles, generals, and armies: individual and situational determinants of victory and casualties." Journal of Personality and Social Psychology 38 (January): 110–119.

_____ (1980b) "Techno-scientific activity and war: a yearly time-series analysis, 1500–1903 A.D." Scientometrics 2 (4): 251–255.

_____ (1979a) "Multiple discovery and inventions: Zeitgeist, genius, or chance?" Journal of Personality and Social Psychology 37 (September): 1603–1616.

_____ (1979b) "Was Napoleon a military genius? Score: Carlyle 1, Tolstoy 1." Psychological Reports 44 (January): 21–22.

_____ (1978a) "The eminent genius in history: the critical role of creative development." Gifted Child Quarterly 22 (Summer): 187–195.

_____ (1978b) "Independent discovery in science and technology: a closer look at the Poisson distribution." Social Studies of Science 8 (November): 521–532.

_____ (1978c) "Intergenerational stimulation, reaction, and polarization: a causal analysis of intellectual history." Social Behavior and Personality 6 (2): 247–251.

_____ (1977a) "Creative productivity, age, and stress: a biographical time-series analysis of 100 classical composers." Journal of Personality and Social Psychology 36 (November): 791–804.

_____ (1977b) "Eminence, creativity, and geographic marginality: a recursive structural equation model." Journal of Personality and Social Psychology 35 (November): 805–816.

_____ (1977c) "Women's fashions and war: a quantitative comment." Social Behavior and Personality 5 (2): 285–288.

———— (1976a) "Biographical determinants of achieved eminence: a multivariate approach to the Cox data." Journal of Personality and Social Psychology 33 (February): 218–226.

———— (1976b) "The causal relation between war and scientific discovery: an exploratory cross-national analysis." Journal of Cross-Cultural Psychology 7 (June): 133–144.

———— (1976c) "Does Sorokin's data support his theory? A study of generational fluctuations in philosophical beliefs." Journal for the Scientific Study of Religion 15 (June): 187–198.

———— (1976d) "Interdisciplinary and military determinants of scientific productivity: a cross-lagged correlation analysis." Journal of Vocational Behavior 9 (August): 53–62.

———— (1976e) "The sociopolitical context of philosophical beliefs: transhistorical causal analysis." Social Forces 54 (March): 513–523.

———— (1975a) "Age and literacy creativity: a cross-cultural and transhistorical survey." Journal of Cross-Cultural Psychology 6 (September): 259–277.

———— (1975b) "Sociocultural context of individual creativity: a transhistorical time-series analyses." Journal of Personality and Social Psychology 32 (December): 1119–1133.

SOROKIN, P. A. (1937–41) Social and Cultural Dynamics (4 vols.). New York: American Books.

———— (1926) "Monarchs and rulers: a comparative statistical study II." Social Forces 4 (March): 523–533.

SUEDFELD, P. and A. D. RANK (1976) "Revolutionary leaders: long-term success as a function of changes in conceptual complexity." Journal of Personality and Social Psychology 34 (August): 169–178.

SUEDFELD, P. and P. E. TETLOCK (1977) "Integrative complexity of communications in international crises." Journal of Conflict Resolution 21 (March): 169–184.

TAAGEPERA, R. (1979) "People, skills, and resources: an interaction model for world population growth." Technological Forecasting and Social Change 13 (January): 13–30.

THORNDIKE, E. L. (1936). "The relation between intellect and morality in rulers." American Journal of Sociology 42 (November): 321–334.

TOLSTOY, L. (1952) War and Peace. Chicago: Encyclopedia Britannica. (originally published 1865–1869)

TOYNBEE, A. J. (1946) A Study of History (2 vols.). New York: Oxford University Press.

WENDT, H. W. and P. C. LIGHT (1976) "Measuring 'greatness' in American presidents: model case of international research on political leadership?" European Journal of Social Psychology 6 (1): 105–109.

WINTER, D. G. (1973) The Power Motive. New York: Free Press.

WOODS, F. A. (1913) The Influence of Monarchs. New York: Macmillan.

———— (1906) Mental and Moral Heredity in Royalty. New York: Hold, Rinehart & Winston.

ZUCKERMAN, H. (1977) Scientific Elite: Nobel Laureates in the United States. New York: Free Press.

CHAPTER 3

GROUPS AND THE INNOVATION PROCESS

JOSEPH E. McGRATH

Groups both help and hinder social change, especially those social changes called innovations. This chapter is an effort to describe some of the key findings from group research that seem to bear on how social systems deal with potential innovations. The first part discusses six relevant topics from group research. The second part offers a social-psychological analysis of what happens to a system when it is faced with a possible innovation. The third section states some implications of the first two sections for innovation in organizations.

Group and Interpersonal Processes that Bear on Innovation: Some Evidence

At least six topics from the group research literature seem directly germane to questions of how organizations deal with potential innovations. They are: group brainstorming; the so-called risky shift in groups; groups as effective systems for performance of certain kinds of tasks; groups as media for negotiating resolution of conflicts; groups as media for influencing individuals; and "groupthink," or certain dysfunctional processes that can occur in groups making decisions under crisis conditions. While these six topics overlap to some degree, each has something to tell us about how innovation may or may not work.

GROUP BRAINSTORMING: ARE GROUPS MORE CREATIVE THAN INDIVIDUALS?

One of the most widely publicized findings of the group research area is, in fact, not a fact at all. Group brainstorming, a technique that gained great popularity a decade or so ago, is based on the assumption that groups are more creative than individuals; that is, they can generate more, and more creative, new ideas or solutions to a problem than the same individuals could working alone. In fact, starting from the very early work of Shaw (1932) and continuing through the work of Lorge, Restle, Davis, and many others (see Davis, 1969, for a good summary), group research has shown that groups are indeed *less* efficient than individuals at solving certain kinds of problems, and are extremely less efficient on a man-hour basis in generating creative or innovative solutions, compared to those same individuals working alone.

A group of, say, four members, using brainstorming rules, will generally generate fewer than half as many ideas (and, on the average, less creative ideas) than those four individuals working separately on the same problem, even when one subtracts out the redundancies among the ideas generated by the four individuals. This is such a robust finding that it is one of the few principles of social psychology that can be demonstrated in front of an undergraduate class with no fear of being embarrassed by an unexpected outcome. The inferiority of groups as a forum for creative problem solving has emerged clearly and without exception from many such demonstrations, as well as from many formal research studies (see Dunnette et al., 1963; Taylor et al., 1958).

Given what we know about pressures toward conforming in groups (discussed later in this section), we should hardly be surprised that a group context is a poor forum for individuals to generate "creative" (that is, unlikely, novel, low-probability) responses. Indeed, we would expect quite the contrary, and if one were writing a prescription for generating good creative ideas on a problem, that prescription might well start: "First, catch yourself some individuals, working alone. . . ." It can be an effective second step to bring the ideas generated by individuals, working alone, into a group setting, as a forum for evaluating and choosing among them, as will be evident in later parts of this section. But asking individuals to work as a group to generate creative ideas is clearly counterproductive, advocates of brainstorming notwithstanding.

GROUPS AS RISKY OR CONSERVATIVE DECISION MAKERS

For centuries, it has generally been taken for granted that groups are likely to make very conservative decisions, because extreme positions of individuals or factions within a group tend to cancel each other out, and the group will often reach a compromise decision that does the least violence to the status quo. Many social observers noted such a tendency, and some developed fairly extensive theories to account for it. From our vantage point of the present, we can see that there was no empirical evidence at all to support this view—or at least not the kind of evidence we would now insist upon before offering such a broad empirical generalization. But there was little questioning of the belief that groups made conservative decisions until the early studies by Kogan and Wallach (1967), which showed that groups reached decisions that were riskier than the alternatives these same persons had chosen for the same problem when working as individuals.

This began a flurry of research, much of it apparently replicating those early findings, and also a rash of theoretical explanations for these counterintuitive results. One of those theoretical explanations was the concept of a "diffusion of responsibility": Groups make riskier decisions because no *one* is to blame for them. This same concept, interestingly enough, had been used earlier as an explanation for why groups reached conservative decisions. Another theoretical explanation for the "risky shift" was the assertion that risk is a value in our culture and, therefore, that no individual would want to appear less risk-taking than his or her peers in making the group decision, even if he or she were in fact much less risk-taking when making individual choices. Hence, group decisions move inexorably toward more risky choices (see Dion et al., 1970, for a review of this area).

The risky shift phenomenon flourished as an active area of research until two things occurred. First, it was discovered that groups shift in the conservative direction on certain items, and that one can concoct items to yield either a risky or a conservative shift. If risk is a positive value for some matters in our culture, conservatism is apparently a positive value for other matters. This clearly alters the nature of the phenomenon to be accounted for, as well as the status of its explanation in terms of risk as a positive value.

The second set of events that shifted the interest in the risky shift was much more careful attention to what went on in decision-making groups at the individual level, and how resulting shifts related to the prediscussion distribution of attitudes among members of a particular group. Such work (Davis, 1969; Zajonc et al., 1972) showed that shifts to either riskier or more conservative positions seemed to mirror what one would expect given the distribution of prediscussion individual opinions, plus reasonable assumptions about the rules of combination by which views of individuals get combined into a single group decision. From this point of view, the counterintuitive risky shift of groups as decision-making entities becomes largely an artifact—both of the content of the problems used, and of the logic of combining prior positions of individuals.

Other work on group choice shifts seems to show a decided tendency for group discussion to lead to *polarization*—that is, for there to be a shift toward a more extreme position on whatever side of the issue's neutral point most group members had been at the outset. The concept of polarization is more than just another way of saying that groups shift toward risk on risky items (that is, on items for which they tended to be on the risky side at the start) and toward caution on cautious items (that is, on items for which they tended to be on the cautious side at the onset).

Myers and his colleagues (Lamm and Myers, 1978; Myers and Lamm, 1976) used the polarization concept to examine the full range of possible explanations for these more general choice-shift phenomena. One explanation that receives strong support, as reflected in the work of Burnstein and Vinokur (1977), hypothesizes that the direction and magnitude of the shift depend on the ratio of pro and con arguments that are presented to members during the group's discussion, and on the salience, credibility, and novelty of those arguments for the individual members. In other words, group discussion has the effect of shifting a group choice in the direction favored by the larger part of the material discussed—tempered, of course, with the caveat that members are likely to reflect in group discussions those arguments that favor the position they themselves already hold. In the naturally occurring case, a shift toward the dominant prior position and a shift toward the direction of the dominant portion of the discussion will almost always be the same. In the experimental case, however, they can be separated. Results seem to support the idea that each is a separate, strong force. This could give some credence to arguments in favor of deliberate policy advocacy debates for decision-making groups.

These recent developments disconfirm the point of view that groups make riskier decisions than individuals. Like group brainstorming, it was another widely held generalization that just was not true. The recent work also made clear that the equally widely held earlier generalization—that groups are conservative decision-making instruments—was equally wrong as a generalization. The sum total of work on choice shifts after group discussion makes it clear that we cannot assume anything to be true about the decision-making proclivities of *all* groups, working on *all* problems, under *all* sets of social conditions. In retrospect, it seems surprising that so many ever thought we could make such sweeping generalizations. Perhaps the successful and rapid spread of belief in the risky shift, and in the efficiency of group brainstorming, is testimony to our yearning for "real" laws and immutable findings in the social sciences, a yearning not likely to be sated soon.

GROUPS AS EFFECTIVE TASK PERFORMANCE SYSTEMS

Although groups are not really very good as generators of creative ideas, and although groups are not really systematically risky or cautious in their decision making, groups nonetheless have a number of potential strengths in making decisions and carrying them out. Groups are effective task performance systems for many kinds of tasks. They offer a basis for an effective division of labor and can offer a diversity of skills, abilities, attitudes, and areas of know-how. On a probability basis, a group is more likely than any one individual to contain any given task-relevant talent. Whether or not such a diversity of talents or division of labor is useful depends, of course, on the nature of the task and how members' efforts combine to yield the group's product on that task.

Steiner (1972) has offered one of the most useful available classifications of tasks in regard to the combination of member efforts (see McGrath, 1984, for a review of such group task classifications). He specifies five types: (a) *additive tasks*, in which the output of members simply sums to provide a group output (as in tasks where the group's production for the day is the sum of the units produced by individuals); (b) *disjunctive tasks*, in which the group solves a problem if any one member can solve it (as when a team wins a race if any one of its entries finishes first); (c) *conjunctive tasks*, in which the group is successful only if all of its members pass some standard (as when a football team is penalized if any one of its members commits an infraction of the rules); (d) *compensatory tasks*, in which performances of members are averaged (rather than summed), and thus the excellence of one member's performance can compensate for a weak performance by another (as when a team runs a relay race); and (e) *complementary tasks*, in which the performances of members, doing different subtasks, are related in varied and complex ways, often requiring tightly coordinated sequencing and timing.

It is on complementary tasks that an effective division of labor in a group is crucial, and it is on these tasks that groups can provide the *possibility*—not, of course, the guarantee—of highly effective performance. Furthermore, it is on complementary tasks, as well as on disjunctive tasks, that diversity among group members in their talents and knowledge can be an advantage (rather than a disadvantage, as such diversity clearly would be for conjunctive tasks). On disjunctive and perhaps additive tasks, the probability of success at a given level or standard is increased as the number of group members increases. But groups pay a stiff price for the gains derived from the diversity of abilities and attitudes that comes with size. Steiner (1972) argues that increases in the number of members leads to both *coordination losses* and *motivation losses* in groups. If a task requires both a diversity of talents and tight coordination among members, as complementary tasks ordinarily would, increasing the size of the work group represents a set of trade-offs with respect to group task performance: an increased range of talents, an increased probability that the group has in it any given needed skill, but increased coordination and motivation losses as well.

A group is likely to be an effective instrument for carrying out a complex task, including implementing an innovation, if the group contains the proper range and mix of abilities, motives, and attitudes for that task (see Hackman and Morris, 1975, for a review of these matters). But a group is not especially likely to adopt new procedures. Groups are far more likely to continue doing what they have been doing in the past. One main reason for such a conservatism of process, the establishment and enforcement of group norms, is discussed in a later part of this section.

INNOVATION AND NEGOTIATION GROUPS

Sometimes a task is given to a group rather than to an individual not because it takes a number of persons to do the job and needs a division of labor, and not because a diversity of talents and opinions will increase the probability that at least one member will have the necessary skills and ideas to deal with the task, but because the nature of the task itself calls for consideration by a diverse group that is somehow representative of the range of views in the broader system. When there are two or more factions who hold sharply divergent

views on a matter considered important by the system or by major
forces in the system, it is sometimes valuable to form a group that
includes representatives of those factions in order to try to generate
a jointly acceptable solution to the matter. These can reasonably be
called "negotiation groups," although that term has some more precise uses in the group research area (see, for example, Morley and
Stephenson, 1977).

Sometimes decision-making groups within organizations are institutionalized in a form that tries to ensure diversity and representativeness with regard to contending subgroups. This is often the case
for policy advisory groups, for example. Not only do such groups
provide a range of views and ideas for a number of potential task-
topics with which that group is likely to deal, but often a decision
coming from such a group is more likely to be accepted as legitimate
by members of all of the contending groups.

Ideally, such groups can develop solutions that are new and better
than the preferred solutions of any one faction—that is, innovations.
In practice, however, there is little evidence that such negotiation
groups are likely to generate or choose markedly creative solutions.
Such groups are likely to "satisfice," with a compromise solution that
leaves much of the status quo in place, rather than to optimize by
choosing a new, innovative approach. Depending on the sharpness
of disagreement among the factions and the crisis status of the system,
they may be satisfied with any solution that can be agreed to without
ripping the system apart. Some factors (for example, the use of a
neutral third party, or of tactics to blur the representativeness of
members' roles) that can help overcome such anti-innovation tendencies are discussed in the final section of this chapter (see McGrath
and Julian, 1963; Vidmar and McGrath, 1970).

GROUPS AS MEDIA FOR INFLUENCING INDIVIDUALS

Much has been said about how groups exert pressure for conformity, and some of it is true. Groups hold power over their members
because they control positive and negative reinforcements valued by
them. Groups to which members are attracted—because they like
the other members, because of reinforcements they receive from the
prestige of being in a group, or because a group gives them access
to valued activities and resources—can influence their members and
often do. Even groups to which members do not have a positive
attraction, but of which they must remain members, have some degree
of influence over their members.

The relation of group members to one another, including these influence relations, can be viewed as an interpersonal flow or exchange. The exchange may involve goods and services, but the crucial exchange from a social psychological point of view is the exchange of rewards and costs—that is, of positive and negative reinforcements. Thibaut and Kelley (1959), in their classic theoretical formulation, lay out the bases of such social exchanges in detail. Some portions of that formulation are useful in the present context.

Persons evaluate their present cost-reward situation within any interpersonal relationship by comparing it to each of two standards. The first standard is a general comparison level (CL), the level of reward they are accustomed to receiving in such social relationships. If their present level of reward is above that comparison level, they view the present situation as positive. The second standard is the level of reward they would expect to receive in the best available alternative situation (including being in no interpersonal interchange). Thibaut and Kelley call that standard the comparison level for alternatives (CL_{ALT}). If an individual's present pay-off level is above the CL_{ALT}, he or she will stay in that relationship; if it is below the CL_{ALT}, he or she will go to a better alternative. It is possible, of course, for an individual to be in a situation that is worse than his or her general CL (thus, a negatively valued situation) but nevertheless better than any currently available alternative (that is, above CL_{ALT}). In this case, the individual will stay in the negatively valued situation (that is, will remain a member of a group to which he or she has a negative attraction). It is equally possible for the individual to leave a positively valued situation (present level above CL) for a still more attractive alternative (present level below CL_{ALT}).

To some extent, such concepts clarify the rather complex relations among group cohesiveness, retention of members versus turnover, and levels of task performance and member satisfaction in group settings. At the same time, they point up several facts germane to the present context: that members stay in groups even when not attracted to them, and that they are subject to some influence exerted by groups they are in, even when they are not positively attracted to the other members. (It is still true, though, that group influence on members is stronger when those members are positively attracted to the group—that is, when that group has high cohesiveness.)

Since they view interpersonal relations as exchanges of rewards and costs, Thibaut and Kelley (1959) show how one member can influence another by making a response (leading to the other's rewards and costs) contingent on the other's behavior (which leads to the first individual's rewards and costs). When two or more persons are engaged in such a contingent reward situation, they are said to have "behavior control" over one another. Such relations are usually, but not necessarily, mutual or reciprocal.

It is often the case, however, that behaviors that will lead to high rewards for one party (individual, group, or faction) are antagonistic to those behaviors that will lead to high rewards for the other party. If each has behavior control over the other—that is, if each can deliver or withhold positive and negative reinforcements, depending on the behavior of the other—then the two parties must contend with one another if either is to be rewarded. Furthermore, any one pattern of interpersonal behavior, even if it is highly rewarding to both parties at the outset, will sooner or later yield diminishing rewards and increasing costs. The parties will become satiated with that particular form of reward. To adjust their behavior to conflicting demands, and to adjust their behavior to shifts in reward value over time, interacting parties develop strategies and practices to optimize the joint pay-off, in the ultimate interest of maximizing their own individual pay-off over the long haul. These strategies and practices include alternation, sequencing, and the like. They become jointly held values—in effect, *group norms.* Thibaut and Kelley (1959) point out that such group norms take on the force of third parties: They can be appealed to in adjudicating disputes, they protect the interests of both the stronger and the weaker parties, and so forth. Such group norms about how individuals should behave, vis-à-vis one another and the task at hand, provide a good focus for discussion of how groups influence their members.

Groups have a big stake in predicting the behavior of members (and vice versa). This is so for a number of reasons, including the need for all members to be able to calculate accurately the rewards and costs they are likely to accrue, and how best to behave to maximize those rewards. Usually, the group's stake in behavior predictability becomes manifest in the form of pressure for consistency in the behavior of a given member when in the same situation on different occasions. Sometimes it involves pressure for similarity in the behavior of different members in a given situation. Equally often, however, it involves pressure for different individuals to do complementary things (each to carry out what is expected of someone in his or her role) rather than to exhibit similar behaviors.

The different and complementary behaviors of different members of a group derive from a shared set of beliefs and attitudes about how various members of the group should behave in given circumstances. That is, all members of the group share expectations about appropriate role behaviors of all group members, themselves included. Even though those norms or role expectations call for a diverse set of behaviors by the different members of the group, the norms or role expectations themselves are shared. Thus, uniformity in attitudes and beliefs, at least about how group members ought to behave and usually about most other matters of consequence to the group as well, is a highly frequent if not inevitable byproduct of the development of norms and their enforcement and reinforcement in groups.

Research over several decades on these matters has made several points clear: (a) Group norms often exert powerful influences on the behavior of group members; (b) such influence can work toward either higher or lower productivity with respect to the group's tasks; (c) norms are more powerful in more cohesive groups and have more influence on the behavior of members who are highly attracted to and/or dependent on the group; and (d) norms operate by and large so as to support what has been (that is, the status quo) rather than to urge new forms of behavior (innovations). How one can arrange matters so that existing group norms are not a barrier to innovation has been the subject of considerable research since Coch and French's (1948) now classic study on overcoming resistance to change in an industrial setting. Suffice it to say that we are, as yet, quite far from having an efficient technology for changing group norms to reduce resistance to innovation, much less for shifting norms so that they might become a positive force for innovation (for reviews of this area, see McGrath, 1978; McGrath and Altman, 1966; for an optimistic view of possibilities, see Hackman and Morris, 1975).

GROUPTHINK AND INNOVATION

Ideas about groups as forums for decision making and conflict resolution, and ideas about forces toward uniformity of behavior by group members are brought together by Janis in his work on *Groupthink* (1972). That term refers to a set of processes, largely dysfunctional, that can occur in groups trying to decide crucial issues. Janis analyzed how those dysfunctional processes operated for President Kennedy and his advisers as they considered and made their decisions about the Bay of Pigs invasion in 1961, as compared to the way in which the same processes operated, less than two years later, in the Cuban missile crisis. In the first case, information not in accord with the prevailing (pro-invasion) view was ignored, discredited, or discounted; individuals failed to express divergent views; and alternatives were ignored or rejected with no attempt to consider them fully. Janis and Mann (1977) call this set of processes "defensive avoidance." The result was a disaster, both militarily and politically, and one that could have been avoided on the basis of information potentially available to the decision makers at that time.

In contrast, during the Cuban missile crisis in October 1962, conflicting views were not only permitted but expressed and encouraged by the decision managers (President Kennedy and his brother Robert). A wider set of informational inputs was sought and reviewed, and the decision managers adopted procedures that forced a search for alternatives (a form of policy advocacy). The resulting policy can be viewed as a compromise, since it was less aggressive than the "hawks" advocated but more aggressive than the "doves" urged. The final plan was not a clear and advocated option at the outset, but more or less emerged from the group proceedings. In any case, the outcome was successful, both militarily and politically, whether or not there were better alternatives that could have been adopted.

One lesson that some have drawn from these analyses is that groups are potentially dangerous and ought not to be involved in crucial decisions. That is the wrong lesson to take from these cases, because many of these kinds of decisions must be addressed by sets of people acting in concert, whether or not they are called a group. There is no evidence that any individual would have arrived at the "right" decision had he or she been acting *alone* in the Bay of Pigs case. (Indeed, what is the "right" decision in that case remains a matter of controversy, even among people who would agree that the course actually followed was the "wrong" decision.) Furthermore, the Cuban missile crisis showed that groups can and sometimes do perform splendidly in crucial decision situations. The lesson to be learned—in general, and for those who are concerned with the adoption of innovations in organizations—has to do with the different ways in which groups can operate: encourage versus discourage dissent; force versus preclude wide information searches; require versus forbid full and fair consideration of an array of alternatives; and the like. These in turn are greatly influenced by the attitudes and intentions of the powerful members of groups, who largely determine whether a group will be open or closed to new ideas—that is, to innovations.

One should also be cautious in making too literal an interpretation of the group processes described for such situations. It is all too easy for researchers, as well as those involved in actual events, to let the post hoc outcomes in part shape their judgments about prior occurrences. Suppose the Bay of Pigs decision had worked—that is, had achieved the goals of its protagonists; or suppose the Cuban missile crisis decision had backfired, as many thought it might at the time. Would either of those outcomes have changed the meaning we give and the efficacy we assign to the group processes that led to those decisions?

The Social-Psychological Context of Innovation in Systems: Some Perspectives

Innovation has a variety of meanings in ordinary usage: creativity, novelty, improvisation, invention, adoption, and/or adaptation. It is used in this chapter to include three of its usual meanings: (a) the *invention* of a new idea, device, and/or procedure; (b) the *adoption* by an operating system of an idea/device/procedure that is new to that system, whether or not it is new in a generic sense; and (c) the *adaptation* of an idea/device/procedure within an ongoing system, after the new idea/device/procedure has already been adopted by that system. All three of these meanings—invention, adoption, and adaptation—fit the general usages of the term "innovation" within this volume.

From the point of view of a social psychologist, the things called innovations are just one special subset of a class of events called social changes. Innovations are distinguished from other social changes in two regards: (a) They are deliberate and intended—or at least they are intended by some of the people involved; and (b) they are considered desirable—or at least are desired by some of the people involved. But whether a given change was intended, desirable, and therefore an innovation depends on whose viewpoint is taken as the point of reference.

Innovations can be regarded as the insertion of a new device, idea, or procedure into an ongoing system, either by adding the new device/idea/procedure to extend the system or, more often, by substituting the new idea/device/procedure to replace an old one that has been part of the system up to that point. "New" here means new to a particular operating system. It does not necessarily mean new to the world, or even new to the sociocultural setting within which that system is embedded. So, in any given case, an innovation can be a new device/idea/procedure that is created at that time and for that system; or, it can be an idea/device/procedure that is adopted, pretty much intact, from some other operating system; or, it can be an idea/

device/procedure that is adopted from some other system but at the same time *adapted* or modified to fit the referent system (Rogers and Kim, Chapter 4, this volume, use *reinvention* as I am using *adaptation*).

INNOVATION AND CHANGE

The topic of innovation is often discussed as if it referred to a unique event that marks the beginning of change and represents the sole sufficient cause of that change. If we regard innovations from a social-psychological perspective, it makes much more sense to view the focal event—the innovation—as just one event within a continuous system-change or social-change process. In other words, innovations have histories, both direct and indirect, and consequences, both intended and unintended.

Consider an example on a rather molar social system level. Henry Ford certainly did not invent the automobile, but in the present use of terms he was responsible for several innovations: the use of an assembly line in auto manufacture (although it had been used earlier for manufacturing weapons and other things); the design of systems with interchangeable parts; and the planned use of mass production in the United States. His production methods were innovative in the sense that they permitted the widespread purchase and use of the automobile and thus changed the American (and international) social and economic landscape. This example also illustrates the cascading and amplifying effects (intended and unintended) that flow from a major innovation-event. The "invention" plus the mass production of the automobile led to a number of further devices/ideas/procedures: massive modifications in the rubber processing, oil refining, and highway construction industries; major social changes in terms of urban living patterns, transportation, and food technology; and, some say, major changes in family patterns and morality. At the same time, the automobile itself can be viewed as a second- or third-order consequence of a whole series of earlier innovations (advances in metal processing; development of the internal combustion engine; the invention of the wheel) and the social/political/economic opportunities and needs that resulted from them (for example, vast distances to travel, loads to haul). In turn, the mass production of the auto helped to create (or at least make manifest) opportunities and needs that led to further innovations, both technical and social.

Some people generally favor change and even equate it with progress, while other people generally oppose change, perhaps equating it with decay. But nobody can seriously favor or oppose all possible changes without regard to the goals and potential consequences of those changes. Whether a particular innovation is to be desired or feared depends on what it is and what it does. Not all possible new ideas or procedures are desirable. Innovation—that is, change—is desirable only in regard to good ideas and effective procedures. But which ideas or procedures are effective is a value question, and the answer is relative to the viewpoint from which the assessment is made.

We can clarify this point by returning to the example of the auto. For over half a century, the invention of the automobile and its consequences were widely hailed as major and highly desirable innovations, with only a few dissenting voices. Except for the alleged negative consequences of the auto on the mating, dating, and sexual behavior patterns of the young (the auto has been viewed as a portable and unchaperoned "courting parlor"), even the major unintended consequences of the auto (such as urban growth and substitution of private autos for public/mass transportation) have been viewed more as positive than as negative social effects. It is only in recent times— because of both the extremely negative environmental impact of auto emissions, and the extremely wasteful uses of now-scarce and costly oil—that many find the automobile the curse, rather than the blessing, of the twentieth century. Many such major changes, and the changes flowing from those changes, may or may not be desirable depending on whose viewpoint is adopted, what criteria of desirability are considered, and even when an assessment is made.

INNOVATION AND CHOICE

Regardless of how the decision to adopt an innovation is made, an invention or innovation always occurs within an ongoing system. It is itself a consequence of preceding changes and conditions in that system and in its "surround" and it is likely to have a cascading set of consequences. In general, the ongoing system works more or less satisfactorily *without* the innovation. Thus, potential innovation must be viewed as a replacement for an extant part of the ongoing, and more or less satisfactory, system. Its value must be assessed in comparison to the more or less satisfactory part of the system that it is to replace. There are times, of course, when the extant system is not working well at all; then it is a system in crisis. Here, a potential innovation must be assessed not so much in comparison to the present system, but in comparison to all available alternatives.

For a potential innovation to be considered good means, in part, that it must be demonstrably better than the part of the present system it would replace. In such cases, there is a danger of making something analogous to type two errors in statistical inference: not adopting a new idea because it does not seem to be much better than the present one, or because proponents cannot prove that it is better without having an empirical tryout. In the case of a breakdown or imminent breakdown of a system—a system in crisis—defining any proposed innovation as "good" implies that it is the best of all available alternatives. The danger here is of making a type one error: adopting a bad scheme out of desperation, and because it seems to be the only one, or the most expedient, alternative (perhaps because it is being touted as such by a vocal and persistent special interest group).

When a system is considering an innovation, the matter is often posed as though it were a quite limited choice: adopting a particular new form versus keeping the present one; or, for the case of a system in crisis, between adopting a particular proposed form versus system collapse. In fact, innovation is always, in principle, a matter of choosing among an array of alternatives. Those alternatives almost always include the present method, perhaps some previous way of doing a task, and one or perhaps more potential innovations that are being recommended (and perhaps lobbied for) by interested parties. The set of alternatives also includes, implicitly, a host of possible other forms that are *not* being actively considered—perhaps because no one is "selling" them, or perhaps because no one has even thought of them.

It is tempting to consider only the few alternatives that are obvious and pressing for attention: the proposed innovation and the status quo. Often there are many other possibilities much better than either the proposed or the present system. It seems crucial, therefore, that a system should always contain some mechanism for carrying out an active search for alternatives, even when the system is not in crisis, and even when no particular new idea is being pushed.

INNOVATION AND THE STATUS QUO

Everyone in a system has a stake in present procedures. Some with a low stake may expect a gain by certain kinds of changes, but all risk losing some or all of their rewards and statuses with any change. Those who favor an innovation must therefore develop a reinforcement system that does three things: (a) reward people who try innovations, whether or not they succeed; (b) insure against losses (such as blame) if the innovation fails; and (c) insure against losses even if the innovation succeeds. Successful innovations can lead to layoffs, higher performance standards, higher job requirements, as well as shifts in the mix of skills needed and therefore in the status of certain occupations. This can be seen in some recent trends in higher education. The importance of budgeting, demands for accountability, and massive increases in paper work have put a premium on financial, accounting, and other fiscal and administrative skills for those who manage universities. This has downgraded the importance of the traditional skills of scholarship, research, and teaching for those in upper academic positions, such as deans, chancellors, and academic vice presidents, that offer high power, high prestige, and high pay. Successful innovations have undoubtedly had positive, but also some negative, effects on those institutions, and they certainly have had negative effects on major sets of persons within those institutions.

When a new procedure is introduced from the top without the active cooperation of personnel at the lower echelons of the system, those lower-echelon personnel will try to get the new procedure under control one way or another. Its unknown and fearful aspects will be rendered known, tamed, and manageable. This will be done, insofar as possible, without major shifts in prior patterns of behavior and relationships. Lower-echelon staff often act in ways that, de facto, nullify, undo, or even reverse the intended effects of the innovation. One needs the cooperation, if not the enthusiasm, of all echelons of system personnel to have an innovation adopted and successfully implemented.

The unhappy fate of "new math" shows what can happen when innovations are integrated into operating systems. The new math was a major innovation in methods for teaching, and in the conceptual basis for organizing principles of mathematics for elementary and secondary school students. It was launched in the early sixties from several experimental programs, including the University of Illinois. It rapidly gained both fame and notoriety. The new math had spectacular success as long as it was being used by teachers who were themselves part of new math projects or else eager, first-generation volunteers. But when it began to be used by in-place classroom teachers who had many years invested in the "old math," the new math ran into difficulties in implementation. Those teachers had only minimal training, and little if any attitudinal preparation, to help them accept and use the new math. Many were less than enthusiastic about any innovation that would require more work on their part, and that would imply a complete overhaul or abandonment of long-valued lesson plans. The miraculous positive effects that had seemed to flow from the new math in its experimental and early implementation phases faded rapidly, while the basic principles on which it was based became diluted, if not undone, at the operating level. The new math soon joined other recent educational innovations as the curse, rather than the savior, of Johnny in his attempts to read, write and "reckon."

Resistance of workers to changes in system processes (that is, innovations) and attempts to overcome such resistance have long concerned social psychologists (for example, Coch and French, 1948), as well as labor-management relations experts. The problem even provided the theme for the successful Broadway musical, *Pajama Game*. All sorts of strategies, ranging from worker participation in decisions to group incentive systems, to threats of layoffs and/or plant closings, have been advocated and tried, with mixed results. But no one has yet suggested a way that is likely to eliminate resistance to change in the status quo, even for systems that are not working very well.

Sometimes innovations are introduced from the bottom rather than the top of a system. These are often treated by higher levels as undesirable variations in standard practices. They are seldom welcomed as evidence of workers' interest in the system's good; they are more often seen as symptoms of laziness, corruption, or a lack of discipline. Yet every works manager or platoon sergeant knows that it is often necessary to depart from the letter of the boss's instructions in order to carry out their spirit. In fact, a leader can have no worse fate than his or her subordinates deciding that they will do exactly, and only, what they are told to do.

One can view both the kind of adapting that the lower levels of an organization do to innovations inserted at the top, and the kinds of deviation-countering actions that managers do in relation to innovations snuck in at the bottom levels, as *counter-innovations*. Both are fairly predictable, though unintended, consequences of an innovation—that is, of a disturbance of the status quo.

How to Use Groups to Help (or Hinder) Innovations in a System: Some Implications

The earlier discussion of key research evidence on group and interpersonal processes can be tied to the discussion of the social-psychological context of innovations to yield some prescriptions about how groups can be used to aid—or to hinder—the invention, adoption, and adaptation of innovations in systems within which those groups are embedded. The three aspects of innovation—invention, adoption, and adaptation—are often viewed as three stages of an innovation process. These three stages correspond quite closely to three types of group task performance processes: the *generation* of ideas or alternatives, the *selection* of correct or preferred alternatives, and the *execution or implementation* of the selected alternative (McGrath, 1984). These three task types require that a group carry out quite different performance processes. A fourth task type, requiring a group to resolve within-group differences in viewpoints or interests, may also become involved in the innovation process, although it is seldom talked about explicitly in the innovation literature. Such negotiation tasks require still another performance process by the group.

Many aspects of group research bear on only one or two of these group task performance processes. Brainstorming, for example, has to do with the first group performance process, generation (or, with the first stage of innovation, which is invention). Material on group risk-taking, on the other hand, refers to the selection or decision-making process (or to the adoption stage of innovation). There is no reason to suppose that groups will be advantageous in all aspects of innovation, nor a hindrance in all of them. Rather, groups, like all other systems, have some strengths and some weaknesses.

From the point of view of facilitating innovations in systems, the main advantages of groups as effective task performance systems lie in their strengths as vehicles for decision making, for problem solving, and for the execution of complex tasks that require a range of talents and a divison of labor. Their main limitations lie in their weakness as a medium in which to generate new ideas (that is, for invention); in their potential for distorting or constraining the decision-making process so that many potentially valuable alternatives are not considered (hence, limiting the adoption of innovative alternatives); in their tendency to compromise and satisfice when trying to resolve within-group differences (thus, choosing alternatives that protect status quo interests); and in their proclivity for developing and enforcing norms that support the status quo (hence, tending to adapt and transform new ideas and procedures to fit old behavior patterns). These strengths and weaknesses of groups are highlighted in the following set of rules or prescriptions for using groups to facilitate innovations in systems.

(1) Design the system to include a component devoted to a continuous, active *search for alternatives,* even when—indeed, especially when—the system is not in crisis. Such a component should deal not only with the invention stage but also with the adoption and adaptation stages of innovation. It should be situated so that its results

are given full consideration at the top of the organization, with as much "lead time" as possible.

(2) *Provide rewards (incentives) for trying innovations,* and make sure that those rewards are not seen as contingent on the ultimate success of the innovation.

(3) *Provide insurance against losses ensuing from an innovation.* It is, of course, important to make sure that the system members know they are insured against losses, including blame, if the innovation fails. It may be even more important that system members know they are insured against losses that can occur when an innovation succeeds. If workers are to embrace an innovation with enthusiasm, they must believe that its adoption will not lead to layoffs, changed standards, or downgraded status.

(4) *Assign the task of generating some new and creative ideas about a problem to individuals, working alone.* Be sure these individuals are working under instructions by which they know that creativity and novelty will be rewarded, and that they are not supposed to try to guess what the boss thinks is a right answer.

(5) *Assign the review and evaluation of a set of ideas to a group.* The outcome of the evaluation process will be affected by (a) the prediscussion distribution of attitudes among group members; (b) the credibility and salience of arguments favoring different alternatives that are brought into the group's deliberations; and (c) whether or not the group contains a small but committed minority, presumably well versed in arguments favoring their position, which persists in the face of majority opposition to support a particular alternative. Consequently, if there is a particular alternative that you want selected—that is, if you have a stake in the adoption of a particular innovation—make sure that the deciding group has at least some members who are strongly committed to that position, armed with many plausible arguments for that alternative, and willing to persist in their support of it.

(6) If the task at hand involves conflict between two (or more) contending factions and is to be settled by a conflict-resolving or negotiation group, some steps that could help that group seek new (that is, innovative) alternatives rather than compromises that support the status quo include:

(a) trying to blur the degree to which negotiation group members see themselves as, and are committed to acting as, representatives of their constituencies;

(b) persuading negotiation group members to see themselves as representatives of the larger system; and

(c) inserting a third-party mediator who is creditably accepted by all factions as neutral with regard to the contending parties and who can focus the negotiation group members on the good of the larger system rather than on gain for their own faction.

(7) In any group trying to choose a course of action, especially in a crisis situation, some steps that will help the group *avoid excessive narrowness of perspective* include:

(a) requiring a wide information search, full consideration of all information, and rewarding such behavior;

(b) encouraging, rewarding, and indeed *requiring dissent* in the group;

(c) making provisions for a *broad search for alternatives*, preferably by people other than those who will evaluate and choose among those alternatives; and

(d) charging some group members with the task of representing and supporting positions other than their own—role-playing the positions of opponents—and rewarding them for how well they represent that other view.

Some of these propositions are, in effect, prescriptions to develop group norms that (a) question the status quo, (b) give positive value to behaviors leading to change, and (c) give positive value to diversity and disagreement. Groups need predictability, but they do not need uniformity over time. Groups need to be able to manage conflicts among members, but they do not need to avoid or suppress such conflicts. Groups want to plan for a future more or less under control, with equal or greater rewards and equal or lower costs. They do not want unplanned change, but they also do not need unchanging conditions, nor unchanging rewards and costs.

Perhaps the key feature in all this is the idea of *perceived control*, a variable that has received much recent study in social psychology and that seems to have quite pervasive effects on interpersonal behavior (see Wortman and Brehm, 1975). Groups and their members need to feel in control of their situation, now and in the future. Unplanned for and abruptly introduced changes—innovations—threaten this control, or seem to threaten it. Undoing that threat, restoring that perceived control, would seem to be the underlying necessary condition to facilitate the process of innovation.

REFERENCES

BURNSTEIN, E. and A. VINOKUR (1977) "Persuasive argumentation and social comparison as determinants of attitude polarization." Journal of Experimental Social Psychology 13 (July): 315–332.

COCH, L. and J.R.P. FRENCH, Jr. (1948) "Overcoming resistance to change." Human Relations 1 (August): 512–532.

DAVIS, J. H. (1969) Group Performance. Reading, MA: Addison-Wesley.

DION, K. L., R. S. BARON, and N. MILLER (1970) "Why do groups make riskier decisions than individuals?" pp. 350–377 in L. Berkowitz (ed.) Advances in Experimental Social Psychology (vol. 5). New York: Academic Press.

DUNNETTE, M. D., J. P. CAMPBELL, and K. JAASTED (1963) "The effect of group participation on brainstorming effectiveness for two industrial samples." Journal of Applied Psychology 47 (February): 30–37.

HACKMAN, J. R. and C. G. MORRIS (1975) "Group tasks, group interaction process, and group performance effectiveness: a review and proposed integration," pp. 45–99 in L. Berkowitz (ed.) Advances in Experimental Social Psychology (vol. 8). New York: Academic Press.

JANIS, I. L. (1972) Victims of Groupthink. New York: Houghton Mifflin.

―――― and L. MANN (1977) Decision Making: A Psychological Analysis of Conflict. New York: Free Press.

KOGAN, N. and M. A. WALLACH (1967) "Risk taking as a function of the situation, the person, and the group," pp. 111–278 in New Directions in Psychology (vol. 3). New York: Holt, Rinehart & Winston.

LAMM, H. and D. G. MYERS (1978) "Group-induced polarization of attitudes and behavior," pp. 145–195 in L. Berkowitz (ed.) Advances in Experimental Social Psychology (vol. 11). New York: Academic Press.

McGRATH, J. E. (1984) Groups: Interaction and Performance. Englewood Cliffs, NJ: Prentice-Hall.

―――― (1978) "Small group research." American Behavioral Scientist 21 (May/June): 651–674.

―――― and I. ALTMAN (1966) Small Group Research: A Synthesis and Critique of the Field. New York: Holt, Rinehart & Winston.

McGRATH, J. E. and J. W. JULIAN (1963) "Interaction process and task outcome in experimentally-created negotiation groups." Journal of Psychological Studies 14 (September): 117–138.

MORLEY, I. E. and G. N. STEPHENSON (1977) The Social Psychology of Bargaining. London: Allen & Unwin.

MYERS, D. G. and H. LAMM (1976) "The group polarization phenomenon." Psychological Bulletin 83 (July): 602–627.

ROGERS, E. M. and R. ADHIKARYA (1979) "Diffusion of innovations: An up-to-date review," pp. 67–81 in D. Nimmo (ed.), Communication Yearbook 3. New Brunswick, NJ: Transaction.

ROGERS, E. M. and J. KIM (1984) "The diffusion of innovations in public organizations," in R. L. Merritt and A. J. Merritt (eds.), Innovation in the Public Sector. Beverly Hills, CA: Sage.

SHAW, M. E. (1932) "A comparison of individuals and small groups in the rational solution of complex problems." American Journal of Psychology 44 (July): 491–504.

STEINER, I. D. (1972) Group Processes and Productivity. New York: Academic.

84   *Innovation in the Public Sector*

TAYLOR, D. W., P.C. BERRY, and C. H. BLOCK (1958) "Does group participation when using brainstorming facilitate or inhibit creative thinking?" Administrative Science Quarterly 3 (June): 23–47.

THIBAUT, J. W. and H. KELLEY (1959) The Social Psychology of Groups. New York: John Wiley.

VIDMAR, N. and J. E. McGRATH (1970) "Forces affecting success in negotiation groups." Behavioral Science 15 (March): 154–163.

WORTMAN, C. B. and J. W. BREHM (1975) "Responses to uncontrollable outcomes: an integration of reluctance theory and the learned helplessness model," pp. 277–336 in L. Berkowitz (ed.) Advances in Experimental Social Psychology (vol. 8). New York: Academic Press.

ZAJONC, R. B., R. J. WOLOSIN, and M. A. WOLOSIN (1972) "Group risk-taking under various group decision schemes." Journal of Experimental Social Psychology 8 (January): 16–30.

CHAPTER 4

DIFFUSION OF INNOVATIONS IN PUBLIC ORGANIZATIONS

E V E R E T T   M.   R O G E R S

J O U N G - I M   K I M

Over thirty-nine years of diffusion research in various fields have produced 3,000 publications on the diffusion of innovations (Rogers, 1983). Most of this past research, however, has been conducted on individuals as innovation decision makers. This high concentration on individual decisions in diffusion research might mislead one to think that innovation usually occurs among individuals, and only rarely in organizations. In fact, innovation is happening most of the time in most organizations. Organization scholars consider the innovation process to be one of the main functions in organizations, along with production and maintenance (Katz and Kahn, 1966: 39; Rogers and Agarwala-Rogers, 1976: 149–150).

During the late 1960s and early 1970s, a number of organization scholars began to study the diffusion of innovations among organizations. Today, about 500 publications, almost 16 percent of the total number of diffusion publications, deal with organizational innova-

AUTHORS' NOTE: The present chapter grew out of several recent research projects on the innovation process in organizations conducted by the authors and various colleagues. The first investigation of the innovation process for GBF/DIME (a computer-based information system promoted by the U.S. Census Bureau to local governments) was sponsored by the National Science Foundation and was carried out with J. D. Eveland, then of the University of Michigan at Ann Arbor. The second investigation, sponsored by the U.S. Department of Transportation's Urban Mass Transit Administration, consisted of twelve in-depth case studies in U.S. cities of the innovation process for Dial-A-Ride. This study, conducted with Kathleen Magill and Ronald Rice of Stanford University, further tested the model of the innovation process. The contribution of these colleagues is gratefully acknowledged, as is a recent review of diffusion research by Rogers and Adhikarya, from which certain of the present ideas are drawn.

tions (Rogers et al., 1977a). Like diffusion research in general, research on the innovation process in organizations is conducted by scholars in various disciplines. Until recently, however, most diffusion studies of organizational innovation focused mainly on organizational innovativeness and were patterned closely after past studies of individual innovativeness. The oversimplified correlates-of-innovativeness research was the most common type of previous diffusion research (Rogers et al., 1979: 1–29). The results were judged to be generally unsatisfactory (Rogers and Eveland, 1978). The study of innovativeness in local public health departments by Mohr (1969) is a good example of the many organizational innovativeness studies. He investigated 93 county-level health departments in Illinois, Michigan, New York, Ohio, and Ontario. The data were gathered primarily by interviews with each health department chief in 1965 to identify the determinants of innovativeness in public organizations. The innovativeness of health departments, the dependent variable, was measured by the number of health innovations that each health department had adopted. Mohr examined independent variables at the individual, organizational, and community level: attitudes of health officials toward innovation, organizational obstacles to innovations, size of the health department, resources available to the health department, community obstacles to innovation, and community size. Mohr performed a correlational analysis of these variables with innovativeness and concluded that innovativeness was a function of motivation, obstacles, and resources.

In the early 1970s, a series of conceptual and methodological criticisms of diffusion research began to appear (Rogers and Shoemaker, 1971; Warner, 1974; Downs and Mohr, 1976; Rogers, 1976). Most criticisms centered on the studies of organizational innovativeness. Possible biases, oversights, and shortcomings of previous studies of the diffusion of innovation were pointed out. The need for a better understanding of the nature of the innovation process in organizations was recognized as a high priority. Downs and Mohr (1976) concluded that diffusion research findings were "unstable" (that is, different results were obtained by different studies of innovativeness). The main paradigm for diffusion studies was questioned, and an alternative model for innovation in organizations seemed to be emerging (Kuhn, 1970). The search for an alternative research paradigm more appropriate for the study of organization innovation thus began.

Recently, several empirical studies of the innovation process in public organizations have attempted fresh approaches, such as a shift from the "variance" approach to a "process" approach,[1] and a change from the "organization" or the "innovation" to an "innovation-application" or an "organization-in-relation-to-an-innovation" as the unit of analysis (Downs and Mohr, 1976; Lambright, 1977; Rogers et al., 1977b; Rogers et al., 1979; Yin, 1978). Concepts and definitions of commonly used variables such as innovation and innovativeness have been modified or reformulated in the context of organizational innovation. In addition, attempts to identify and test variables useful for studying organizational innovation, such as reinvention,[2] have been made.

The present chapter discusses a number of issues central to the diffusion of innovations in organizations in order better to understand the status of research in this field. It also examines the flaws and shortcomings in previous research on innovation in organizations.[3] For all its shortcomings, the classical model of diffusion provides a useful starting point for our discussion.[4]

The Classical Model of Diffusion

Although the origins of general diffusion research trace from the German-Austrian and the British schools of diffusionism in anthropology, and from the French sociologist Gabriel Tarde (1903), the specific study of the diffusion of innovation began in the late 1930s when two sociologists, Bryce Ryan and Neal Gross (1943), investigated the spread of hybrid seed corn among Iowa farmers. The hybrid corn study set forth a new approach to the study of communication and change that was soon emulated by an increasing number of scholars in a wide variety of scientific fields. Subsequently, the amount of research activity in the field of innovation diffusion has increased at an exponential rate. Of more than 3,000 publications on the diffusion of innovations, about two-thirds are empirical research reports. The remainder comprise bibliographies, theoretic writings, and syntheses. Through these studies we have learned a great deal about the way innovations are diffused among such varied groups as peasants, physicians, housewives, Australian aborigines, industrial plant managers, and in private/public organizations.

The four main elements in the classical model of the diffusion of innovations are (1) the *innovation*, (2) *communication channels*, (3) *time*, and (4) the *members of a social system*.

THE INNOVATION

An innovation is an idea, practice, or object perceived as new by an individual or other relevant unit of adoption. It matters little whether or not and idea is "objectively" new as measured by the lapse of time since its first use or discovery. If the idea is perceived as new and different to the adopting unit, it is an innovation.

Newness in an innovation need not just involve new knowledge. Someone may have known about an innovation for some time but not yet developed a favorable or unfavorable attitude toward it, let alone adopted or rejected it. The "newness" aspect of an innovation may be defined in terms of knowledge, persuasion, or a decision to adopt.

It should not be assumed that the diffusion and adoption of all innovations are necessarily desirable. In fact, there are some studies of harmful and uneconomical innovations that are generally not desirable for either individuals or their social system. Further, the same innovation may be desirable for one adopter in a particular situation but undesirable for another potential adopter in a different situation.

It is a gross oversimplification to assume that all innovations are equivalent units of analysis. Whereas it may take an educational innovation such as the "new math" only five or six years to reach complete adoption, another innovation such as team teaching may require several decades to reach widespread use. An innovation's characteristics as perceived by its potential users will affect its rate of adoption. Five attributes frequently studied are:

(1) *Relative advantage* is the degree to which an innovation is perceived as better than the practice that it supersedes. The degree of relative advantage may be measured in economic terms, but often social prestige factors—convenience and satisfaction—are also important components. Its "objective" advantage matters less than whether or not the innovation is perceived by the adopting unit as being advantageous.

(2) *Compatibility* is the degree to which an innovation is perceived to be consistent with the existing values, past experiences, and needs of the potential adopters. The adoption of an incompatible innovation often requires the prior adoption of a new value system.

(3) *Complexity* is the degree to which an innovation is viewed as difficult to understand and use.

(4) *Trialability* is the degree to which an innovation may be tested on a limited basis.

(5) *Observability* is the degree to which the results of an innovation are visible to others.

In general, innovations that are perceived by receivers as having greater relative advantage, compatibility, trialability, and observability, as well as less complexity, will be adopted more rapidly than others. These are not the only qualities that affect adoption rates, but past research indicates that they are the most important characteristics of innovation in explaining rates of adoption.

COMMUNICATION CHANNELS

Communication is the process by which messages are transmitted from a source to a receiver, often with a view to modifying the receiver's behavior. The communication channel is the means by which the message gets from the source to the receiver.

Diffusion is a subset of communication in which the messages are concerned with innovations. The essence of the diffusion process is the interaction by which a new idea is communicated. In its most elementary form, the process involves: (1) an innovation, (2) an individual or other unit of adoption that has knowledge of the innovation, (3) another individual or unit that does not have knowledge of the innovation, and (4) a communication channel connecting the two units. The nature of the information-exchange relationship between the source and the receiver determines the conditions under which a source will or will not transmit the innovation to the receiver; further, it influences the effect of the transfer.

A general finding from past diffusion investigations is that mass media channels can be effective in creating awareness/knowledge of a new idea, but interpersonal networks carry messages about an innovation that convince individuals to adopt it. Even when scientific evidence about an innovation's results is available to potential adopters, they depend more heavily on subjective evaluations by peers.

TIME

Time is one of the most important considerations in the process of diffusion, since it is involved in (1) the innovation-decision process, (2) the relative innovativeness of the individual or other relevant unit of adoption, and (3) the innovation's rate of adoption in the social system.

The innovation-decision process is the mental process through which an individual unit of adoption progresses from initial awareness of an innovation, to a decision to adopt or reject, and finally to confirmation of this decision. We conceptualize four main functions in the process: (1) knowledge, (2) persuasion (attitude formation and change), (3) decision (adoption or rejection), and (4) confirmation.

The innovation decision can take a negative turn—that is, the final decision can be to reject, rather than to adopt, an innovation. Also, after the adoption decision is made, an adopter may decide to discontinue use of an innovation. The last step in the process is confirmation, a stage where the receiver seeks reinforcement for the adoption or rejection decision he or she has made. Occasionally contradictory messages reaching the receiver about the innovation may lead to discontinuance after adoption, or to adoption after previous rejection. Discontinuances also occur for other reasons, including replacement of the innovation with an improved idea.

Innovativeness is the degree to which an individual or other relevant unit of adoption is early relative to other members of a social system in deciding to use an innovation. Adopters may be classified as: (1) innovators, (2) early adopters, (3) early majority, (4) late majority, and (5) laggards. The measurement of innovativeness and the classification of a system's members into adopter categories are based on the time when an innovation is adopted.

A third way that the time dimension relates to diffusion involves an innovation's rate of adoption, or the relative speed with which it is adopted by members of a social system. This rate is usually measured by the time required for a certain percentage of the system's members to adopt the innovation, so the adoption rate is measured for an innovation or for a system rather than for an individual. As we pointed out earlier, innovations that are perceived by receivers as having greater relative advantage, compatibility, trialability, observability, and less complexity have a faster rate of adoption than others. There are also differences in the rate of adoption for the same innovation in different social systems.

MEMBERS OF A SOCIAL SYSTEM

A social system is a collectivity of units which are functionally differentiated and engaged in joint problem solving with respect to a common goal. The members or units of a social system may be individuals, informal groups, complex organizations, or subsystems. The social system analyzed in a diffusion study may consist of all the farmers of an Ohio county, all the peasants in a Latin American village, all the married women in a Korean village, staff and patients in a mental hospital, medical doctors in a large city, members of an Australian aborigine tribe, or all the regional and local government agencies in the standard metropolitan statistical areas in the United States. Each unit in the system can be functionally differentiated from every other. All members cooperate to the extent of seeking to solve a common problem or reach a mutual goal, and this sharing of an objective binds the system together.

The social system is important because its structure affects the innovation's diffusion patterns in several ways, and the system itself constitutes a set of boundaries within which innovations are diffused. For our purposes, the important aspects to consider are how the social structure affects diffusion, the roles of opinion leaders and change agents, and, finally, types of innovation decisions.

Social Structure and Diffusion

To the extent that the members in a social sytem are differentiated, structure exists within the system. Social structure develops through the arrangement of statuses or positions in the system. A formal organization such as a government agency has a well-developed, formal social structure, consisting of titled positions, which gives those in a higher-ranked status the right to give orders to those of lesser rank and to expect the orders to be carried out. Even an informal grouping has some degree of structure inherent in the interpersonal relationships among its members which determines who interacts with whom and in what circumstances. Naturally, both formal and informal social structures have an effect on human behavior and how it changes in response to communication stimuli.

Diffusion and social structure are interrelated in a complex fashion. The social structure of a system acts to impede or facilitate the rate of diffusion and adoption of innovations through what are called "system effects." The norms, social statuses, hierarchy, and so on of a social system influence the behavior of individual members of that system. System effects are the influences of the system's social structure on the behavior of individual members of the social system. Evidence from several studies indicates that system effects may be as important in explaining individual innovativeness as are such individual characteristics as education, social status, and the like. Diffusion may also change the social structure of a system in the sense that many innovations are of a restructuring nature. The adoption of quality control circles in a manufacturing firm changes the company's social structure by adding a new set of statuses. The initiation of a research and development unit within an industrial firm and the departmentalization of a public school are also restructuring innovations. In many instances, the restructuring affects the rate of future innovation diffusion within the system.

Opinion Leaders and Change Agents

Very often, the most innovative member of a system is perceived as a deviant from the social system and is accorded a somewhat dubious status and low credibility. This member's role in diffusion, especially in persuading others of the innovation, is therefore likely to be limited. At the same time, other members of the system function as opinion leaders, providing still others in the system with information and advice about innovations.

Opinion leadership is the ability to influence informally—and fairly often—individual attitudes or behavior in a desired way. Thus, opinion leadership is a type of informal leadership rather than a function of the individual's formal position or status in the system. Opinion leaders are usually members of the social system they influence. In some instances, however, individuals with influence in the social system are professionals who represent external change agencies.

A change agent is a professional who influences innovation decisions in a direction deemed desirable by a change agency. The change agent usually seeks to have new ideas adopted but may also attempt to slow down the diffusion and/or prevent the adoption of undesirable innovations. Change agents often use opinion leaders in a social system to prime the pump of planned change; however, there is no research evidence that opinion leaders can be "worn out" by change agents who overuse them. Opinion leaders may be perceived by their peers as too much like the change agents and thus lose credibility with their former followers.

Types of Innovation Decisions

The social system has yet another important kind of influence on the diffusion of new ideas. Innovations can be adopted or rejected by individual members of a system, or by the entire social system. The relationship between the social system and the decision to adopt an innovation may take one of several forms:

(1) Optional decisions—choices to adopt or reject innovations—are made by an individual independent of the decisions of other members of the system. Even in this case, the individual's decision is undoubtedly influenced by the norms of his or her social system and by his or her need to conform to interpersonal influences from the group. The decision of an individual to begin wearing contact lenses instead of eyeglasses, an Iowa farmer's decision to adopt hybrid corn, and a woman's adoption of birth control pills are examples of optional decisions.

(2) Collective decisions are choices to adopt or reject innovations that are made by consensus among the members of a system. All must conform to the system's decision once it is made. An example is fluoridation of a city's drinking water. Once the community decision is made, the individual has little practical choice but to accept fluoridated water.

(3) Authority decisions are choices to adopt or reject innovations that are made by a relatively few who possess power, status, and/or technical expertise. The individual's attitude toward the innovation is not the prime factor in his or her adoption or rejection; this individual is simply told of and expected to comply with the innovation decision made by those in authority. Relatively few research studies have been conducted of this type of innovation decision, which must be very common in an organizational society such as the United States today. In all authority decisions we must distinguish between the decision maker, who is one (or more) individual(s), and the adopter or adopters, who carry out the decision by implementing the innovation. In the case of optional and collective decisions, these two roles (of deciding and adopting) are performed by the same individual(s).

Collective and authority decisions are more common than optional decisions in organizations like factories, hospitals, schools, labor unions, and government agencies, in contrast to such areas as agriculture and family planning, where innovation decisions are usually optional. Generally, the fastest adoption rate is by authority decisions (depending, of course, on whether the authorities are innovative or not). In turn, optional decisions can be made more rapidly than collective decisions. Although made most rapidly, authority decisions are more likely than others to be circumvented in the process of their implementation and may eventually lead to a high rate of discontinuance. Where change depends on compliance under public surveillance, it is not likely to continue once the surveillance is removed.

The type of innovation decision for a given idea may change or be changed over time. Automobile seat belts, during the early years of their use in the United States, were installed in private autos largely as optional decisions. Then, in the late 1960s, many states began to require by law installation of seat belts in all new cars. In 1968 a federal law was passed to this effect. An optional innovation decision then became a collective decision.[5]

These three types of innovation decisions may, of course, occur in sequential order so that an optional decision, for example, cannot be made until a prior collective decision has been made.[6] Contingent decisions are choices to adopt or reject which can be made only after a prior innovation decision, and therefore are essentially a sequential combination of two or more of the three types we have just discussed.

Research on Innovation in Organizations

In recent years, an important advance in diffusion research has occurred in the area of organizational innovation processes. The scope of this newer type of diffusion research can be expressed in a question: How are innovations adopted and implemented in organizations, and to what effect?

HISTORICAL BACKGROUND

In the late 1960s and early 1970s, the classic model for the diffusion of innovations was applied to the study of innovation in organizations. As noted earlier, most of this early research was simply an extension of the classic diffusion model. It looked at the determinants of organizational innovativeness, defined as the degree to which an organization is relatively early in adopting new ideas compared with other similar organizations.

The research usually consisted of a correlational analysis of cross-sectional survey data of innovativeness in a sample of several hundred organizations. This rather stereotypic methodological approach provided some insight into the characteristics of innovative organizations but very little understanding about intraorganizational innovative behavior was generated.

Although the organization was the unit of analysis, the unit of observation (that is, of data gathering) was usually the individual, typically the chief executive of the organization (such as a school superintendent, a county health officer, a hospital administrator, or a factory manager). These individuals were treated just as the farmers had been in the Ryan and Gross (1943) study of hybrid corn diffusion. As Yin (1976) has pointed out, the individual-oriented classical diffusion model was too directly applied to the study of organizational innovativeness. In the very early organizational innovativeness studies, not much attention was paid to organizational structural variables or to other distinctive aspects of organizations as decision-making units. During the late 1960s and early 1970s, greater emphasis was placed on organizational structure as a class of independent variables, but such dimensions did not covary very highly with the dependent variable of innovativeness (see, for instance, Hage and Dewar, 1973; Mohr, 1969; Mytinger, 1968; and Gordon et al., 1974).

About 400 studies of organizational innovativeness were identified in a review of the literature (Rogers et al., 1977a), and this number had grown to approximately 500 by 1981 (Rogers, 1983). Most of the earlier studies dealt with a rather limited range of organizations, especially public schools and private firms. Since the late 1960s, studies of innovativeness in public organizations have begun to blossom. Among the public organizations studied in the United States were county health departments, hospitals, municipal fire departments, city governments, and other government agencies. The innovations investigated have shifted from modern math, instructional television, and health program innovations to "rapid water," GBF/DIME, Dial-A-Ride, downtown transit malls, impact attenuators, Godzilla trash collectors, computers, and methadone maintenance. Many of the later (post-1970) organizational innovativeness studies were conducted in public organizations.

Radnor and his colleagues (1978: 3–4) suggest some reasons that diffusion research attracted organization scholars from various academic disciplines and pointed them in the direction of innovation research:

(1) A diffusion approach seemed to promise a way for federal agencies that had invested in research on some topic to have the results utilized by state and local governments or by private organizations to solve a particular social problem.

(2) By tracing an innovation's rate of diffusion through a system in time and/or space, diffusion research can give life to a behavioral change process.

(3) The classical diffusion model, as a conceptual paradigm with relevance for many disciplines, allowed scholars to repackage their empirical findings in the form of higher-level generalizations. Downs and Mohr (1976) stated, "Innovation has emerged over the last decade as possibly the most fashionable of social science areas." Various behavioral science disciplines are involved in the study of innovation, including in recent years scholars of organizational behavior. "The popularity is not surprising. The investigation by innovation research of the salient behavior of individuals, organizations, and polities can have significant social consequences. [These studies] imbue even the most obscure piece of research with generalizability that has become rare as social science becomes increasingly specialized" (Downs and Mohr, 1976).

(4) The methodology implied by the classical diffusion model (in studying innovativeness) is clear-cut, straightforward, and relatively facile.

The Paradigm Shift in the 1970s

Despite its appeal to many scholars, the classical diffusion model has been blamed for restricting theoretic advance in the field of innovation in organizations. In the mid-1970s, a number of major criticisms of such diffusion research began to appear (Rogers and Shoemaker, 1971; Warner, 1974; Rogers and Agarwala-Rogers, 1976; Downs and Mohr, 1976; Mohr, 1978; Radnor et al., 1978).

The new school of diffusion research no longer emphasizes the overly stereotypic classical diffusion model. Rather, it uses theoretical and methodological approaches more appropriate to the new context of innovation in organizational settings. This represents a shift from the classical diffusion model in several ways. For example, the perceived characteristics of innovation, such as relative advantage, comparability, complexity, and so on vary depending on the basis of the potential adopting unit. The effects of different organizational determinants of innovation and the organization change (Downs, 1978: 2). The use of an "innovation-decision design" is suggested in place of the "multiple innovation design" (Downs and Mohr, 1976)—that is, study of the innovation process instead of organizational innovativeness.

Second, the "bottom line" for the innovation process in organizations is *implementation* (including institutionalization of a new idea), not just the adoption decision. Third, there is the realization that the adopter can also play an active, creative role in the innovative process, in matching the innovation with a perceived organizational problem, possibly including modification and reinvention of the innovation. An innovation should be conceived of not as a fixed, invariant, and static quality in the innovation process, but as a flexible and adaptable concept that is consecutively defined and redefined through increasing specification as the innovation process gradually unfolds. It was realized that the diffusion and adoption of all innovations is not necessarily advantageous for everyone in a given system. The same innovation may be desirable for one adopter but not for another potential adopter, depending on their respective situations (Rogers and Shoemaker, 1971: 21). Therefore, each innovation must be carefully studied in terms of its burdens, as well as its benefits, within the context of different potential adopters (Gold, 1978: 27). Previously, diffusion scholars tended to display a pro-innovation bias.

Finally, instead of an overdependence on a survey approach to gathering cross-sectional data about the correlates of innovativeness, diffusion researchers began to engage in more in-depth case studies of the innovation process in organizations. The case study approach exemplified what Mohr (1978) calls a "process" model, as compared to the variance model that characterized past studies of innovativeness. This newer research approach allowed diffusion scholars to pursue different theoretical interests (the process of innovation in an organization). The turn away from the highly structured and quantitative methods of investigating organizational innovativeness began in the 1970s when more qualitative, hypothesis-generating case studies of the innovation process in organizations began to be conducted.

Certainly, innovation is a process, a sequence of decisions and behavior changes over time. But past research designs almost never adequately allowed analysis of the temporal aspects of innovation that would be necessary to explore its process nature adequately. Very little past research included data at more than one observation point, and almost none at more than two such points. Therefore, almost all past research is unable to trace the change in a variable over "real" time; these investigations deal only with the present tense of innovation behavior. Diffusion and innovation thus become, in the actuality of research operations, an artificially halted snapshot.

Cross-sectional survey data cannot answer many of the "why" questions about innovation. The one-shot survey provides the grist for description, of course, and enables a type of correlational analysis; various independent variables are associated with the dependent variable of innovativeness. But little can be learned from such a correlational approach about *why* a particular independent variable covaries with innovativeness.

Mohr (1978) points out the confounding of variance and process approaches in past diffusion research.[7] A variance approach deals with variables and their associations. It deals with "snapshots" rather than "movies." The time-ordering among the independent and dependent variables is considered unimportant. Therefore, a variance approach is "state-oriented" rather than "process-oriented."

In contrast, a process approach specifies a series of events and a set of assumptions and rules determining the occurrences of each event in the series, hence providing an understanding of an over-time process. The time-ordering of the events involved in the process is critical.

In short, past diffusion research has lacked this process orientation. As noted earlier, few past studies have investigated the innovation process in organizations. We believe there is more long-term payoff in both theoretical and policy terms from improved knowledge of the innovation process than from the correlates-of-innovativeness approach alone. We recommend much greater attention to investigation of the innovation process in organizations and much less to determining correlates of organizational innovativeness, a shift from the variance approach to a process approach. We recommend a turn from the highly structured, quantitative, and hypothesis-testing studies of innovativeness to less structured, more qualitative, and hypothesis-generating approaches for analyzing the innovation process in organizations.

Instability of Diffusion Research Findings

A major theoretical criticsm of diffusion research comes from Downs and Mohr (1976), who concluded that "the most alarming characteristic of the body of empirical study of innovation is the extreme variance among its findings." In a later volume, Mohr (1978: 1) suggested that "the field of innovation research is thus actually overburdened with a plethora of interesting results whose relation to one another is so problematic as to produce more confusion than clarity." Downs and Mohr (1976) attribute this instability of empirical diffusion findings to "a lack of clarity on several conceptual issues." They point out that, of 38 generalizations cited by Rogers and Shoemaker (1971), 34 (almost 90 percent) were found to be "unstable."

Their point seems to be overstated. When a generalization is drawn at an abstract level, it will inevitably lack complete support from research results derived from particular conditions. Therefore, what is at issue is in part the degree of specificity (or abstractness) of research-based generalizations. Would not one be suspicious of perfect (100 percent) stability of research findings about a proposition? Is this "instability" of empirical findings unique to diffusion research?

Downs (1978: 3–4) described this instability in diffusion research findings as common in cross-academic discipline research and attributed it to the complex interactions among variables: "As requirements for accuracy and research integration have increased, a host of disciplines have discovered that contradictory findings are the result of nonsimple interaction and that the formulation of simple, contingent generalizations about relative impacts is impossible."

The diversity of disciplinary affiliations of scholars studying innovation in organizations may be one of the sources of instability. Diffusion scholars thus are studying different research questions with a variety of discipline-related assumptions, terminology, and research methods. This heterogeneity of disciplines may contribute to the "unrest and uncertainty" of diffusion research today. There is also doubt that this wide variety of disciplinary viewpoints, theories, and research approaches is an advantage (Radnor et al., 1978: 7–8).

Downs and Mohr (1976) claimed that the use of the organization or the innovation (independently of each other) as the unit of analysis is one of the main sources of instability in past research findings. They suggested (1976: 706) that the pairing of an innovation and an organization be taken as the unit of anlaysis: "The unit of anlaysis is no longer the organization, but the organization with respect to a particular innovation, no longer the innovation, but the innovation with respect to a particular organization." They strongly recommended using an "innovation-decision design"[8] with "an organization in relation to an innovation" as the unit of analysis. Employing this design, the sample size becomes the number of innovations times the number of organizations. For example, when studying the adoption of 10 innovations by 100 organizations, we would have a sample of 1,000 (10 × 100) innovations in relation to organizations.

Rogers et al. (1977b, 1979) used the "innovation-application" as the unit of analysis. The term "application" is equivalent to what Downs and Mohr (1976) called "an organization in relation to an innovation."

In past research, the innovation studied was viewed as static and invariant, a very dangerous reification (Downs and Mohr, 1976; Downs, 1978). An innovation is a set of elements and relationships that represent the characteristics of what the innovation is and how it is used, not a single, invariant, and unitary entity. "Customization of an innovation, as it passes through the innovation process, is an important dynamic; reinvention of the technological innovation may occur in this innovation process" (Rogers et al., 1979). *Specification* is the movement through the innovation process from the innovation as a general concept to its expression as a specific organizational set of behaviors regarding the innovation. An innovation is specified by an organization as it moves from awareness to initiation and from implementation to institutionalization (Rogers et al., 1979).

All these criticisms of past diffusion research tell us to shed the overemphasis on organizational innovativenss and to focus more heavily on investigating the innovation process in organizations.

METHODOLOGICAL PROBLEMS IN STUDYING
ORGANIZATIONAL INNOVATIVENESS

In the organizational innovativeness studies, a primary focus was usually on attributes of organizational structure as determinants of innovativeness. This viewpoint grew out of the previous work of such organization scholars as Lawrence and Lorsch (1969), who argued that organizations must develop structures appropriate for their milieu. The weight given to structural variables in explaining innovativeness may also have been a reflection of the scholarly disciplines that were becoming involved in organizational innovativeness research: sociology, political science, business management, public health, and social psychology.

Organizational innovativeness scholars used the organization as their main unit of analysis, a type of research methodology that was commonly utilized in studies of organizational behavior. This design, of course, assumed that most organizations operate as relatively autonomous units, with the organization's leaders making decisions for the organization, and with only minimum influence on such decisions coming from external sources. Thus, the organizational innovativeness studies looked within, rather than outside of, the organization for the primary explanation of innovation.

Because of the sample size (often 100 or more organizations), the typical organizational innovativeness study had to follow a highly quantitative approach. Independent variables such as centralization and formalization were measured for each organization. The dependent variable of innovativeness was typically measured as a composite score, composed of the adoption of from 10 to 20 innovations. The innovation process for each such innovation was thus merged through aggregation into an overall innovativeness score for each organization. As a result, differences among the innovations were lost. The cross-sectional approach to data analysis also meant that time as a variable was mainly obscured (except to the extent that the time dimension was captured in the innovativeness variable). Thus, the "process" (that is, over-time) aspects of the innovation process could not be measured.

In fact, most organizational innovativeness studies could not have been designed more appropriately to preclude understanding the innovation process in organizations. They were appropriately designed and conducted to determine the characteristics of more and less innovative organizations, but the results showed mainly that "attributes of organizational structure are by no means the sole determinants of innovation adoption" (Kervasdoue and Kimberly, 1978). The relatively modest correlations of organizational structure variables with innovativeness at least helped to establish the futility of understanding innovation in organizations through innovativeness surveys.

The question troubling any diffusion scholar who depends solely on data from the top leader in an organization is how fully such information can describe the organization's innovation behavior—probably not very.[9] The remedy, of course, is to follow a multiple-respondent data gathering design, as Bingham and Frendreis (1978) did, or better still a multimeasurement approach in which interview, archival, and other data are gathered.

Such an in-depth approach requires a smaller sample of organizations. While there would then be less basis for generalization of the research results, in return the approach would provide more reliable data and permit greater flexibility in tracing the nature of the innovation process in each organization. This research design follows a process approach rather than a variance approach (Mohr, 1978). The researcher learns more about less, rather than less about more.

The Innovation Process in Organizations

A MODEL OF THE INNOVATION PROCESS

Most recent investigations of the innovation process in organizations follow a relatively unstructured, open-ended, case-study approach to data gathering. Essentially, they consist of "tracer studies" of the innovation-decision process for a single innovation in an organization. These investigations typically are guided by a general model of the innovation process.

In the model guiding the authors' present research, innovation is viewed as a process of gradually specifying the operational details about an innovation as a system. In this sense, an innovation is not a single, unitary entity, but rather a set of elements and relationships that represent the characteristics of what the innovation is and how it is used.

The innovation process consists of a gradual specification of the new idea in five general stages, each characterized by a particular range of decisions to be made at that point. Later stages in the innovation process usually cannot be undertaken until earlier stages have been settled, either explicitly or implicitly. Thus there is a sequence to the following five stages in the innovation process:

I. Initiation Subprocess

(1) *Agenda-setting:* A general organizational problem that may create a perceived need for innovation is defined by members of the organization.

(2) *Matching:* A specific problem from the organization's agenda and an alternative solution (that is, an innovation) are brought together, and their fit is considered by members of the organization.

II. Implementation Subprocess

(3) *Redefining:* The innovation is defined in terms relevant to the particular organization and its perceived problem, as the technological innovation is modified during its implementation to fit these specific conditions. At this stage, a certain degree of reinvention may occur.

(4) *Structuring:* Organizational structures directly relevant to the innovation are altered to accommodate the innovation. For example, a new organizational unit may be created to manage and maintain the innovation.

(5) *Interconnecting:* Relationships between the innovation and the rest of the organization are clarified, so that the innovation eventually loses its separate identity and becomes an ongoing element in the organization's activities. This absorption of the innovation is sometimes called institutionalization or routinization (Yin, 1976, 1978).

The five steps in the innovation process can be divided into two main subprocesses, initiation and implementation, on the basis of the decision to adopt the innovation. *Initiation* consists of all the information gathering, conceptualizing, and planning for the adoption of the innovation in an organization leading up to the decision to adopt. *Implementation* consists of actually putting the innovation into use in an organization. In many cases, the initiators of an innovation in an organization are a different set of individuals than the implementors. Past diffusion research on organizational innovativeness largely centered on the decision to adopt, ignoring the study of implementation.

This use of the innovation application as the unit of analysis is consistent with the recommendation (mentioned previously) by Downs and Mohr (1976) on the basis of their critical review of innovation research: "It is helpful to employ an innovation-decision design, a consideration of the unit of analysis as an organization in relation to an innovation." What we term an application is what Downs and Mohr (1976) call "an organization in relation to an innovation." Organizations often adopt not a specific blueprint for an innovative activity but a general concept, the operational meaning of which gradually unfolds in the specification process of adopting and implementing a new idea.

REINVENTION

Component elements in an innovation are often modified, adapted, and changed when the innovation is implemented by various adopters as they fit the innovation to the distinctive conditions of their organizational situations.

Reinvention is the degree to which an innovation is changed by the adopter in the process of adoption and implementation after its original development (Rogers, 1978). The concept of reinvention is relatively new in research on innovation in organizations, and its recognition poses certain questions about the conduct and meaning of past research on this topic.

Most scholars have made a distinction between invention and innovation. *Invention* is the process by which a new idea is created or developed, while *innovation* is the process of adopting an existing idea. This difference, however, is not so clear-cut when we acknowledge that an innovation is not necessarily a fixed entity as it diffuses within a system; in fact, a new idea is frequently redefined in the process of its implementation by an adopting organization.

For most of the past four decades of research on the diffusion of innovations, these were regarded as invariant, essentially unchanging in the process of their diffusion and adoption. This research stance, in retrospect, now seems surprisingly oversimplified. The existence of reinvention was simply ignored; it was "noise" in the analysis, as it was then structured. Further, the degree of reinvention may have been rather low in the case of agricultural innovations like hybrid corn and 2,4-D weed spray due to the genetic, chemical, and biological nature of these innovations.

The current focus on reinvention was encouraged by Charters and Pellegrin (1972), who recognized the occurrence of reinvention (although they did not use the term per se). These researchers traced the adoption and implementation in four schools over a one-year period of the educational innovation of "differentiated staffing." They concluded:

> Differentiated staffing was little more than a word for most participants (that is, teachers and school administrators), lacking concrete parameters with respect to the role performance of participants, their modes

of interdependence and relationship, and generally the conduct of the instructional process. . . . The innovation was to be invented on the inside, not implemented from the outside.

Future Research on Reinvention

We suggest the following lines for future inquiry about reinvention:

(1) What does the S-curve of adoption, or a measure of the rate of adoption of an innovation, really mean if a high degree of reinvention occurs? If each innovation-adoption is different in certain crucial respects, an important (but previously unrecognized) source of variation is present in the diffusion process, casting some doubts on previous research findings (or at least suggesting the need for recasting previous results in light of the variable nature of each innovation-adoption).

(2) When is reinvention appropriate (such as in matching an innovation to an organization's problem), and when is it dysfunctional to the adopting unit?

(3) How can one best measure the degree of reinvention as a conceptual variable?

(4) How do the diffusion policies of innovation-support organizations (like the federal government) encourage or discourage the degree of reinvention that occurs among adopting units?

Conclusions

This chapter describes how studies of innovation in organizations grow out of earlier research on the diffusion of innovations among individuals. At first, investigations of innovativeness in organizations followed the classical model of diffusion too closely, slowly substituting the organization for the individual as the unit of analysis. Then, since the mid-1970s, tracer studies of innovation process in organizations were conducted following a five-stage model and concentrating on the implementation of an innovation as well as the factors leading to the decision to adopt. These more recent studies recognize the possibility of the innovation's reinvention during implementation as it is modified to fit the conditions and problems of the organization.

These newer approaches to investigating the diffusion of innovations in organizations promise to provide useful understandings of how new ideas are adopted by organizations, with implications for those who manage such organizations, and for government agencies and others who seek to introduce innovations into these organizations. The present viewpoint does not see organizations only as passive recipients of new ideas that are introduced from external sources, but also as active shapers of innovations as they are adapted and modified to fit an organization's circumstances.

NOTES

1. Mohr (1978: 3) defined a "variance" approach as centering on determining the covariance among a set of variables without determining their time-order. In contrast, a "process" approach seeks to determine the time-ordered sequence of a set of events.

2. *Reinvention* is the degree to which an innovation is changed by the adopter in the process of adoption and implementation after its original development (Rogers, 1978: 3).

3. We will focus on the innovation process in *public* organizations in this chapter because almost all past research on the diffusion of innovations in organizations has been conducted in public organizations. Whether these results and approaches are also appropriate for private firms is still an open question. Certainly there are important differences between public and private organizations (such as the profit-orientation of the latter) which are expected to affect the innovation process. Roessner (1977), however, questions whether public organizations are empirically less innovative than private organizations, even though they are intuitively expected to be so. Some understanding of innovation in private organizations is provided by Rogers and Larsen's (1984) study of semiconductor firms in the Silicon Valley of Northern California.

4. The main ideas in the following section are adapted from Rogers and Shoemaker (1971).

5. In another sense, an optional decision was still required by the automobile driver or passenger to use the belts—that is, to fasten them when getting in the seat. The collective decision in 1968 led to a rapid (100 percent) installation of the belts but not to a parallel increase in the use of the safety devices.

6. Of course, there are also many innovation decisions which are difficult to categorize in that they fall between these three types; nevertheless, the three types are heuristically distinct.

7. The distinction between these two approaches resembles that between the "etic" and "emic" research approaches discussed by Osgood et al. (1957), Pike (1967), and Harris (1968). In etic research, the investigator structures the respondent's responses in terms of the investigator's own categories and codes. Emic research is characterized by allowing the respondent to provide the categories and codes in which his or her responses are classified.

8. Downs and Mohr (1976: 706, 712–713) define the innovation-decision design as "essentially a single-innovation design, which explicitly recognizes that a great many organizational characteristics can be validly measured only in relation to a particular innovation."

9. How fully a leader's information describes an organization's behavior depends on how many individuals in the organization are actually involved in an innovation decision. Not many individuals are involved in most such decisions in public organizations, as suggested by the available evidence (Rogers et al., 1977b, 1979; Bingham, 1976). In most cases, the chief executive is not directly involved. Depending solely on

106

Innovation in the Public Sector

his or her perceptions of the innovation process would, therefore, give a dangerously incomplete picture.

REFERENCES

BINGHAM, R. D. (1976) The Adoption of Innovation by Local Government. Lexington MA: D. C. Heath.
——— and J. P. FRENDREIS (1978) "Innovation characteristics and the adoption of zero-base budgeting: agreement and conflict in city administration." Paper presented at the 36th annual meeting of the Midwest Political Science Association, Chicago.
CHARTERS, W. W., Jr., and R. J. PELLEGRIN (1972) "Barriers to the innovation process: four case studies of differentiated staffing." Educational Administration Quarterly 9 (Winter): 3–14.
DOWNS, G. W., Jr. (1978) "Complexity and innovation research," in M. Radnor et al. (eds.), The Diffusion of Innovations: An Assessment. Evanston, IL: Northwestern University, Center for the Interdisciplinary Study of Science and Technology.
——— and L. B. MOHR (1976) "Conceptual issues in the study of innovation." Administrative Science Quarterly 21 (December): 700–714.
GOLD, B. (1978) "Some shortcomings of research on the diffusion of industrial technology," in M. Radnor et al. (eds.), The Diffusion of Innovations: An Assessment. Evanston, IL: Northwestern University, Center for the Interdisciplinary Study of Science and Technology.
GORDON, G. et al. (1974) "Organizational structure, environmental diversity, and hospital adoption of medical innovations," pp. 53–75 in A. D. Kaluzny et al. (eds.), Innovation in Health Care Organizations: An Issue in Organizational Change. Chapel Hill: University of North Carolina, School of Public Health.
HAGE, J. and R. DEWAR (1973) "Elite values versus organizational structure in predicting innovation." Administrative Science Quarterly 18 (September): 580–597.
HARRIS, M. (1968) The Rise of Anthropological Theory. New York: T. Y. Crowell.
KATZ, D. and R. L. KAHN (1966) The Social Psychology of Organizations. New York: John Wiley.
KERVASDOUE, J. de and J. R. KIMBERLY (1978) "Are organization structures culture-free? The case of hospital innovation in the U.S. and France," pp. 77–95 in A. Neghandi and B. Wilpert (eds.), Cross-Cultural Studies on Organizational Functioning. Kent, OH: CARI Press.
KUHN, T. S. (1970) The Structure of Scientific Revolution (2d ed.). Chicago: University of Chicago Press.
LAMBRIGHT, W. H. (1977) "Innovating in urban mass transit: The Syracuse Dial-A-Bus," pp. F1–F46 in W. H. Lambright (ed.), Adoption and Utilization of Urban Technology: A Decision-Making Study. Syracuse, NY: Syracuse Research Corporation.
LAWRENCE, P. R. and J. W. LORSCH (1969) Organization and Environment: Managing Differentiation and Integration. Homewood, IL: Richard D. Irwin.
MOHR, L. B. (1978) "Process theory and variance theory in innovation research," in M. Radnor et al. (eds.), The Diffusion of Innovations: An Assessment. Evanston, IL: Northwestern University, Center for the Interdisciplinary Study of Science and Technology.

_____ (1969) "Determinants of innovation in organizations." American Political Science Review 63 (March): 111–126.

MYTINGER, R. (1968) Innovation in Local Health Services: A Study of the Adoption of New Programs by Local Health Departments, with Particular Reference to Newer Medical Care Activities. Washington, DC: U.S. Government Printing Office, PHS Publication 1664–2.

OSGOOD, C. E., G. J. SUCI, and P. H. TANNENBAUM (1957) The Measurement of Meaning. Urbana: University of Illinois Press.

PIKE, K. L. (1967) Language in Relation to a Unified Theory of the Structure of Human Behavior (2d ed.). The Hague: Mouton.

RADNOR, M. et al. (1978) "Research on the diffusion of innovations: a reappraisal," in M. Radnor et al. (eds.), The Diffusion of Innovations: An Assessment. Evanston, IL: Northwestern University, Center for the Interdisciplinary Study of Science and Technology.

ROESSNER, J. D. (1977) "Incentives to innovate in public and private organizations." Administration and Society 9 (November): 341–365.

_____ (1978) "Re-invention during the innovation process," in M. Radnor et al. (eds.), The Diffusion of Innovations: An Assessment. Evanston, IL: Northwestern University, Center for the Interdisciplinary Study of Science and Technology.

_____ (1976) "Where are we in understanding the diffusion of innovations?" pp. 204–222 in W. Schramm and D. Lerner (eds.), Communication and Change: The Last Ten Years and the Next. Honolulu: University Press of Hawaii, East-West Center.

ROGERS, E. (1983) Diffusion of Innovations, 3d ed. New York: Free Press.

_____ and R. ADHIKARYA (1979) "Diffusion of innovations: an up-to-date review," pp. 67–81 in D. Nimmo (ed.), Communication Yearbook 3. New Brunswick, NJ: Transaction.

ROGERS, E. and R. AGARWALA-ROGERS (1976) Communication in Organizations. New York: Free Press.

ROGERS, E. and J. LARSEN (1984) Silicon Valley Fever: Growth of High-Technology Culture. New York: Basic Books.

ROGERS, E. with J. D. EVELAND (1978) "Diffusion of innovations perspectives on national R&D assessment: communication and innovation in organizations," pp. 275–297 in P. Kelly and M. I. Kranzberg (eds.), Technological Innovation: A Critical Review of Current Knowledge. San Francisco: San Francisco Press.

ROGERS, E. with F. F. SHOEMAKER (1971) Communication of Innovations: A Cross-Cultural Approach. New York: Free Press.

ROGERS, E., L. WILLIAMS, and R. B. WEST (1977a) Bibliography of the Diffusion of Innovations. Monticello, IL: Council on Planning Librarians, Exchange Bibliography, nos. 1420–1422.

_____ (1977b) The Innovation Process in Public Organizations: Some Elements of a Preliminary Model. Ann Arbor: University of Michigan, Department of Journalism.

ROGERS, E. et al. (1979) The Innovation Process for Dial-A-Ride. Stanford, CA: Stanford University, Institute for Communication Research.

RYAN, B. and N. C. GROSS (1943) "Diffusion of hybrid seed corn in two Iowa communities." Rural Sociology 8 (March): 15–24.

TARDE, G. (1903) The Laws of Imitation (tr. E. C. Parsons). New York: Henry Holt.

WARNER, K. E. (1974) "The need for some innovative concepts of innovation." Policy Sciences 5 (December): 433–451.

YIN, R. K. (1978) Changing Urban Bureaucracies: How New Practices Become Routinized. Lexington, MA: D. C. Heath.

———— (1976) "The routinization of new technology in local services." Washington, DC: The Rand Corporation.

PART II

Innovation in Practice: West Germany

CHAPTER 5

INNOVATION IN WEST GERMANY'S PUBLIC SECTOR

THOMAS ELLWEIN

Recent discussions in both academic and political circles in the Federal Republic of Germany on innovation in the public sector have proceeded from two perspectives. The first focuses on events immediately after 1945 and asks, To what extent was there ever a "zero hour," that is, a point at which developments in postwar West Germany could proceed *ab ovo?* To what extent did postwar politics and economics take their cue from longstanding German traditions? The second perspective concerns reform efforts in the 1960s and 1970s. These, it is widely held, did not fulfill expectations and have, in almost all instances, led nowhere. As a result, the argument continues, the average citizen is tired of reform.

The extent to which politics and economics in the three Western zones of occupation—later the Federal Republic of Germany—grew out of German tradition cannot be conclusively determined. That these traditions played a significant part, however, cannot be denied. In fact, both politics and economics could and indeed had to rest on the legal, organizational, and circumstantial situation that existed before 1945 (see Hammerschmidt, 1965; Bracher, 1970; Löwenthal and Schwarz, 1974; Winkler, 1979; Ellwein and Bruder, 1984).

Among the elements of tradition, three deserve specific mention, since they significantly affected the development of the administrative system. They also help to determine how innovations come about in the public sector.

First, Germany has never been a centralized state. The functions of the state have always been divided between its territorial units (*Länder*) and the central authority (the *Reich,* later the *Bund*). There was no precise separation of jurisdictions, but rather an intermingling of tasks. This necessitated complicated negotiations between the central and *Land* governments, negotiations at once facilitated and complicated by the fact that in the Länder the federal government has no administrative organization of its own. In West Germany the federal government has sole control over only the foreign service, defense forces, customs, and some aspects of financial administration. This practice actually dates back to the structure of the first federal state in Germany, when individual Länder already had such highly developed administrative systems that no federal system could be superimposed on them. The result today is not only that the federal and Land governments must negotiate with each other, but they also depend on each other in carrying out executive functions. The administrative power that resides with the Länder gives them a great deal of influence over the federal government. This is clearly shown in the role played by the *Bundesrat* (Federal Council) in Bonn. The Bundesrat is not a parliament but rather a political body, composed of representatives of the Land governments, that makes decisions by majority vote and may, in certain circumstances, take a stand significantly different from that of the *Bundestag* (Federal Parliament) (see von Beyme, 1979; Ellwein, 1983; Sontheimer and Röhring, 1977; on federalism, Deuerlein, 1972).

Second, local autonomy is limited. The federal and Land governments define generally, and in many cases specifically, which tasks are to be the responsibility of a local community. They also use the local administrative apparatus to implement their own functions. Local communities thus find their activity closely circumscribed by the state, which leaves them limited discretion in adapting laws and regulations to local conditions. Since they are not permitted to collect taxes, they must rely on allocations from the federal and Land governments. In their authority over local administration, however, including the administration of federal and regional law, they regain a portion of the power they might have under an ideal form of communal autonomy. Even here, a clear division of functions does not exist; many tasks are carried out by both local and Land authorities, while others, such as road construction, are performed by local communities, the Länder, and federal authorities.[1]

Third, laws have a carefully defined and special function in German society. The Federal Republic carried over a German tradition, according to which laws have a threefold function: (a) They distinguish the public from the private sphere by defining the rights of the state with respect to the citizen; (b) they enable the federal government to instruct the *Länder* about how to carry out federal legislation, and similarly they are instruments of the Land governments vis-à-vis the local authorities; and (c) laws are the primary instrument available to the parliament and cabinet for directing the administration. The German constitution does not permit the state to do anything affecting the citizen without legislative action. Every directive within the political system from a higher level downward also rests on laws. Moreover, since all state activity depends almost entirely on laws, it is also almost entirely open to judicial review. The citizen may go to court against the local government or the state, a Land against federal authorities, a community against its own Land. Such recourse via the law, which originated in Germany during the nineteenth century, is often considered more effective than appealing to political institutions (Ellwein and Görlitz, 1968; Böckenförde, 1958; Maihofer, 1973; Noll, 1973).

Since most civil undertakings are based on laws enacted after the federal and land governments have reached agreement, it is in legislation that evidence for innovations and reforms must normally be sought. A law, however, brings about merely the basic decision. Whether or not that decision prevails and what effect it has must be looked into separately. One may then find that what the law intended has been fully realized, or that steps to adapt or change it have been initiated, or that the law is only formally observed.[2] In any case, no matter what the degree of implementation, the innovations and reforms leave some imprint.

During the 1960s, the issue of reform became a predominant topic (Luhmann, 1971a, 1971b). A great many reforms, or experiments proclaimed as reforms, were attempted, but in fact the resulting changes were limited and brought about a certain amount of disillusionment (Schwan and Sontheimer, 1969; Greiffenhagen, 1978). To understand this apparent contradiction requires an understanding of the starting point for such reform efforts. For one thing, there have been more far-reaching changes since the creation of the Federal Republic than in almost any previous time in German history. Examples may be found in the development of social security and the expansion of systems of public health, education, and public transportation. This expansion of public services is clearly shown by such indicators as the growth of the civil service, increased governmental shares of national income, and the redistribution of social wealth. At the same time, fundamental reforms have been the exception, because existing structures have impeded true reform in most policy areas.

Innovation: Delimiting the Issue

The following survey of innovation in the administrative system of the Federal Republic focuses on the special features of German federalism, local autonomy, and the German tradition of government by law. It also takes into account the debates of the 1960s and 1970s carried on mainly within the scholarly community. What makes this task problematic is the difficulty of delimiting the subject in a meaningful way. Since a comprehensive review of the direct and indirect functions of the administrative system is impracticable, this chapter proceeds pragmatically to deal with selected structures and processes within the framework of the debate of the last two decades.

An important difficulty requiring such a pragmatic treatment is the fact that innovation takes place within a system, irrespective of whatever may have preceded it by way of the development and diffusion of processes or inventions (Rogers with Shoemaker, 1971; Badura et al., 1978; Bruder, 1980). It may strengthen the existing system (innovation as norm, innovation as routine) or modify it (innovation as adaptation). The former derives observably from a direct or indirect decision by the legislature, cabinet, ministry, or some other decision-making unit. The latter also stems from such a decision, but external analysts may find it more difficult to trace the actual innovation to the original decision.

Innovation by adaptation is hard to distinguish from social change or general changes in an organization. Still, such a distinction should be made for pragmatic reasons. Change includes developments affecting administrative language patterns, relations between an agency and the public, and even the consequences of technical innovations for an administration. Innovations, by contrast, whether based on an unequivocal decision or more ambiguous processes of adaptation,[3] are intended as improvements. (This view of innovation approximates the common usage of the term *reform*, which will be used here in such a sense.)

What follows is a descriptive account of innovation—that is, efforts at improvement—in the Federal Republic's public sector. It concludes with some suggestions for analysis and evaluation that may permit a more comprehensive examination of conditions for innovation in the West German political system.

Structural Innovation

COMMUNAL TERRITORIAL REFORM

When the Federal Republic of Germany was constituted in 1949, both government and administration were confronted with established frontiers without and the division of federal states (*Bundesländer*) within. During the 1960s, the Länder decided to reexamine the boundaries and size of local communities and hence the territorial infrastructure of the subordinate state authorities. In the counties or districts (*Landkreise*), such state authorities were at the same time representatives of communal associations (*Gemeindeverbände*). The move toward a merger was motivated mainly by planning difficulties. Postwar conditions had brought about a high rate of mobility among the population, and consequently large-scale relocations. Both phenomena caused grave problems, especially within and toward the edges of densely populated areas, and tempted the communities to exploit for their own purposes difficulties at the centers of concentration. Apart from planning problems, the question was raised as to whether or not the trend toward migration into high-density areas might not possibly be eased by expanded urbanization. This led to regional zoning on the one hand and, on the other, to a desire to strengthen administrative powers at the local level. To achieve this goal, a minimum size for each community, or administrative association of communities, was considered indispensable (Schimanke, 1978; Wrage, 1975; Tiggemann, 1977).

Conditions for territorial reform in eight of the Länder—the remaining three, being city-states, need not be considered here—were unequal due to size and because, in some cases, there had always existed offices that administered jointly some aspects of certain smaller communities. Nevertheless, the general development was similar. It was hoped that each community would have an average minimum size of 5,000 inhabitants. At the outset, incentives were established for voluntary association among communities; later, comprehensive legislation was to complete the reform. To date, with the process not yet completed, there has been substantial progress in meeting the goal. The total number of communities has been reduced from about 24,000 to a third that number in 1976 (see Ellwein, 1983).

On closer inspection, this territorial reform turns out in fact to be an administrative reform, because its two principal purposes—rational use of communal planning authority, and strengthened local administrative potential—were aimed at the overall administrative system. During the initial discussions, it was agreed to set aside for the moment the question of whether one ought to strengthen local autonomy (that is, enable communities to play their full part within an integrated pattern of federation, Länder, and local communities) or else view them as a counterbalance to the central authority and thus make it possible for *all* local governments to function as independent powers in a decentralized system. The large cities had always been able to do this to a certain extent. The final decisions made in this regard were closer to the first model.

The West German "Basic Law," as the constitution is termed, postulates a "uniformity of living conditions" as a goal of public policy. Differences in the education system, for instance, which are constitutionally in the sphere of competence of the Länder, meet with criticism rather than acceptance as a normal consequence of federalism. In those regards requiring national legislation and hence generalization, however, the leveling effect is usually accepted without opposition. In contrast to local communities, which were being merged by subnational levels of government and in which local pride made organized resistance to territorial reform not only possible but sometimes even successful, counties rarely offered organized resistance (except in those county seats where residents feared the elimination of government offices or a loss of jobs). County reform was thus administrative in a double sense: because it reformed administrative structures, and because it was carried through in the administration itself, where popular consent or dissent plays no decisive part.

Through these reforms, the administrative system no doubt became more efficient, at least initially. But increasing the size of local communities also meant a larger, more professionalized communal workforce (Ellwein and Zoll, 1973a, 1973b). Honorary and part-time officials, usually more independent and less sensitive than professionals to directives from superiors, have been all but eliminated. As a result, most local administrations have become large enough to differentiate their functions and specialize their personnel. This has contributed to professionalization and improved relations, both formal and informal, among specialists at different levels. In counties, the situation is similar. By and large, every two county administrations were consolidated, and this in turn initiated a process of internal differentiation and specialization that enhanced bureaucratic efficiency. That these developments have had their costs in terms of ties between community personnel and the citizenry is also clear (Ellwein, 1976, 1978, 1979b).

In fine, territorial reform, apart from its secondary effects on society and the political system as a whole, must be seen as a lasting structural change in the administrative system. Such an innovation has far-reaching consequences. Realized through legislation and subject to judicial review, it can be termed successful because, compromises on details notwithstanding, the innovation itself was not stifled. Even the compromises may be seen as part of a process of innovation by which administrators and politicians preserve or improve their ability to anticipate resistance and, without yielding on matters of principle, accept changes in details. Essentially, this was possible because the innovation process took place mainly in the administrative system itself (see Schimanke, 1978, on Baden-Württemberg). Resistance thus came mostly from within the system. It could be overcome because the demand for reform came from above and was, therefore, sustained by the instruments of power wielded by Land ministries over their own subordinate officials, as well as local communities.

Although earlier discussions among scholars and publicists had taken place on the need for reform, the process of innovation rested almost exclusively on initiatives from within the system. What decision makers had to digest before arriving at ideas for change were essentially internal experiences. They were *not* adapting the system to environmental conditions.[4] Opinions may differ, however, over the question of whether or not the territorial reform anticipated future environmental needs. I would argue that the administrative system obtained increased power, thereby bolstering its relative autonomy within the political system, and that the reasons advanced internally as well as externally were based on anticipated future needs.

FUNCTIONAL REFORM

Territorial reform in the Federal Republic could be neither discussed nor implemented without dealing with the question of whether or not the existing civil service structure and division of functions among administrative levels continued to be appropriate. The anticipated problems were examined at an early stage under the rubric of "functional reform" (Hoffmann, 1973). The debate over whether functional or territorial reform ought to have priority remained inconclusive. In general, territorial reform was carried out through extensive legislation and according to precisely calculated time schedules. Functional reform required several stages and has not been finished to this day.

Functional reform includes three constellations of innovation (Thränhardt, 1978; Wittkämper, 1978). The first is a general check on areas of responsibility previously established by law and their distribution within the administrative system. This scrutiny began in the 1950s with the aim of weeding out obsolete laws. Bavaria, for instance, streamlined its laws in 1957. The 177 volumes (with 110,000 pages) of official laws and decrees (*Gesetz- und Verordnungsblatt*) published after January 1802 were replaced in January 1958 by four volumes (*Bereinigte Sammlung*) with only 2,700 pages (Bayern, Staatskanzlei, 1968: 7). Other Länder and the federation followed suit. This process of weeding out the obsolete provided an opportunity not only to make the codes of law more rational, but also to create commissions that could reexamine jurisdictions. Although it proved impossible to reduce the number of jurisdictions, the commissions could at least clarify their spheres of competence.

Despite the fact that any state activity in West Germany is based on legislation, all attempts to get a grip on these jurisdictions or even to arrange them in a logical system have failed (Ellwein, 1976: esp. 84ff.). Only the relations between the federation and the Länder have become clearer, thanks to the Basic Law and the obligation to amend that document whenever significant changes occur. Waves of such reforms took place in the 1960s when the recommendations of the Troeger Commission were implemented (Kommission für die Finanzreform, 1966). The proposals outlined a decade later by a committee set up by the Bundestag have not yet been adopted (Enquête Kommission, 1977).

The second type of innovation comprises all the efforts for administrative reorganization. Primary among these were the elimination of small offices and the establishment of larger administrative units; it also involved the internal centralization of numerous functions, including such diverse tasks as establishing car pools and sharing personnel and legal counsel. Such decisions are usually made in accord with the organizational authority of the governmental unit involved (Böckenförde, 1964). They are, therefore, not readily visible, although a first impression may be gained from such things as the fact that, in Bavaria, about a third of all finance and land survey offices were eliminated between 1948 and 1968 (Bayern, Staatskanzlei, 1968: 7).

The third type of innovation consists of what is normally called internal administrative reform. Included here are personnel guidance and collegial responsibility sharing, encouraging individual staff members to use independent judgment, as well as administrative simplification in the sense of designing less complex forms, streamlining the reporting system, facilitating financial transactions, and so forth (Sachverständigenkommission, 1957). It is difficult to draw limits in this area, for we are concerned here less with tangible decisions than with a general change of climate (that is, more with structural than process innovations, which will be discussed below).

In contrast to territorial reform, functional reform is not easily identified. Nevertheless, it does exist. The transfer of functions, organizational modification, delegation of authority, and a good many measures aimed at optimizing the use of available resources do occur. Moreover, in this regard the political leadership seems to be under a certain amount of pressure. After having insisted in the 1960s on the need for administrative reform and simplification (see Bayern, Staatskanzlei, 1968; Projektgruppe, 1969; Hegelau, 1977), it must now show results. The 1970s saw mounting criticism of bureaucracies and bureaucratization. Citizen initiatives sprang up, some of them quite vigorous in *inter alia* expressing doubt as to the rationality, efficiency, and good sense of what the administration does. Politicians react to such pressure with the slogan, "getting close to the citizens," and appoint committees charged with working out further proposals. Yet no one can claim that there has been any great functional reform; at best, one might speak of tentative steps in the direction of reform.

Functional reform as an innovatory process faces the difficulty that its procedures are not exactly clear-cut. To the degree that it was brought about by laws and decrees, it has been extensive and successful, but efforts to modify procedures and attitudes are almost impossible to evaluate. That the climate generally has improved in the civil service can only be conjectured. One may assume that differences of status and rank play a lesser role today than in the past. That the individual civil servant's room for discretion has increased cannot, however, be assumed, at least judging from a few available empirical studies (Grunow et al., 1978). Altogether, it is hard to escape the impression that, although external pressure has affected the administrative system, practically all reforms have sprung from internal initiatives. Coming from below, these innovations have not attracted powerful support, especially since a strong interest in direct administrative action has evidently continued to assert itself in both federal and Land ministries.

GOVERNMENT REFORM

The Länder governments that were set up shortly after the end of the war, as well as the federal government somewhat later, were organized according to patterns that had become well established in nineteenth-century Germany. These patterns were the subject of criticism even before 1933. In the immediate postwar years, such reservations gave way to more pressing needs. Criticism flared up once again, however, as state activities entailing a substantial inflation of bureaucracy steadily intensified and the government apparatus became increasingly cumbersome. Of primary interest here was the federal government; detailed studies on Länder governments are still a rarity (but see Dillkofer, 1977; Katz, 1975). Some critiques contained proposals for change, and some of these proposals were actually accepted by committees set up to explore avenues for reform (Projektgruppe, 1969).

Regardless of results, therefore, it is possible to speak of an innovation process in government organization. One may also distinguish here between organizational (or structural) innovation and procedural (or process) innovation, although in practice they are closely connected. The introduction of certain planning procedures, for instance, was frustrated for organizational reasons (Mayntz and Scharpf, 1973; Schatz, 1973; Murswieck, 1975). Finally, leaving aside the question of the extent of bureaucratic developments that take place in both and are conditioned by each other, it is possible to distinguish between government and administration, with the former superordinate at any level of organization.

In the discussion about desirable changes in government organization at the federal level, several issues very quickly came to the fore: the number of ministries, an important issue then as now, since the constitution provides for equal status of all federal ministers; the status of the federal cabinet and chancellery, especially in coordinating policies; the excessive burden on those responsible for each ministry's political direction, which creates a bottleneck between themselves and their usually steadily expanding ministries; within each ministry, the cumbersome bureaucracy of specialized offices (*Referate*) with their strict separation of responsibilities; and, finally, due to the strong position of these offices, the difficulty of distributing rationally the fluctuating volume of work. For many years it was common practice in Bonn to increase the number of employees in an overburdened office rather than to draw staff members from some other office that might not have enough work.

Government reform takes place in the public limelight. This is due in part to the generality of knowledge about administrative developments. With the exception of those dealing with particular scandals or extraordinary bungling, for instance, most complaints lodged about the administration are of a general nature, based on the sheer growth of the civil service. Similarly, reforms (or what passes for reforms) are invariably scrutinized in the light of earlier discussions in numerous professional or general publications (Hochschule, 1967, 1973; Lepper, 1973; for surveys of the literature and debate, Ellwein, 1968, 1979c; on the parliamentary secretary of state, Wahl, 1971).

Several changes that were made legislatively are by and large uncontroversial: Work in the cabinet was made more efficient by establishing committees; the number of federal ministries was reduced once again in 1969; ministers obtained parliamentary secretaries of state; planning units, with instructions to cooperate with one another, were set up in the office of the federal chancellor and in the ministries; ministries experimented to a certain extent with their specialized offices, such as integrating some of them or adding hierarchical levels of organization by forming groups of offices; and more frequent studies were made, on the strength of which, for instance, the central services were better integrated, overlapping responsibilities reduced, and special temporary units established to handle unusual political or administrative workloads (Hegelau, 1977; Mayntz and Scharpf, 1973). Without touching the fundamental structure of government, which is guaranteed by Article 65 of the Basic Law, there have been important changes in the detailed operation of government. Together, they have partly counteracted the effects of growing numbers of both ministries and ministerial units, as well as the greater volume of governmental responsibilities. There can be no denying the fact that the government has shown itself capable of learning and innovating, even though it would be rash to speak of the kind of governmental reform that has so frequently been called for.

At the same time, two further quesions must be asked: Did the government sufficiently absorb the ideas being discussed, and did the extent of changes actually achieved correspond to what was recognized as being needed? Both questions are answered in the negative by many, because the primary problem in West German governmental organization—overload—has not yet been resolved. Moreover, there is practically no evidence that the responsible decision makers are prepared to define precisely the difference between governmental and administrative matters, and then to leave all essentially administrative tasks to the administrative services. Rather, the ministries have tended to fall victim to that administrative specialization which they themselves had fostered. The ever-increasing number of special authorities and units of experts has created an ever-increasing need for coordination. As a rule, this need cannot be satisfied by the general administration (Sonderarbeitskreis, 1973; Wagener, 1976), weakened as it is today even in its center of power, the provincial executives (Fonk, 1967). Coordination must thus proceed from the bottom upwards. Increasingly, the ministries have gained primary jurisdiction, even over policies of limited scope.

The expansion of special offices at the expense of the general administration affects governmental organization as well. Central direction is frustrated at an intermediary level and, since the ministries have more and more contact with special offices at subordinate administrative levels, these segmented and specialized units both interrupt and inflate hierarchical relations. The process is intensified by the existence side by side of both the federal and Land governments. The former, in broad areas lacking an administrative apparatus of its own, feels cut off from certain information and often tries to make up for this by instituting its own administrative activities or setting up administrative bodies in disguise—law firms, for instance, which dispense public funds, or groups of experts who influence the use of these public funds (Becker, 1978).

Reform mandated by laws and decrees and a propensity to innovate with respect to the structure of ministries coexist with an equally discernible tendency to accept and, without examination, adapt to existing circumstances. Traditional structures are surprisingly tenacious. This became most evident, perhaps, when the effort to set up intraministerial planning groups, especially for political planning, encountered the resistance of both ministerial officials harboring the widespread view that everyone in the ministry should be part of the staff, and of careerists blocking the promotion of other staff members. Discrimination against such special groups, irrespective of what they were called in various federal ministries, soon produced a generally retrogressive trend (Mayntz and Scharpf, 1973; Murswieck, 1975; Böhret, 1978).

This record shows no clear-cut mode of innovation in governmental organization. Modifications were achieved through both routine measures and processes that were virtually imperceptible. No comprehensive strategy for change existed. Among the changes, we find both successes and marked failures. Innovative ideas and proposals originated inside and outside the organization. They sought both to adapt to and contend with environmental needs. The movement of the late

1960s toward planning, for instance, was really an attempt to improve the responsiveness of the system by providing better information and early coordination.

REFORM OF CIVIL SERVICE STATUTES

After 1945 there was a great deal of discussion, much of it instigated by the occupation powers, about the German tradition of a professional civil service. It resulted, as a similar discussion in 1919 had, in the continuation of this institution and its entrenchment through the guarantees provided in Article 33 of the Basic Law. The post-World War II situation was significantly different from that of 1919, however, mainly because the civil service was substantially larger. Indeed, the need for qualified civil servants was so large in the late 1940s and 1950s that it was impossible to educate sufficient numbers of potential applicants or provide advanced training for those already in the civil service. Filling the need required co-opting ever more employees without civil service status who could perform the same functions as civil servants. It was primarily the administration's desire for greater efficiency that prompted this expansion. It also diluted, however, the civil service's traditional linkages to the state—the absolute loyalty given to the state by civil servants, for example, in exchange for absolute job security and other benefits. A practical consequence was an increase in the number of professional qualifications required for public service, which in turn made it more and more difficult to lay down legally based conditions of employment for civil servants (Wiese, 1972; Laux, 1978).

Any changes that have occurred have taken place in the context of a long-standing debate on two sets of issues. One set concerns the necessary statutory response of the civil service to the new situation (and other social changes). This includes the possibility of relaxing the special legal bonds tying the civil servant to the state; bringing civil service salaries into line with general income levels; creating a vast number of new positions, partly to improve career chances and salaries, partly to maintain internal differentiation within the service; and, finally, differentiating the civil service to accommodate not only its traditional members (lawyers, teachers, the intermediary service in general, and some special groups such as forest rangers and locomotive engineers) but also many new professional groups that have entered public service. Through changes of this sort, the civil service could adjust to new demands being made on it without changing its original legal structure. Since the structure of the civil service as a whole is based on law, such continuous adjustments have required commensurate changes in relevant legislation. Wage agreements with unions, too, are made for employees and workers in the public service on the basis of civil service status. In other words, legislative action and union agreements are mutually interrelated.

The other part of the debate notes that, in view of the fundamental changes that have taken place, holding on to earlier civil service statutes would merely exacerbate existing contradictions. Accordingly, in this view, reform is necessary. In the late 1960s the clamor for reform became so loud that the federal government acceded to the Bundestag's request to appoint a committee of independent experts to study the "position and functions of the public service in the state and society of today" (Studienkommission, 1973: 1). The committee's charge was to "submit proposals for promoting the development of a modern public service." The report issued by the committee yielded a wealth of reform proposals, all of which, however, took a middle road. Its thrust was that the constitutional principles governing the civil service (Article 33 of the Basic Law) ought to be retained, but that the civil service should be substantially unified and status differences eliminated.

Despite marginal successes with respect to personnel planning and counseling, the reform initative as a whole failed. Indeed, given the general mood of the time and such decisions as the selection of committee members,[5] some might even conclude that its work was doomed to failure (Luhmann, 1971a; Koch, 1975). A prerequisite to any large-scale reform is the substantial revision of Article 33 of the Basic Law. Such a revision would in turn require a two-thirds majority in both the Bundestag and Bundesrat—that is, effectively, consensus among the Social Democrats (SPD) and Christian Democrats (CDU/CSU), who are sharply at odds on central issues.

The result has been that the contradictions in the public service sector have remained. The voluminous statutes have been modified in many respects, to be sure. They have been adjusted to meet the demands of individual associations, internal administrative requirements, and external influences, such as the need for more part-time positions in the public service (a need that affects some civil service jobs). Fundamental changes, however, were avoided. In the German legal system, which stresses cooperation between lawmakers and their social partners, tacit changes are not possible. At the same time, procedures for bringing about changes have led nowhere. Nothing deserving the name reform has occurred with respect to the public service.

Process Innovations

Innovation, it was suggested earlier, has a double meaning. It includes what we commonly call reform, which is the consequence of decisions deliberately made and therefore implying both intention and action. Innovation is also, however, a developmental process. It leads, on the one hand, to the emergence and diffusion of ideas, techniques, proposals, and the like and, on the other hand, to the adoption of such ideas by a system that displays a capacity to learn and thus to survive (Deutsch, 1963). Such adaptation occurs at both the level of the system, which develops appropriate processes, and at the level of individual members of the system who are prepared to learn, change habits, and experiment. As the previous section has indicated, structural innovations in the West German administrative system derive for the most part from the intentional use of established, formal procedures. The organization of the federal government is more susceptible to the influence of informal events and procedures.

Methods and processes are in a somewhat different situation. These too require substantial formal legitimation—that is, innovations must lead to formal decisions. Yet much can only be understood by looking at various kinds or levels of administration, individual administrative authorities, sections of such authorities, or even individual officials. Despite limited empirical research on the subject (and recognizing that the "administrative system" under consideration is only a theoretic concept), it seems clear that there are various styles of administration in the Federal Republic. They differ from sector to sector within the administration as a whole. They also differ at various levels of administration, as well as from Land to Land and in West Germany's several thousand local communities.

INFORMATION AND INFORMATION PROCESSING

When administrative structures were first developed, there was less information to process than today. In 1880 the Prussian minister of the interior had twelve section heads working for him. It was easily possible for them to report to him once a week. The minister also met his section chiefs and talked to them outside office hours. By comparison, today the interior minister of one of the larger German Länder, while having a smaller scope of responsibility, may have between fifty and one hundred section chiefs under him. Unless these structures are changed, the increasing amount of information will become a problem. The minister cannot possibly absorb, let alone comprehend, everything produced by his subordinates. And this ministry is but one organization of which the minister is a member. Each and every one of them hopes to keep him informed and through this information influence his actions.

In the absence of any fundamental organizational reform in the Federal Republic, information-processing needs have not been dealt with adequately. Proposals for introducing anything new can be considered only if they require no organizational changes. An example of this principle is "management by discussion." It plays an important role in the administrative system, because in many cases the only way to get things done is through a regular exchange of information between the chief and his colleagues. "Management by delegation," by contrast, presupposes organizational change and is nearly impossible to institute within the framework of the existing structure. Not only was that structure established by law, but the political system also ensures that only the minister is responsible to the Bundestag. In other words, better information processing is possible if changes of attitude are sufficient; it fails when organizational changes are required. It is along these lines that further analysis would be useful. It may show that smaller changes usually depend exclusively on the nature of the organizational authority in question. In the 1980s the ministries are more generously staffed at the higher echelons than they were in 1949; furthermore, the staffing of the provincial executives has grown in response to the proliferation of information.

COORDINATION

A second administrative process that typically involves action is coordination. At least two sorts of coordination exist: coordination on a single level of administration, and coordination between different levels.

Single-level Coordination

Coordination on a single level is widely viewed as a necessity in the Federal Republic. Two aspects have received special attention in the general discussion: the existence side by side of general and specialized administrations, and the coordination of sectoral policies at the governmental level. Coordination is needed whenever special administrative offices—such as the forest service and, later, water resource management agencies—are created to perform some specialized task, using their own procedures, conceptual approaches, tools of analysis, jargon, publicity, and so forth, and demanding their own executive independence. Frequently, when issues requiring some expertise have to be decided authoritatively rather than jurisdictionally, this cannot be done at the same level across administrative offices. Coordination must be sought at the next higher level. Greater differentiation in the administrative system leads inevitably to additional coordinative needs within the hierarchy.

At the governmental level there are several instruments for coordinating sectoral policies. These include proclamations and programs, budget consultations, cabinet committees, and interministerial committees. In addition, ministries are obligated to inform their central authority (federal chancellor's office or executive offices of the Länder) promptly about future measures so that if coordination is needed, provision can be made for it. Similarly, sections within a ministry must indicate which other sections ought to participate so that problems may be aired and resolved in a timely fashion. Such instruments of coordination at the governmental level in the Federal Republic have been refined to a remarkable degree. Important formalized decisions, as well as changed attitudes, have contributed to this. While individual analyses show a time lag in developing and applying coordinative mechanisms, the trend has been toward fewer difficulties in this regard, and toward greater anticipatory behavior. This cannot be said, however, of policy areas in which functional agencies are directly competitive. Programmatic conflict requires resolution, not coordination.

Multilevel Coordination

The federal government, Länder, and cities and towns all have different, if overlapping, responsibilities. Jurisdictional coordination between Länder and communities is largely achieved at the Land level through legislation, financial planning, and legal as well as subject-matter oversight. The federal-Land relationship is somewhat different. Here, too, the legislature plays a role as the maker of federal laws, in the development of which the Länder participate through the Bundesrat. In addition, there are in some fields programs (for example, the federal zoning program) and planning (such as the comprehensive education plan) in which the federal government and the Länder both participate, according to Article 91 of the Basic Law, and others in which they work along parallel lines (as in highway construction).

Such parallelism necessitates a high degree of coordination. In the federal-Land relationship, this has resulted in a nearly perfect form of "democracy by negotiation," in which decisions require the consent of all concerned. Such a procedure poses the danger, of course, that a minority can block the majority and thus render the system incapable of making decisions (Crozier, 1970; Lehmbruch, 1969, 1976). Democracy by negotiation must be seen against the background of extensive, constitutionally designated concurrent powers which the federal government and the Länder may only exercise more or less in common (Scharpf et al., 1976, 1977). Legal interpretations and practices have steadily expanded the area of concurrent jurisdiction, which in turn has required enhanced capacities for coordination. The effect of the latter may be to push toward including still other political matters in the realm of interlaced policymaking.

The growth of reliance on consensual decision making has a number of causes: the special form of federalism inherent in the Basic Law, the widespread expectation of constitutionally guaranteed "uniform conditions of life," a distinct desire for harmony, the fact that there is political and economic interaction without regard to Land boundaries, and a trend toward internal equalization through the Federal Republic's integration into the European Community and its dependence on the world market. All these phenomena and developments favor, on the whole, centralization. They make federalism, in the sense of a division of state functions, appear questionable. That the political system has reacted and adapted to these phenomena and developments (Thieme, 1970; on the constitutional changes of 1969, Kommission für die Finanzreform, 1966) reveals its capacity to learn. It also suggests that any evaluation of innovation depends on the analyst's initial normative position.

Coordination and Political Differentiation

Coordinative efforts are complicated whenever the administrative system reacts negatively to inevitable increases in political differentiation. This contradiction may be illustrated by the existence side by side of procedures for "coordination from above" and "coordination from below" (see Scharpf et al., 1976: 61). Remarks on this problem will be confined here to an abstract consideration of Land-community relations.

On the Land level, political goals are defined and ways found to realize them. This process may take different forms. One form results from directives. Local communities, for example, must handle their sewage disposal in a manner prescribed by law, or else they will be fined. At best, the Land will assist individual communities by subsidizing the construction of proper facilities. A second form comprises various incentive programs, which are financed by the Land to encourage local communities to promote certain activities, such as sports or tourism. A third form results from programs addressed not to local communities alone, but which in some circumstances are apt to affect them. The promotion of public housing projects is an example. Subsidies may flow to cities and towns to be passed on to local construction companies; they may also go to independent developers, with the provision that the communities must pick up the financial burdens as soon as the housing projects reach a certain size.

As a rough distinction, we might say that "coordination from above" means that the Land must harmonize its programs so as to assure smooth local functioning, whereas "coordination from below" means that the communities must be sufficiently autonomous to choose freely among programs and then work out a comprehensive development program of their own appropriate to local conditions. Since the former poses an excessive demand for the Land, and the latter entails the risk of conflicting programs in various localities, a mixed system has developed. The Land now attaches to its programs administrative provisions that subject the communities to supervision and the possibility of enforced coordination (for example, by requiring that a housing development plan include some infrastructural planning, or a zoning plan some landscape planning). In this way, the Land maintains its right to intervene without taking full responsibility for coordination. A measure of "coordination from below" is also ensured, since the communities have some freedom to act even if they cannot do whatever they wish locally. To date, it has not been possible to have simultaneously obligatory and occasionally subsidized community activities along with the chance to choose among Land programs and to react to the programs selected by others.

This situation once again points to the multiplicity of possible evaluations. The Land, in moving from general directives to program implementation, has expanded its control while reducing its own decision-making problems. This may be viewed as an innovation of procedure. Moreover, the Land has made more certain the implementation of its own programs—again a procedural innovation. In the process, however, these steps have made the degree of interaction in the system even more complicated. Partial innovation may thus imperil both structures and processes.[6]

PLANNING AND DECISION MAKING

If we look at the actual process of planning and decision making, it is possible to ascertain which novel techniques and ideas were adopted by the administrative system, and which enlarged the possibilities of theoretical planning (by which is meant the prior conception of policies rather than the planning involved in implementation). A glance at the observable world reveals a rapid diffusion of planning techniques and substantial educational training in planning. Moreover, the planning processes both at the regional level and by subject matter have been institutionalized. To a certain extent, too, a planning organization has been built in part cross-sectorally among existing organizations and in part parallel to them (for relevant literature, see Buse and von Dewitz, 1974; Greiffenhagen, 1978).

According to the literature, an original rejection of planning in principle was followed in the 1960s by a euphoric attitude, only to yield later to weary resignation. Such a judgment is valid only if one also accepts its underlying premises. Usually it refers less to the development of planning techniques than to planning policies themselves—that is, to the often bewildering conglomeration of active versus reactive, long-range versus short-term, broadly conceived versus narrowly specific policies—in short, policies with a long view, as against those based on the art of "muddling through." As far as planning techniques and the ready acceptance of planning are concerned, however, one may speak of a march of triumph. It started out with medium-term financial planning, continued with forecasts of future tasks incumbent on local communities and special branch planning with a high information value, and ended up in comprehensive planning, primarily at the Land level. The Länder, it is true, do not always have fully mature planning techniques, because they still focus too much on specific factors (such as population growth) to achieve their purposes fully (Böhret, 1975).

The administrative system's capacity for planning is generally conceded to be greater today than a decade ago. The decision-making process has also changed. Nowadays more decisions are discussed in a wider context, and a great many more are placed into decision frameworks or even time schedules laid down long before. The reason the public may be so unaware of this change is that often extremely short-term decisions become necessary. And a growing number of planning mistakes may simply indicate that much more planning in a quantitative sense is taking place. Planning capacities and possibilities are judged more soberly today than before, and there is more skepticism about the whole array of prognostics, as well as possibilities for ascertaining which needs can be provided for in political planning.

LEGISLATION

As in nearly all similar industrial societies, politics in the Federal Republic of Germany has changed during the last few years. Directives as well as interdictions no longer carry the same impact, while private citizens are increasingly influencing public and private decisions. The tradition of providing the funds to carry out public policies in education and public health, highway construction, defense, and internal security has expanded to include cross-sectional tasks such as nationwide planning.

A policy change of this kind requires better information, better coordination, and withal planning. Despite a number of problems, innovations in these regards have been successful. They have altered both self-administration and federalism, noticeably in the shift of functions, rather imperceptibly at times as far as processes are concerned. Existing structures have proved capable, at least initially, of absorbing the impact, changing processes, and meeting increased demands. An unequivocal failure, however, was the attempted revitalization of the legislative process by which most of the important decisions are finalized; this also frustrated endeavors to clarify the significance and functions of the law.

Two sets of events are relevant here. First, since the 1960s there has been talk in the Federal Republic of a parliamentary reform that would also reform the legislative process. The Bundestag was to be relieved of the superabundance of laws so that it might have time to consider and conduct public debates on the really important bills (for literature, see Bermbach, 1973). Second, complaints from the public about the deluge of laws have been rampant since 1950. The complaints are directed against both the sheer volume of laws and the increasing detail with which each legal point is spelled out. The structure and number of paragraphs in the income-tax law have not changed since 1949, for example, but the number of printed lines has increased tenfold (Bull, 1979). As new and supplementary legislation mushroomed, laments have become more pointed and dramatic. The result has been that politicians feel increasing pressure to justify what they are doing.

Several innovations and noninnovations in the administrative system merit attention. Since neither the federal government nor the Länder have succeeded in modifying parliamentary rules that permit their legislatures to deal with less important bills by a less elaborate procedure, they have fallen back on adaptation: What seems of little importance is hardly debated. Formal procedures are therefore not

changed at all. Federal and Land governments are accused with
mounting intensity of drafting too many laws. It is unlikely, however,
that parliament will invest the executives with more authority to issue
decrees, or that the need for directives to the subordinate administrations will be filled other than by laws, even though the consequences of bureaucratization and overbureaucratization of the
administrative system are also encountering mounting criticism.

The rule of law is thus a two-edged sword. Those who draft programs discovered long ago that carrying them out may require subsidies to encourage specific cities or companies to take action. They
cannot say this openly, of course. Rather, they must create the conditions in which those for whom supporting funds are intended will
actually apply for them. Sometimes this is possible, but more frequently not. In the latter event, the appropriated funds may indeed
be disbursed, but in a way that fails to attain the original goal. Instead,
like a garden sprinkler, the government appears to be showering funds
indiscriminately on those who can make good use of them and those
who cannot. "Equality" replaces potential use for the desired purpose
as the principle governing resource allocation. Seen from another
perspective, the sprinkler effect, a favorite object of political attack,
is often the inevitable consequence of tying political programs to a
legal system devoted to the principle of general equality, combined
with that system's formalism and the pretention that pragmatic measures must nonetheless be seen in their wider context.

A look at the legislative process provides insight into innovations
in a more specific sense. For example, most laws are addressed exclusively or in part to the administration. They therefore include
implementing regulations and procedures that tend toward increasing
differentiation. As a result, a law on administrative procedures was
demanded and even drafted as early as the 1950s. But it was not
passed until the 1970s, at a time when differentiation and specialization had advanced to such a degree that this attempt at a unified
administrative procedure no longer held any promise of achieving its
goal. Generally speaking, there is just as much room for improvement
in legislation as a process as there is in its technical and structural
content. But such improvements, although discussed, were usually
not carried out because of the pressure on legislators for an accelerated output. In this respect, neither the government nor the administration has proved to be capable of innovating.

Another topic, the function of law, could also be dealt with in
connection with innovation. But should it be? In answering this question, one must distinguish between the law as a function of the political

system subject to change and adaptation, and law as a fundamental structural and functional component, which in the final analysis could only be changed permanently if the system as a whole were changed. Law as a function could be adapted to external developments and to the internal needs of the system to such a degree that it would move away from its ideological origins in the conception of government by law—that is, as general and abstract acts of legislation. It would be difficult to discover any innovative potential here. Indeed, if we insist on strict principles, we shall have to admit that an analysis of innovation in and the innovative capacity of systems is simply not possible, since we have entered the domain of political science and the theory of the state.

A Summary

HOW INNOVATIONS ARE PERCEIVED

An examination of innovative capacity in larger fields of action, not just in small or clearly defined "systems" (in the sense of General Systems Theory) points up a peculiar imprecision in the concept of innovation. This imprecision is only slightly diminished by the distinction made here between innovation and adaptation. Any administrative system is familiar with adaptive processes, such as adopting suggestions from the outside (for example, in the form of new planning techniques) or informal procedural changes of a minor sort (such as shortening official channels by sending a copy merely to one's immediate superior), all of which are mixed up almost indistinguishably with procedural changes that require formal approval.

Genuine innovations—those that can be unequivocally identified as such because of their timing, origin, participants, decision makers, or direct consequences—are more easily understood as such than are those that result from gradual processes of change. The latter may appear to be innovations only because they are defined as such by the analyst, as is the case with improved techniques for gathering and storing information.

The proof of nonambiguity lies in the process of realization. The system itself decides what is not ambiguous. The most unequivocal innovation in the administrative system of the Federal Republic has undoubtedly been territorial administrative reform—a "reform of the century," as far as local communities and counties are concerned. By comparison, increased administrative responsibilities seem much less unequivocal. They may be due in part to new legislation, and to an intensification of already existing tasks. One might also argue that fundamental change caused the jump in administrative activities after 1949, whereas territorial reform was merely its (adapting) consequence. An analysis of these questions ought to include the reform debate in general. Until now this debate has centered on the issue of what appeared to be unequivocal; long, drawn-out processes have been relegated to the background. This also meant that we learned less and less about how far such processes are determined by general social change and how far by political decisions. For the present we can only point out some of these connections. They show that it is not yet possible to subject the administrative system as a whole to the rigors of a theoretic analysis. Analyses of innovation must take more limited fields as their starting points.

INNOVATION AND SUCCESS

This chapter began with the observation that the administrative system of the Federal Republic of Germany is structured in various ways, both horizontally and vertically. Vertically, there are several ways in which lower levels may influence higher ones, and vice versa. From this fact we may posit the hypothesis that *the success of structural innovations within the administrative system of the Federal Republic increases as the number of levels in the system and the unequivocal nature of its hierarchical relations decrease.* A supplementary hypothesis suggests that *processes of innovation that work their way down the hierarchy and are supported from above have a greater chance of being successful.*

These hypotheses find support in the cases cited earlier, since as a rule structural innovations were possible simply as a result of directives (such as closing an office) and did not encounter resistance worth mentioning. Structural innovations initiated at a higher level (such as territorial reform) and requiring the cooperation of a relatively autonomous partner could also be realized. However, the amount of time and the means required in this case (including negotiations, incentives for a voluntary merging of communities, and so forth) were greater; the simple directive did not as a rule come into the picture until the end. Similar observations may be made about other functional reforms. Conversely, structural innovations requiring decisions by equal partners (for example, federation and Länder, or federal ministries among themselves) have failed or progressed very slowly. Other failures, such as the attempt to reform the civil service statutes, involved a personal and functional mixture of the administrative system and outside influences (in this case, by civil service associations and political parties).

These observations lead to a second supplementary hypothesis: *Structural innovations are more likely to succeed if their realization depends on internal considerations.* External factors have hardly any weight of their own; whatever influence they exercise stems from their foothold within the organization.

Another hypothesis, which takes into account the structural level, hierarchy, and instruments, suggests that *structural innovations in the administrative system of the Federal Republic may not be realized against or without the higher echelons of the ministerial bureaucracy.* Supporting this contention is the fact that every case study included here refers to a core group that always plays a role in an organization. This core is not formed by the political leadership in the narrow sense, which would react differently to public pressure. Otherwise it would be difficult to explain the relative intransigence and stability of that level of the administrative system which has brought about structural innovations while exempting itself from them.

In the area of process innovations, similar hypotheses may be formed, with slight variations. Turning immediately to a comprehensive one: *Process innovations have a better chance the less they touch the hierarchical position of the leading ministerial groups.* To the extent that this is accurate, it shows that all process innovations depend on the learning capacity of the core of the political leadership. For this reason there may be a great deal of progress in the field of information processing, development of finer instruments for coordination, acceptance of planning concepts and techniques, and thus a closer exchange with scholars and scientists. This does not, however, increase the efficiency—or, if the emphasis is quantitative, the speed—of coordination between the federal government and the Länder. Moreover, it does not clarify whether structural or process innovation has taken place in the relations between minister and staff, on the one hand, and the higher ministerial bureaucracy on the other. The notorious overburdening of the former with decision making leads to a gain in power and influence by the latter. Shifts in responsibility between federation and Länder are tolerated as long as they leave the basic spheres of influence untouched. In fact, it can even be shown that the ministerial bureaucracy of the Länder profits from a relatively enhanced position of the federal bureaucracy.

Legislative problems belong in a formal sense to the realm of process innovations. The hypothesis that follows from this is that, since the balance of power between parliament and government on the one hand and, on the other, government and high-level bureaucracy is demonstrated in the legislative process, and since the leadership function of these three centers of power depends decisively on their legal position, *the very structure of the system precludes any innovation if it affects the legislative process or the function of the law in principle.* What is needed and may be possible is a reinterpretation of the content of the law to adapt these three power centers to a changed environment.

This suggests a further supplementary hypothesis: *The form of a law partly predetermines its contents; conditional programs, therefore, generally function better than finalized ones.* If this hypothesis is correct, an analysis of this program area would show that, when law and money are involved, the latter is usually employed less effectively because the juridical bases for using it are insufficient. Also unclear is the extent to which financial resources can, shall, and must be attached to programs in the form of laws, thus subjecting them to judicial review.

The following points should be included when examining this hypothesis:

—the function of hierarchy in making ministerial leadership positions secure even against the political head of the ministry;

—the ineffectivenss of attempts to change ministerial structures that predetermine policies by recruiting personnel along political party lines;

—the linkage between law as an instrument that directs the administration and the hierarchical structure of that administration;

—endeavors to obtain comparable hierarchical structures through planning and structuring the budget, and the limits of such efforts; and

—the part played by partisan political programs in the relations between the political leadership and the leading civil service group in the ministries.

WEIGHT OF THE MINISTERIAL BUREAUCRACY

A preliminary description of processes of innovation, both attempted and achieved, shows that the higher levels of the federal and Land ministerial bureaucracies are the intransigent core which can either promote or obstruct almost all innovation or adaptation. Without elaborating on the interaction patterns between this bureaucratic core of the administrative system and the political leadership, and without wishing to deny the leadership function of the government, it is clear that the core plays a dominant role inasmuch as it determines the effectiveness of the system. The political leadership, because it must use this efficiency optimally (that is, by increasing the output of the system vis-à-vis program realization), does not retain sufficient free time to check and improve system-immanent conditions for such program realization. To the extent that innovations or adaptations occur, they are initiated by the bureaucratic core (possibly because they increase its influence), are taken over by it, or else founder due to resistance.

All of this suggests that it would be useful to develop and realize, on the basis of the present preliminary study, a comprehensive analysis of the structures and processes of the administrative system in the Federal Republic with a view to discovering the conditions for innovation and adaptation. This might produce some interesting ideas about program and goal innovations. It might also lead to conclusions about indispensable elements of the administrative and thus the political system: special characteristics of federalism, the position and function of the law, and the possibility that self-administration is partially susceptible to leadership but also finds relief in "coordination from below," which requires both coordination and negotiation as well as a larger bureaucratic apparatus.

This is an analytic, not a critical, theory, since we have not focused on those aspects of the system which give rise to the criteria to develop such a critical theory. At least one critical implication should nonetheless be mentioned: If the administrative system is highly autonomous—that is, if it innovates and adapts largely without heeding public criticism, suggestions, or wishes—then some clear-cut conclusions about the position of the political leadership in that system are indicated. It also reveals that expectations about governmental performance are geared to efficiency rather than primarily the means or manner by which it is achieved. The Federal Republic of Germany is first and foremost an efficient state, and only secondarily one aimed at integrating society. In this sense, it may be vulnerable.

NOTES

1. For an empirical study of local political and administrative processes, see Zoll (1974). Unexcelled although somewhat unwieldy bibliographies have been published by the Deutsches Institut für Urbanistik (DIFU) in West Berlin.

2. Renate Mayntz and Helmut Wollmann have made valuable contributions in this area; see Böhret (1978) and Wollmann (1980).

3. Ellwein (1978), in describing this parallelism in administrative development, distinguishes between reform operations that can be identified with precision, and processes of change that may entail—by a diffusion of ideas, among other things—innovations as well as adaptations; see Gawthrop (1969, 1971).

4. This must be emphasized even though external factors were, of course, among the reasons advanced for territorial reform. The Bavarian State Ministry of the Interior (Bayern, Staatsministerium des Innern, 1968: 6), for instance, has noted that the rural citizen expects conveniences similar to those available in the cities—namely, public institutions as well as officials with "special knowledge and a substantial degree of expertise." If these and other demands were not satisfied, then there would be migration to the cities and a further deterioration of communal self-governance. In fact, little has changed in rural migration patterns. Communal administrations have been more professional, to be sure, but they cannot keep up with the new trend toward specialization. Moreover, the small communities are entirely at the mercy of the specialized authorities and thereby handicapped in their capacity for self-administration.

5. Appointed to the committee were three parliamentarians, five university professors, two industrial managers, five active civil servants, and one representative of the German Federation of Trade Unions (*Deutscher Gewerkschaftsbund*), German Employers Union (*Deutsche Angestellten-Gewerkschaft*), and the German Cities Association (*Deutscher Städtetag*). The appointments were aimed at a political balance, but the slight majority that evolved in favor of relatively uniform public service conditions approximating civil service status seemed built in from the start.

6. The question may well be asked as to whether or not the multiplicity of influences on local communities does not really give them an unintended freedom of action or even a chance for anarchical behavior, so that excessive rationalization actually produces the opposite of the desired results. This is related to the American reform discussion at the end of the nineteenth century which asked how to build a rational and professional administration out of an almost anarchically atomized one (see, for example, Waldo, 1948; and, more specifically related to our topic, Danielson, 1976).

REFERENCES

ALEMANN, U. von and R. G. HEINZE [eds.] (1979) Verbände und Staat: Vom Pluralismus zum Korporatismus: Analysen, Positionen, Dokumente. Opladen: Westdeutscher Verlag.

BADURA, B., W. BRUDER, and M. WALZ (1978) Informationsverhalten in komplexen Organisationen. Konstanz: Werkstattbericht (unpublished).

Bayern, Staatskanzlei [ed.] (1968) Verwaltungsreform in Bayern: I. Aus den Arbeitspapieren der Berater des bayerischen Ministerpräsidenten für Fragen der Verwaltungsreform. München: Bayerische Staatskanzlei.

Bayern, Staatsministerium des Innern (1968) "Bestandsaufnahme und Vorschläge zur kommunalen Gebiets- und Verwaltungsreform." München: Staatsministerium des Innern (mimeo).

BECKER, B. (1978) "Zentrale nichtministerielle Organisationseinheiten der unmittelbaren Bundesverwaltung: Eine dimensionale Strukturanalyse." Verwaltungsarchiv 69 (1, April): 149–202.

BERMBACH, U. [ed.] (1973) Hamburger Bibliographie zum parlamentarischen System der Bundesrepublik Deutschland 1945/1970. Opladen: Westdeutscher Verlag.

BEYME, K. von (1979) Das politische System der Bundesrepublik Deutschland: Eine Einführung. München: R. Piper.

BÖCKENFÖRDE, E.-W. (1964) Die Organisationsgewalt im Bereich der Regierung: Eine Untersuchung zum Staatsrecht der Bundesrepublik Deutschland. Berlin: Duncker & Humblot.

_____ (1958) Gesetz und gesetzgebende Gewalt: Von den Anfängen der Deutschen Staatslehre bis zur Höhe des staatsrechtlichen Positivismus. Berlin: Duncker & Humblot.

BÖHRET, C. [ed.] (1978) Verwaltungsreformen und politische Wissenschaft: Zur Zusammenarbeit von Praxis und Wissenschaft bei der Durchsetzung und Evaluierung von Neuerungen. Baden-Baden: Nomos-Verlagsgesellschaft.

_____ (1975) Grundriss der Planungspraxis: Mittelfristige Programmplanung und angewandte Planungstechniken. Opladen: Westdeutscher Verlag.

BRACHER, K. D. [ed.] (1970) Nach 25 Jahren: Eine Deutschland-Bilanz. München: Kindler Verlag.

BRUDER, W. (1980) Sozialwissenschaft und Politikberatung: Zur Nutzung sozialwissenschaftlichen Informationen in der Ministerialorganisation. Opladen: Westdeutscher Verlag.

_____ and T. ELLWEIN [eds.] (1980) Raumordnung und staatliche Steuerungsfähigkeit. Politische Vierteljahresschrift, Sonderheft 10. Opladen: Westdeutscher Verlag.

BULL, H. P. [ed.] (1979) Verwaltungspolitik. Neuwied: Luchterhand Verlag.

BUSE, M. J. and D. von DEWITZ (1974) Bibliographie zur politischen Planung/ Bibliography on Political Planning. Baden-Baden: Nomos-Verlagsgesellschaft.

CROZIER, M. (1970) La société bloquée. Paris: Editions du Seuil.

DANIELSON, M. N. (1976) "The politics of exclusionary zoning in suburbia." Political Science Quarterly 91 (Spring): 1–18.

DEUERLEIN, E. (1972) Föderalismus: Die historischen und philosophischen Grundlagen des föderativen Prinzips. München: Paul List Verlag.

DEUTSCH, K. W. (1963) The Nerves of Government: Models of Political Communication and Control. New York: Free Press.

DILLKOFER, H. (1977) Die Organisation der Innenministerien: Eine sozialwissenschaftliche Analyse. München: Sozialwissenschaftliches Institut der Bundeswehr.

ELLWEIN, T. (1983) Das Regierungssystem der Bundesrepublik Deutschland (5th ed.). Opladen: Westdeutscher Verlag.

_____ (1979a) Gewerkschaften und öffentlicher Dienst: Zur Entwicklung der Beamtenpolitik ders DGB. Opladen: Westdeutscher Verlag.

_____ (1979b) "Konfrontation oder Kooperation—Zu den Grundmustern kommunaler Politik," pp. 3–16 in O. Krabs (ed.) Verwaltung und Planung im Wandel. Köln: Grote Verlag.

_____ (1979c) "Organisationsprobleme in Ministerien." Die Betriebswirtschaft 39 (1b): 73–87.

_____ (1978) "Evaluierung von Organisations- und Verwaltungsreformen," pp. 68–85 in U. Bermbach (ed.) Politische Wissenschaft und Politische Praxis. Politische Vierteljahresschrift, Sonderheft 9. Opladen: Westdeutscher Verlag.

_____ (1976) Regieren und Verwalten: Eine kritische Einführung. Opladen: Westdeutscher Verlag.

————— (1968) "Probleme der Regierungsorganisation in Bonn." Politische Vierteljahresschrift 9 (June): 234–254.

————— and W. BRUDER [eds.] (1984) Ploetz-Bundesrepublik Deutschland. Freiburg: Ploetz-Verlag.

ELLWEIN, T. and A. GÖRLITZ (1968) Parlament und Verwaltung. Vol. 1: Gesetzgebung und politische Kontrolle. Stuttgart: W. Kohlhammer.

ELLWEIN, T. and R. ZOLL (1973a) Berufsbeamtentum—Anspruch und Wirklichkeit: Zur Entwicklung und Problematik des öffentlichen Dienstes. Düsseldorf: Bertelsmann Universitätsverlag.

————— (1973b) Zur Entwicklung der öffentlichen Aufgaben in der Bundesrepublik Deutschland. Annex vol. 8 of the Studienkommission für die Reform des öffentlichen Dienstrechts. Baden-Baden: Nomos-Verlagsgesellschaft.

Enquête Kommission Verfassungsreform des Deutschen Bundestages (1977) Beratungen und Empfehlungen zur Verfassungsreform. Pt. 2: Bund und Länder. Bonn: Presse- und Informationszentrum des Deutschen Bundestages.

FONK, F. (1967) Die Behörde des Regierungspräsidenten: Funktionen, Zuständigkeiten, Organisation. Berlin: Duncker & Humblot.

GAWTHROP, L. C. (1971) Administrative Politics and Social Change. New York: St. Martin's.

————— (1969) Bureaucratic Behavior in the Executive Branch: An Analysis of Organizational Change. New York: Free Press.

GREIFFENHAGEN, M. [ed.] (1978) Zur Theorie der Reform: Entwürfe und Strategien. Heidelberg and Karlsruhe: Müller, Juristischer Verlag.

GRUNOW, D., F. HEGNER, and F. X. KAUFMANN (1978) Steuerzahler und Finanzamt. Frankfurt/Main and New York: Campus-Verlag.

HAMMERSCHMIDT, H. [ed.] (1965) Zwanzig Jahre danach: Eine deutsche Bilanz 1945–1965. München: Kurt Desch.

HEGELAU, H. (1977) "Die Arbeit der Projektgruppe 'Regierungs- und Verwaltungsreform,'" pp. 166–188 in Wissenschaftszentrum Berlin (ed.) Interaktion von Wissenschaft und Politik: Theoretische und praktische Probleme der anwendungsorientierten Sozialwissenschaften. Frankfurt/Main and New York: Campus-Verlag.

Hochschule für Verwaltungswissenschaften (Speyer) [ed.] (1973) Organisation der Ministerien des Bundes und der Länder. Berlin: Duncker & Humblot.

————— [ed.] (1967) Die Staatskanzlei: Aufgaben, Organisation und Arbeitsweise auf vergleichender Grundlage. Berlin: Duncker & Humblot.

HOFFMAN, F. (1973) Entwicklung der Organisationsforschung. Wiesbaden: Betriebswirtschaftlicher Verlag Gabler.

KATZ, A. (1975) Politische Verwaltungsführung in den Bundesländern, dargestellt am Beispiel der Landesregierung Baden-Württemberg. Berlin: Duncker & Humblot.

KOCH, R. (1975) Personalsteuerung in der Ministerialbürokratie: Eine theoretisch-empirische Studie zur Möglichkeit organisatorischer Neuerungen. Baden-Baden: Nomos-Verlagsgesellschaft.

Kommission für die Finanzreform (1966) Gutachten über die Finanzreform in der Bundesrepublik Deutschland. Stuttgart: W. Kohlhammer, Deutscher Gemeindeverlag.

LAUX, E. [ed.] (1978) Das Dilemma des öffentlichen Dienstes. Bonn: Schriften der Deutschen Sektion des Internationalen Instituts für Verwaltungswissenschaften, vol. 4.

LEHMBRUCH, G. (1976) Parteienwettbewerb im Bundesstaat. Stuttgart: W. Kohlhammer.

_____ (1969) "Konkordanzdemokratien im internationalen System," pp. 136–163 in E.-O. Czempiel (ed.) Die anachronistische Souveränität: Zum Verhältnis von Innen- und Aussenpolitik. Politische Vierteljahresschrift, Sonderheft 1. Opladen: Westdeutscher Verlag.

LEPPER, M. (1973) "Die Basiseinheit in der Organisation von Ministerien," pp. 125–136 in Hochschule für Verwaltungswissenschaften (Speyer) (ed.) Organisation der Ministerien des Bundes und der Länder. Berlin: Duncker & Humblot.

LÖWENTHAL, R. and H.-P. SCHWARZ [eds.] (1974) Die zweite Republik: 25 Jahre Bundesrepublik Deutschland—eine Bilanz. Stuttgart: Seewalt Verlag.

LUHMANN, N. (1971a) "Reform des öffentlichen Dienstes: Zum Problem ihrer Probleme," pp. 203–256 in N. Luhmann, Politische Planung: Aufsätze zur Soziologie von Politik und Verwaltung. Opladen: Westdeutscher Verlag.

_____ (1971b) "Reform und Information," pp. 181–202 in N. Luhmann, Politische Planung: Aufsätze zur Soziologie von Politik und Verwaltung. Opladen: Westdeutscher Verlag.

MAIHOFER, W. [ed.] (1973) Begriff und Wesen des Rechts. Darmstadt: Wissenschaftliche Buchgesellschaft.

MAYNTZ, R. and F. SCHARPF (1973) Planungsorganisation: Die Diskussion um die Reform von Regierung und Verwaltung des Bundes. München: R. Piper.

MURSWIECK, A. (1975) Regierungsreform durch Planungsorganisation: Eine empirische Untersuchung zum Aufbau von Planungsstrukturen im Bereich der Bundesregierung. Opladen: Westdeutscher Verlag.

NOLL, P. (1973) Gesetzgebungslehre. Reinbek (bei Hamburg): Rowohlt Verlag.

Projektgruppe für die Regierungs- und Verwaltungsreform (1969) "Erster Bericht zur Reform der Struktur von Bundesregierung und Bundesverwaltung." (mimeo)

ROGERS, E. M. with F. F. SHOEMAKER (1971) Communication of Innovations: A Cross-Cultural Approach. New York: Free Press.

Sachverständigenkommission (1957) "Bericht der Sachverständigenkommission für die Vereinfachung der Verwaltung beim Bundesministerium des Innern." Unpublished report.

SCHARPF, F., B. REISSERT, and F. SCHNABEL [eds.] (1977) Politikverflechtung II: Kritik und Berichte aus der Praxis. Kronberg/Ts.: Athenäum-Verlag.

_____ [eds.] (1976) Politikverflechtung: Theorie und Empirie des kooperativen Föderalismus in der Bundesrepublik. Kronberg/Ts.: Athenäum-Verlag.

SCHATZ, H. (1973) "Auf der Suche nach neuen Problemlösungsstrategien: Die Entwicklung der politischen Planung auf Bundesebene," pp. 9–67 in R. Mayntz and F. Scharpf (eds.) Planungsorganisation: Die Diskussion um die Reform von Regierung und Verwaltung des Bundes. München: R. Piper.

SCHIMANKE, D. (1978) Verwaltungsreform Baden-Württemberg: Verwaltungsinnovation als politisch-administrativer Prozess. Berlin: Duncker & Humblot.

SCHWAN, A. and K. SONTHEIMER [eds.] (1969) Reform als Alternative: Hochschullehrer antworten auf die Herausforderung der Studenten. Köln and Opladen: Westdeutscher Verlag.

Sonderarbeitskreis der Ständigen Konferenz der Innenminister der Länder (1973) Mittelinstanzbericht: Neuordnung der staatlichen Mittelinstanz. Unpublished report.

SONTHEIMER, K. and H. H. RÖHRING [eds.] (1977) Handbuch des politischen Systems der Bundesrepublik Deutschland. München: R. Piper.

Studienkommission für die Reform des öffentlichen Dienstrechts (1973) Bericht der Kommission. Baden-Baden: Nomos-Verlagsgesellschaft.

THIEME, W. (1970) Föderalismus im Wandel: Analyse und Prognose des Verhält-
nisses von Bund und Land Nordrhein-Westfalen von 1949 bis 1975. Köln: Carl
Heymanns Verlag.

THRÄNHARDT, D. [ed.] (1978) Funktionalreform—Zielperspektiven und Probleme
einer Verwaltungsreform. Meisenheim-am-Glan: Verlag Anton Hain.

TIGGEMANN, R. (1977) Die kommunale Neugliederung in Nordrhein-Westfalen:
Möglichkeiten und Grenzen der Anwendung landesplanericher Entwicklungskon-
zeptionen und Instrumentarien auf das Zielsystem der Gebietsreform. Meisenheim-
am-Glan: Verlag Anton Hain.

WAGENER, F. [ed.] (1976) Verselbständigung von Verwaltungsträgern. Bonn:
Deutsche Sektion des Internationalen Instituts für Verwaltungswissenschaften.

——— (1969) Neubau der Verwaltung: Gliederung der öffentlichen Aufgaben und
ihrer Träger nach Effektivität und Integrationswert. Berlin: Duncker & Humblot.

WAHL, R. (1971) Stellvertretung im Verfassungsrecht. Berlin: Duncker & Humblot.

WALDO, D. (1948) The Administrative State: A Study of the Political Theory of
American Public Administration. New York: Ronald.

WIESE, W. (1972) Der Staatsdienst in der Bundesrepublik Deutschland: Grundlagen,
Probleme, Neuordnung. Neuwied and Berlin: Luchterhand Verlag.

WINKLER, H. A. [ed.] (1979) Politische Weichenstellungen im Nachkriegsdeutsch-
land 1945–1953. Göttingen: Vandenhoeck & Ruprecht.

WITTKÄMPER, G. W. (1978) Funktionale Verwaltungsreform. Bad Godesberg:
Godesberger Taschenbuch-Verlag.

WOLLMANN, H. [ed.] (1980) Politik im Dickicht der Bürokratie: Beiträge zur Im-
plementationsforschung. Leviathan, Sonderheft 3. Opladen: Westdeutscher Verlag.

WRAGE, V. (1975) Erfolg der Territorialreform: Auswirkung der territorialen Neugliederung der Gemeinden in ausgewählten Kreisen Nordrhein-Westfalens. Berlin:
Duncker & Humblot.

ZOLL, R. (1974) Wertheim III: Kommunalpolitik und Machtstruktur. München: Ju-
venta-Verlag.

CHAPTER 6

INNOVATION IN WEST GERMANY
Retrospect and Prospects

HERBERT KÖNIG

The following reforms in the public sector of the Federal Republic of Germany (FRG) may be classified as innovations:

(1) *Financial reform,* which, in the mid-1960s, aimed at balancing political power and financial resources between the individual states (*Länder*) and the federal level. Only certain parts of this reform have produced convincing results. Still problematic are such matters as shared tasks and cost-sharing in certain sectors (for example, financing local transportation, urban construction, and hospitals).

(2) *Reform of budgetary statutes.* In 1967–69 the government tried to adapt the budgetary law to the needs of the fiscal policy according to the tradition of John Maynard Keynes. Primarily juridical in form, however, it did not tackle the political and programmatic issues of primary concern in this volume.

(3) *Territorial reform at the communal level.* This reform, which took place throughout the 1970s, sought to create powerful local authorities by reducing the number of communities from about 25,000 to 8-9,000. While possibly strengthening the planning capacity of subnational units, the effort to increase their efficiency neglected or completely overlooked important elements of concern to social science.

(4) *Functional reform.* Beginning in the mid-1970s and following upon the territorial reform, the government instituted measures to delegate power from the top downward and to incorporate special units into more general institutions. (a) Restructuring vertical lines of responsibility did not follow the principle of subsidiarity in order to bring government closer to the citizens; (b) horizontal reform has barely touched the relationship between the general interior and special administrations, and was by and large undertaken without any

theoretical foundation. (c) To date the government has only been successful in weeding out redundant or unnecessary legislation.

5. *Reform of civil service statutes* in the first half of the 1970s: Like the budgetary reform, this has been primarily juridical.

6. *Reform of bureaucratic structures and procedures:* This set of reforms remains in effect incomplete down to the present day. The key issues of procedure and content have hardly been touched. Some of the directives supplementing the Common Standing Order for federal ministries are unclear from a theoretical perspective and have little practical relevance.

Need for Guiding Principles

Innovations in the public sector need the support of guiding principles. One such idea is *subsidiarity,* which is rooted essentially in Christian social teachings. It was specifically introduced into the discussion of state and social structures through the encyclical *Mater et magistra.* Not surprisingly, this principle has been realized only conditionally in the real world of politics, for its complexity and the fact that it varies with the task at hand make its conceptual interpretation extremely difficult. A theoretic foundation is absent altogether in this field.

Another guiding principle for such innovations could be the proposition that *actions of public authorities ought to be directed at the groups they hope to reach.* This is especially relevant for recent discussions of the "deluge of laws," a situation that many feel can be contained only if either the officials producing legislation are removed from the "production line" or, what is more sensible, the total volume of existing laws is limited to the receptivity level of those to whom they are addressed. This latter suggestion finds support in the argument that any legal norm not accepted by those to whom it is supposed to apply is not only useless but even destructive of civic values, since it creates uncertainties in the minds of citizens. Such a situation also undermines the authority and reliability of the political and administrative system itself.

The *primacy of politics,* as opposed to that of administration in general and the budget in particular, is another guiding principle deserving of attention. Political considerations did not prevail after 1945 in the FRG when local levels of government moved increasingly toward administrative governance. Legislation on the constitutional structure of local authorities in counties, cities, and smaller communities all but removed from local legislative bodies any responsibility for parliamentary debate and even governing. Today they are merely bodies that replace the proper administrative magistrates—district presidents, mayors, or whatever—in making administrative decisions, often of the most trivial sort. A similar situation characterizes the state parliaments. They have lost so many of their parliamentary functions that their debates not infrequently drift off into irrelevancies or inappropriate directions.

It might be possible to counteract such a loss of political substance. Among other things, state parliaments should be required to debate both local problems in their states and the impact federal actions have on the local level. Even if they could not change the decisions at the federal level, they could at least offer informed advice.

Public Policymaking Process

More generally, a problem-oriented approach is necessary. One step would be to require that, before the stage of decision making is reached, there be a period during which the various levels of government conduct joint discussions on the nature of a common problem within the framework of a structured pattern of problems. Where the administration instead has introduced a hierarchy of goals or objectives, their possible effect causes some uneasiness (primarily because of their means-end implications). It is a blind alley with no exit other than clear-cut differentiation within the structure of problems—a differentiation that should have been set up in the first place in the form of a structured definition of the problem. Goal-oriented or, respectively, objective-oriented planning initiatives have also proved to be totally ineffective because quantitative methods were used to evaluate the attainment of goals (objectives) when only the qualitative aspects of the policies were of any interest (König, 1977, 1979a-c).

Such considerations constitute a new field for the science of administration. To approach it, however, requires the creation of a broad set of social scientific tools, without which no one would even seek to structure problems, let alone try to analyze or explain their causes.

Closely linked to this problem-solving orientation is the need to shift our concern from the *economy* of public action to its *efficiency*. But even thinking in terms of input-output relationships is less important than moving from this kind of orientation (toward efficiency) to the consideration of *efficacy* (impact)—that is, the relationship

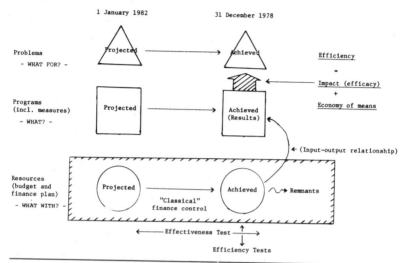

FIGURE 6.1: Finance Control and Political Achievement Control

between documented results on the one hand and, on the other, problems solved.

If the fiscally oriented resources level responds to the question of the wherewithal of public activity (Figure 6.1), and if action-level programs (including their individual provisions) represent the "what" of federal, state, or local action, then the problems answer the "what for" question of public analyses, public concepts, and normative or budgetary public action (see Bohne and König, 1976). In the last analysis, effectiveness may be measured by juxtaposing program and reality. In moving from one level to another, of course, efficiency tests (in the widest sense of the term) may be used.

A great deal of criticism has been aimed in recent years at the prevailing federative system (see Scharpf et al., 1976, 1977). It is not enough, however, merely to insist on the idea of a *cooperative federalism*. What is needed are concrete conceptions, including insights from the economic theory of federalism as well as the interactive concepts of organizational sociology. Of major significance here would be the principle of subsidiarity.

On the micro level—that is, within an individual organizational unit irrespective of its political action level—*the budget* is but one among many fields of systematic structuring in governmental and administrative action. Moreover, the budget is generated from both political agendas for action, even though these may not always be explicitly enunciated, and the concretization of such agendas in the form of incipient organizational categories. The budget itself relays action determinants to personnel planning and data to financial control offices. This relationship is shown in Figure 6.2.

Those handling the budget strive vigorously to reach beyond the elaborate network of corresponding action fields to control what is happening in the forefront of the budget-making process. However understandable and even excusable this may be, one of its structural aspects merits attention. It can be seen clearly in the case of planning-programming-budgeting systems (PPBS). The PPB system, thoroughly reasonable in its conception but weakened and misused in practice, was ultimately wrecked by three *contradictory structures*— programmatic, organizational, and budgetary. Those concerned with decision making on zero-based budgeting will sooner or later face the same dilemma. It takes no great gift of prophecy to predict that this dilemma contains the seed of failure for ZBB, despite its more modest scope. And, of course, budgetary decision making is not essentially dissimilar from political decision making.

In the Federal Republic of Germany, the problem inherent in this kind of *structural dilemma* first became acute with the reorganization of the Federal Ministry of Food, Agriculture, and Forests. At that time, structural congruity was achieved between programs and the organization. The budgetary structure, however, was not included in the package. In the state (*Land*) of Lower Saxony, the entire decision-making system was reorganized according to categories derived from political agendas, with each program clearly distinguishable. By tying each level to its problem, full control of political activity becomes feasible. The critical aspect in all this is that only through such *congruence* of programmatic, organizational, and budgetary structures can organization and budget, which are supposed to be in the service of politics, be prevented from pushing out on their own.

Central to innovative policymaking is the *capacity to steer political programs*. It is closely related to the parallelism between the political and budgetary decision processes mentioned earlier. It is precisely these two lines of procedure that must be intertwined in such a way that they secure for politics its rightful priority. This demand is addressed to any center of governance, including the offices of the federal chancellor, minister-presidents in the states, and mayors, as well as any individual department at the federal or local level.

Political steering gives a new accent to the relationship between "classical" coordination on the one hand and, on the other, those units that are sometimes called planning sections, dealing with overlapping problems as well as medium-range or long-term analyses. It

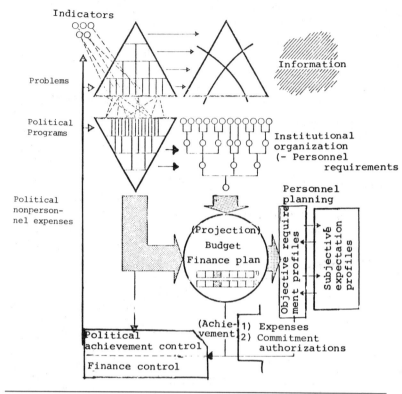

FIGURE 6.2:   Formative Fields of Governmental and Administrative Action

could happen that the classical mode of coordination of departments by the centers of governance will prove to be a waste of time and will therefore be abandoned, to be replaced by purely problem-oriented scrutiny.

If the latter course of action is taken, the departmental structure at the ministerial level will be confronted by a central administration that is no longer geared to the needs and interests of complementary departments but rather to problems. It will therefore become an exceedingly difficult partner for those departments carrying on as usual.

A Comparative Framework

Finally, we should consider the innovative aspect of comparative systems analysis, as well as some contributions by international and key national thinktanks. As important as their work may be, their efforts will bear fruit only to the extent that the seeds reach fertile soil. For example, numerous international proposals on national innovations have been lost because they slipped through the insensitive screens of departmental structures in receiving countries, all of them member states and therefore financial supporters of the idea-producing institutions. The same situation obtains with respect to national thinktanks, especially when they have no immediate access to the political leadership of a government or department.

A possible solution could be to engage the leading, politically responsible directors in the thought processes involved in systematic innovation. Since they have little or no time for this, however, the hope remains to train their closest collaborators. If this cannot be done, innovation may become effective by "subversion"—that is, by focusing the training for innovative capacity on the coming generation of leading governmental officials.

REFERENCES

BOHNE, E. and H. KÖNIG (1976) "Probleme der politischen Erfolgskontrolle." Die Verwaltung 9, 1: 19–38.

KÖNIG, H. (1979a) Dynamische Verwaltung: Bürokratie zwischen Politik und Kosten (2d ed.). Stuttgart: Verlag Bonn Aktuell.

—— (1979b) "Problemfindung als Ausgangspunkt für öffentliches Handeln," pp. 19–45 in Bundesakademie für öffentliche Verwaltung (ed.), Ziel- und ergebnisorientiertes Verwaltungshandeln: Entwicklung und Perspektiven in Regierung und Verwaltung. Bonn: Carl Heymanns Verlag.

—— (1979c) "Zur Typologie integrierter Planungs- und Budgetierungssysteme," pp. 219–240 in H.-C. Pfohl and B. Rürup (eds.), Anwendungsprobleme moderner Planungs- und Entscheidungstechniken. Königstein/Ts.: Hanstein-Verlag.

—— (1977) "Zur Neuorientierung von Zielgruppierungen in der öffentlichen Verwaltung." Verwaltung und Fortbildung 5, 2: 71–92.

SCHARPF, F., B. REISSERT, and F. SCHNABEL [eds.] (1977) Politikverflechtung II: Kritik und Berichte aus der Praxis. Kronberg/Ts.: Athenäum-Verlag.

—— [eds.] (1976) Politikverflechtung: Theorie und Empirie des kooperativen Föderalismus in der Bundesrepublik. Kronberg/Ts.: Athenäum-Verlag.

COMMENT ON THE CHAPTERS
BY ELLWEIN AND KÖNIG

WOLFGANG ZEH

The chief question regarding innovation in the public sector is, Can innovation be invented, managed, or controlled by politics or politicians? In the Federal Republic of Germany in recent years, there have been a number of innovations in the public sector. This was especially true after 1969, when the majority of the Bundestag changed from Christian-conservative (Christian Democratic/Christian Social Union) to social-liberal (Social Democratic/Free Democratic). The first cabinet of Chancellor Willy Brandt initiated the legislative period with a declaration on "policies of internal reform." Since then, a remarkable number of newly designed policies have been undertaken, as Ellwein shows in his chapter in this volume.

Today, a great many people feel that the outcome of these reform policies has not lived up to expectations, and that innovativeness has faded away. Is there no longer a demand for innovation? Or is it that the need still exists, but the public sector is unable to transform the need into action? Perhaps both innovation and innovativeness ebb and flow cyclically, as Simonton suggests in his chapter. If so, should or could government stabilize innovativeness as a process?

Professor McGrath says, and I think he is correct, that the question of whether or not a change is desired is always a question of perspective. Whose perspective decides for or against the implementation of a change? Whose perspective counts ultimately? Presumably, that of a top politician.

One reason for this is that innovative policy in the FRG depends on legal regulations, and that regulations in turn depend on constitutional law—both considerably furthered by the jurisdiction of the Federal Constitutional Court. Legal regulations (or laws) are required for even the smallest change in the public sector, the organization of public authorities, and the like. Even the payment of government officials is regulated by law, as are the methods of public financial planning. If the legal route is not followed to the letter, inevitably someone will institute legal proceedings, and judges will declare null and void the offending administrative act or decree.

Accordingly, only parliament can experiment with new ideas. But parliamentary decisions are determined by the top politicians of the majority party, especially the chancellor and his cabinet. They decide whether or not something will be done. If an innovation is to be enacted into law, it must be important enough to touch on the interests of those at the very top of the political hierarchy.

A second reason for the Federal Republic's reliance on initiatives from the top is the political nature of communication in the public arena. If innovations are generated and discussed in groups or teams, social know-how may in fact play an important role, as Kochen suggests. However, access to the kind of interactions that are meaningful in the implementation of innovations is not a product of social know-how but politically distributed or mediated. It depends on a person's multiple functions, jobs, and roles. Politicians accumulate those functions, not to overload their capacities, but rather to gain access to new sources of important information. An additional function means greater access to relevant interaction; the loss of a function means a loss of information. The result is competition for membership in bodies that control relevant information.

The more binding the results produced by a group, the higher will be the level of the partners interacting in it. This politically mediated access to information determines to some degree the consequences of the communication process—that is, innovation becomes a function of how top-level personnel perceive the need for change. These personnel have a rather special view of such necessities, as well as different bargaining terms.

The experience of a relatively ambitious innovation project illustrates this relationship. The Commission of Inquiry on Constitutional Reforms, set up by the Bundestag after about 25 amendments to the Basic Law had been enacted, was charged with the task of thoroughly scrutinizing that document. The commission was to determine whether or not a more comprehensive reform was needed, especially in the area of federal-state relations. The commission comprised Bundestag members, top officials of the states (*Länder*), and some well-known university professors. With one exception, all were lawyers. After five years of discussion, the commission reported that in most crucial points the Basic Law did not need to be changed. The small number of recommended amendments were relatively insignificant and did not change the status quo. The commission's report makes very good reading, but its usefulness for innovation is limited—a direct result,

I would suggest, of the political and legal mix of the commission's membership.

Thus the perspectives of top politicians prevail not only in parliament, which generates the inevitable legal regulations, but also in the interactions that generate the ideas. We might argue that these politicians—or at least some of them—are elected by the people to make political decisions, and that therefore this situation is perfectly acceptable. The question nonetheless remains of whether or not they can detect the need for change fast enough.

Where does this capacity to think in innovative terms originate? It may derive from one's standing as the parliamentary opposition. After all, the interest in obtaining power is as great as the interest in holding on to it; and, since the opposition has less to lose and does not have as good control of the policy circumstances as does the government, why not be on the lookout for new issues? Being in the opposition, however, does not always encourage innovativeness. Before the reformation of the government in late 1982, the CDU/CSU opposition was not very different from the government in power. The opposition parties controlled the majority of the individual states and hence the federative structure of the Bundesrat, which is co-responsible with the Bundestag for both legislation and administration and therefore has a veto right over the decisions made in Bonn. It followed that, to the extent that it governed the Länder, the opposition was influenced by federal politics and hence not really prepared to run any risks by fighting for innovations in the public sector.

In the final analysis, perhaps only a crisis can generate the call for innovation that many observers feel is needed. Crises seem to come in cycles. Maybe innovations do, too, and perhaps politics must fail in trying to stabilize both crises and innovativeness: If the first are needed to produce the second, the second cannot avoid the first. Are they simply two sides of a single coin?

CHAPTER 7

TECHNOLOGY POLICY IN THE FEDERAL REPUBLIC OF GERMANY

FRIEDER NASCHOLD

A number of economic and political indicators have signaled in recent years that the Federal Republic of Germany, like other industrialized countries, is facing a host of policy crises. Macroeconomic policies have not been able to deal effectively with high unemployment, sluggish growth accompanied by a considerable rate of inflation, and, for the first time, deficits in the balance of payments. The changes in basic conditions wrought by a new division of labor in the world economy are endangering the fundamental mechanisms of a social system that has been acclaimed both at home and abroad as the "German model." There is evidence that the party system is disintegrating, that nonparliamentary and new sociopolitical groups are multiplying, and that the union movement is being destabilized by high unemployment and industrial rationalization.

Other countries, caught up in a similar dilemma, have reacted to this highly problematic situation with a wide variety of counterstrategies, including attempts to decouple themselves from the world market, reliance on austere monetary and fiscal measures, and accelerated modernization of the national economy in an effort to break into the world market. The Federal Republic of Germany has relied heavily on a combination of austerity in the domestic market and aggressive modernization in the export sector. This is where research policy and technology policy play an important role.

The historical stages in the development of government research and technology policy in the Federal Republic coincide with the various macroeconomic and macropolitical constellations. General and indirect support was given to research and technology during the

period of economic and political restoration. Direct funding as selective, sectoral policy gained importance under the modernization
policies of the Social Democrats. As economic prosperity began to
level off and the first signs of long-term economic stagnation started
to appear, as the preeminence of the Social Democratic party began
to wane and friction began to build within the country's leadership
circles, the strategy of socially oriented technology policy was conceived. This concept, which links forced economic and technological
modernization with efforts to include the union movement in the
societal shaping of technology and work organization, has been noted
as an innovation in government policy at the international level as
well.

The following pages will attempt to explain and appraise the conception and implementation of socially oriented technology policy as
an example of innovative corporatist policy. The chapter begins with
a brief sketch of some basic conditions and structural features of the
economy and politics in the Federal Republic and then explains the
most important elements and mechanisms involved in socially oriented technology policy. It concludes with a preliminary overall assessment of this policy.

Basic Economic and Political Conditions

THE ECONOMY

Within the Western capitalist system, the Federal Republic of Germany is considered to be the second-ranking superpower with the
third largest gross national product, the highest rate of exports, and
substantial foreign trade surpluses and currency reserves. This strong
position in the world market is based most of all on the specific
sectoral structure—the specialization of the German national economy primarily in the capital goods industry represented by machine
building, the automotive industry, electrical engineering, and chem-
icals. Through these sectors the German economy as a whole is highly
integrated into the world market. Half the total turnover, one-quarter
of the total production, one-third of all investments, one-quarter of
all employees, and a good third of all profits are accounted for over-
seas. Overall economic development is largely determined by the
profit and expansion strategies of the export sectors, which include
a constant honing of competitiveness on the international market,
the primacy of foreign trade over domestic trade, of export over

consumption, of wage and price stabilization over growth buoyed by purchasing power, and of modernization over employment.

These structures provided for considerable improvements in the standard of living by the mid-1970s, but they came under special pressure to adjust and innovate when the export-oriented sectors themselves were hit by massive distortions such as the oil crisis and the expansion of Japanese export-oriented industry.

PRODUCTION TECHNOLOGY

Since the 1970s the broad, long-term thrust of new production techniques has increased the pressure to adapt, especially in the FRG's dominant export-oriented sectors. And it is precisely in those areas—specifically in machine building, to which we shall return later—that competition in the world market is intensifying, particularly with the United States and Japan. Four central problems of production technology and economics can be identified:

(1) the rapid introduction of microelectronics to the products of the machine building sector (for example, CNC machine tools) and the production procedures involved (such as flexible manufacturing systems and flexible assembly systems);

(2) the reintegration into production of construction and development, which were the functional domains in plants that had been increasingly decentralized as the division of labor expanded in the world market;

(3) the return of skilled workers to the production level of plants as a move away from the Taylorist polarization of qualification; and

(4) the horizontal and vertical integration of the functional dynamics in plants as a whole on the basis of the new information technologies.

Such changes amount to a profound restructuring of the classical organization of the factory and of work.

In terms of technology policy, the following questions had to be answered: Can and should these technical and economic problems be dealt with by the firms on their own and to what extent should there be government support? A further problem was how to win acceptance of these far-reaching changes in product and production structure with their manifold social consequences for employees and unions.

BASIC POLITICAL CONDITIONS

The political-economic system of the Federal Republic of Germany can be characterized by the following four points:

(1) a very fragmented state apparatus that is dependent in matters of economic policy on the consensus of numerous, relatively autonomous

institutions, including the government administration, parliamentary committees, the central bank, and the states (*Länder*), among others;

(2) high economic and political integration of the working class, and representation of corporate and union interests;

(3) a relatively stable system of industrial relations, with a small number of strongly centralized unions based on the principles of the unified labor union; and

(4) a tripartite system of cooperation among the state, companies, and unions that functions as a "fragmented corporatism" and tries to regulate vast areas of economic and social policy by conducting negotiations, primarily at top levels.

Until the 1970s these specific political structures supported a relatively successful package of economic and social policies: restrictive financial and fiscal measures at home, an income policy keyed to growth in productivity, a monetary policy based on the undervalued Deutschmark, an aggressive trade and export policy, and the practice of promoting technology with indirect subsidies.

The question that now arises is, To what extent do the Federal Republic's policy structures have the institutional capacity for innovation needed to adapt policies to the changing situation of the world market? Can a corporatist political structure, like the Federal Republic, cope better with technical and economic shifts and sociopolitical changes than political systems with different structures, such as Italy, France, and England? These political and strategic, as well as scientific and theoretical issues, will be pursued below.

Toward a Socially Oriented Technology Policy

Until the early 1970s, research and technology policy in the Federal Republic was based to a great degree on the principle of autonomous, endogenous development of technological innovations. Assistance consisted largely of general and indirect support for technology through an extensive network of government investment incentives. In the 1950s this concept aimed essentially at encouraging the utilization of existing technology and creating an infrastructure of scientific institutions. In the interest of "closing the technological gap," general support was supplemented in the 1960s by indirect aid in four areas—nuclear energy, air and space travel, electronic data processing, and marine research.

The first signs of international crisis (at the beginning of the 1970s) made it desirable to improve these policies. New technology (microelectronics) became the main focus. It was based on the assumption that technological development can be shaped to a large extent by social and political forces, and that government can take a more active role in the process.

As a result, the research and technology pursued by the government was transformed into a sectoral approach and became increasingly involved in directly subsidizing projects in individual factories. This direct support of technology developed by firms was combined with a governmental advisory policy and the practice of stipulating conditions in return for government aid. The new policy of direct support for projects introducing new technologies in export-oriented sectors of the economy thus became a response to changes in the basic macroeconomic and technological conditions of the world market.

Government policy on subsidizing the development of technology followed similar lines in several Western industrialized countries. The specific policy innovation in the Federal Republic of Germany was its evolution into a socially oriented technology policy. Five aspects should be noted:

(1) Although it was necessary for government to encourage the development of technology and the organization of work on the new technological basis of microelectronics, it was also seen as both necessary and possible to articulate a policy on averting the negative consequences of technological development.

(2) To accomplish this, government was to establish a legally binding link between its financial assistance on the one hand, and social criteria for the shaping of technology and work organization on the other, that would take into consideration the possible effects on employees (for example, stress, qualification, and employment).

(3) Of special significance was the inclusion of the work force, works councils, and unions at the different levels of developing and applying technology as part of the government's assistance package. Social integration of the labor movement and early management of conflicts were fundamental goals, but this did not preclude other developments that might, at least in the state-supported sectors, spawn and strengthen an opposing force that could restrict the primacy of corporate decisions on the development and use of technology.

(4) A concept of this sort also involves a change in the structure of government. Direct support of socially oriented projects means decentralizing and dispersing on a regional basis and into the plant. It means developing a network of competencies among the government, firms, unions, and scientific community in order to initiate, steer, and implement decentralized factory projects.

(5) Direct support of socially oriented projects also involves changing union policy. It means expanding traditional policy on the wage system and working conditions by having union experts participate in the numerous advisory and decision-making bodies at the plant and collective bargaining levels that deal with investment in technology and by strengthening union factory policy on the social determination of how technology is to be used.

Socially oriented technology policy is based on a specific constellation of diverse sociopolitical interests. Firms, particularly middle-sized ones, wished to overcome problems with respect to flexibility, productivity, and quality by introducing flexible production technologies. They also hoped to solve their labor problems by reducing stress and changing qualifications of workers.

Reformist circles among the Social Democrats hoped that the new policy would restabilize the party's electoral support among workers and establish an alliance with small and middle-sized firms. Among the unions, an awareness grew of the limits to the control strategies available within the industrial relations system in the face of the massive thrust toward modernization. They tried therefore to gain influence over corporate investment planning by exerting pressure on and cooperating in certain areas of the state apparatus—in this case the Ministry for Research and Technology—in addition to pursuing their strategies within the industrial relations system. All these various interests led to an "unstable equilibrium of compromise" that formed the labile sociopolitical basis for a technology policy oriented to the needs of society.

Functions and Effectiveness of Socially Oriented Technology Policy

Socially oriented technology policy has centered on essentially two programs: *improvement in the quality of work life* and *production technology*. Together they have an annual budget of well over $66 million. The most important areas of concentration have been: (1) research and development in the areas of occupational safety and health, as well as the reduction of stress; (2) research and development concerning retraining; (3) development and use of operative systems (industrial robots), with particular attention to aspects of stress and retraining; and (4) development and use of flexible production and assembly systems, with special attention to humane work organization and retraining.

The guiding principles and procedural structures of both programs are based on the following practices:

(1) The government makes decisions on the allocation of funds and stipulates the conditions of its aid.

(2) A central advisory body (committee of experts), composed of an equal number of technical experts and representatives from both parties of the industrial relations system, provides advice, recommends the goals of the program, and suggests how the program should be conducted.

(3) An application by a firm for financial and scientific support must contain the desired social criteria and must be formally approved by the firm's works council.

(4) All applications are first discussed by a set of review boards in which employers, unions, and technical experts are equally represented. The members then formulate a final position.

(5) An accepted project is usually directed by a commission in which the company management and the works council are represented equally, and is carried out by a number of working groups composed of technical and social science researchers, members of the works council, and union advisers.

(6) Wage issues are handled separately by the industrial relations parties.

(7) The results of the project are acted on through employment agreements and counseling, as well as various forms of advanced training of the work force on the one hand and, on the other, market processes and government laws.

The government, unions, and independent scholars have conducted interim analyses of the effectiveness of the programs carried out as part of a socially oriented technology policy. Several preliminary conclusions can be drawn on the basis of these analyses.

First of all, three types of project results have been observed. The first type was associated with projects the essential effect of which was the economic survival of the firm (referred to as *Reparaturhumanisierung*). The second type came out of projects in which the firms involved were able to achieve important rationalization goals vis-à-vis their competitors on the world market with relatively little reference to social criteria. The third type of results had to do with projects in which technological innovations were achieved with relevant social criteria in mind. An example of this last type is the development of a flexible manufacturing system in machine building that, in addition to providing technological innovations, was successfully able to incorporate social criteria such as decentralized electronic data processing, alternative ways of steering the system, extensive retraining for the work force by horizontally merging key professional fields in mechanical engineering, the beginnings of vertical rotation and mobility, promotion to higher wage groups, as well as a more developed form of remuneration.

Second, even though the wide variety of projects makes general statements very difficult, in my judgment the effects of *Reparaturhumanisierung* and direct rationalization at the plant level are the most prevalent. In other words, projects yielding results that are truly oriented to the needs of society are relatively rare.

Third, while the direct effects of the program have so far been fairly modest, the indirect effects have been considerably greater. Socially oriented technology policy has spurred much discussion and debate in the plant and among the public at large about heretofore largely taboo aspects of developing alternative technology and the social structure of work. Within the unions, too, it has encouraged a mobilization that cannot be underestimated and has intensified union demands for a stronger voice in matters relating to technology and organization of the work place.

Finally, positive project results did not come about because of the corporatist policy structures, but rather in spite of them. A more socially oriented technology policy was achieved only where the unions involved themselves in the compound corporatist structures and at the same time continued to develop autonomous union demands, achieve a high degree of mobilization in the plant, establish their consultative role in specific projects, set up advanced training, create autonomous and decentralized areas of conflict in the plant, bring about horizontal linkages among these fields of conflict, and cultivate alliances with the academicians in the fields of technology and social science.

Limits to Socially Oriented Technology Policy

Keeping in mind the ambivalent results produced in the past by socially oriented technology policy, I shall try to formulate a concluding assessment of my initial question: In view of the pressure to modernize exerted by the world market, to what extent do the Federal Republic's policy structures have the institutional capacity for innovation?

Past programs have had a few representative and transferable successes in projects and, more particularly, have had the indirect effect of initiating a good deal of discussion and debate about the problems involved with a technology policy that is controlled by society. Many signs over the last year or two have indicated, however, that this new type of policy is increasingly devolving into mere symbolic gestures, and that it is regressing to a policy of government-subsidized modernization and rationalization having no significant effect on the structure of society. The requirement for the participation of the works councils is being confined to formal procedures. Decentralizing tendencies within the state apparatus are losing force and a return to classical, centralized hierarchies becomes visible. The government's practice of controlling policy by tying its support to stipulated conditions has developed into "indirect, specific" forms of support. Moreover, attention to the needs of society was not extended to other research programs of the Ministry of Research and Technology, such as the one established for information technology.

This regression or involution of the new policy is no doubt closely linked to increased tension over the economic situation caused by high unemployment, decreasing returns, and other factors. The equilibrium achieved by compromise within the political formation, which led to support of new types of policy, is threatening to disintegrate under the pressure of economic recession. The reformist forces in the ruling party are losing ground. The inherent dynamics of classic government bureaucracy are becoming stronger, and the circles representing the capital that support the programs increasingly ignore social criteria and the participatory rights of the work force. In the face of growing political and strategic dilemmas, the unions are withdrawing to their traditional battlefields and are resorting to their traditional instruments. New sociopolitical relationships could not be developed, extended, and stabilized in a way that would enable them to withstand the hostile economic climate and political counterattacks.

The corporatist structures in the Federal Republic of Germany have contributed to policy innovation through the concept of socially oriented technology policy. However, this concept was successful only to the extent that individual projects managed to decentralize the compound corporatist system, thereby opening it up. On the whole, however, it was not possible to decentralize decision making on technology in the sociopolitical sense. The approaches to socially oriented technology policy were the product of a particular historical phase and the specific political and economic configuration of the Federal Republic. The conditions that existed then and raised hopes for success are today deteriorating more and more. For the unions, it has meant the ambivalent experience of carrying on disputes within the state apparatus, while at the same time having to follow their classic political strategies, which must be based on union autonomy.

The original thrust of socially oriented technology policy led to an expansion of government policy in the area of corporate investment developments. In the final analysis, however, it did not lead to a new dimension in politics.

PART III

Innovation in Practice: Comparative Studies

CHAPTER 8

POLITICS OF EDUCATIONAL REFORM

H A N S   N.   W E I L E R

The study of educational innovation seems to have reached the point of saturation. So many books, articles, and bibliographies have been written that one major North American educational publisher will no longer consider manuscripts with "innovation" in the title. In education as in other fields, "innovation has emerged over the last decade as possibly the most fashionable of social science areas" (Downs and Mohr, 1976: 700). We must now sort the fad from the fertile and the superficial from the profound.

Innovation and Reform

The scholarly obsession with "educational innovation" reflects a similar and equally consuming preoccupation of decision makers and policymakers throughout the industrialized countries of Western Europe and North America during the last decades. While this interest in innovation stemmed from a genuine recognition of major weaknesses and deficiencies in existing educational systems, many "in-

AUTHOR'S NOTE: Work on the original paper and this revision was supported in part by the National Institute of Education (NIE) under Grant OB NIE-G-78-0212. Additional funds for the author's research project on education and legitimacy have come from the Spencer Foundation and the Ford Foundation. The analyses and conclusions do not necessarily reflect the views of any of these organizations. Valuable comments on an earlier draft of this chapter were made by participants in the December, 1979, seminar on the comparative study of innovation at the *Wissenschaftszentrum* in Berlin, especially Karl Deutsch, Dietrich Goldschmidt, Theodor Hanf, and Richard Merritt. Additional comments were provided by Wolfgang Zapf and my colleagues at Stanford's Institute for Research on Educational Finance and Governance (IFG), including research assistants Leslie Eliason, Margot Kempers, Diana Kirk, and Hernando Gonzalez.

novations" were as faddish and extraneously motivated as the studies of innovations. The attractive political symbolism of "reform" and "innovation" (Naschold, 1974: 21–22) led countries like the Federal Republic of Germany and the United States to devote substantial resources to innovative programs in education. As a result, both necessary and unnecessary activities were labeled "innovations," as demonstrated by a recent inventory of innovations in the public schools of New York City alone (Rogers, 1977). Projects ranged from entire alternative schools to a multisensory approach to bilingual pre-algebra for Spanish-speaking children, and to the "Archdiocese Drug Abuse Prevention Program."

Not surprisingly, a phenomenon of this nature, size, and complexity presents a rather murky picture. Deliberately or by default, no consistent definition of "innovation" in education emerges from the literature. Significant innovation for some is a reinforcement of the status quo, or a minor technical or procedural adjustment for others. Most "definitions" remain conspicuously vague, ranging from "the adoption of means or ends that are new to the adopting unit" (Downs and Mohr, 1976: 701) to "any change which represents something new to the people being changed, . . . usually . . . a change which benefits the people who are changed" (Havelock, 1973: 4). Given the complexity of innovation as an object of study, a more useful definition is needed.

Using Robinsohn's distinction (1970: viii), this discussion will not deal with single, highly specific, and localized measures designed to improve existing educational programs without significantly affecting the substantive and/or ideological orientations of policy nor transcending realities of economic wealth, social structure, and political power. Instead, we shall explore reform as a more encompassing set of policies which are (1) likely to affect in rather profound ways an educational system as a whole or important parts of it, and (2) designed both to reflect and advance relatively clear and politically salient ideas about the future of society and education's role. The political economy of reform in education (rather than the more technical and procedural notion of educational "innovation") has become the focus of recent theoretical debate involving such varied positions as those of Dahrendorf (1976), Becker (1971, 1976), von Hentig (1970), Galtung (1980), Husén (1974), Bourdieu and Passeron (1977), Offe (1975), House (1974), Lenhardt (1977), Katz (1975), Carnoy and Levin (1976), and many others.

The line between "innovation" and "reform" is thus hard to draw with any precision. We exclude "organizational" or "planned" change in educational institutions in the tradition of Gross et al. (1971), even though this field has produced some interesting studies as well as a massive prescriptive literature, albeit of widely varying quality (for example, Havelock, 1973; Zaltman et al., 1977; Owens and Steinhoff, 1976).

For our purposes, educational reform refers to the initiation, modification, implementation, and/or nonimplementation of policies designed to change the "social product" of the educational process along the lines of ideological and political priorities of certain groups in society. With this understanding in mind, the terms "innovation" and "reform" are used interchangeably in this chapter.

Comparative Study of Educational Innovation

While some writings on educational innovation can claim a significant level of generality, the overwhelming majority deal with one particular educational and political system, reflecting the general state of affairs in the study of social intervention in other areas such as health and urban renewal (for some notable exceptions, see Heidenheimer et al., 1975; Heclo, 1974; Liske et al., 1975; Ashford, 1978). Several international organizations have responded to the surge of attention by launching or supporting research on educational innovation in a multinational context. The work of the International Bureau of Education (IBE) in Geneva (see, for example, Blanc and Egger, 1978; Diez-Hochleitner et al., 1978), the Organisation for Economic Cooperation and Development in Paris (OECD, 1971), or the International Institute for Educational Planning (IIEP) in Paris (Adams, 1978) reflects the intensity of effort and the limitations of juxtaposing case studies of individual countries. Little is known about the effects of national or subnational contexts on the way innovations are initiated, implemented, modified, or prevented.

Many questions remain unanswered by the comparative analysis of educational policy. Does the degree of centralization in the policymaking process affect innovation attempts? Does public opinion or administrators' attitudes toward conflict affect the implementation style of new ideas? Does the collective history of a country's social policy efforts lead to discernible patterns of promoting equal educational opportunity? How does the distribution of economic power and the pattern of alliances between economic power and political influence affect the success of certain kinds of educational innovations? To date such studies are limited to a few cases, including Heidenheimer's (1974) analysis of educational reform (comprehensive schooling) in two social democratic systems (Sweden and West Germany) and Peterson's (1973) comparison of educational reform in England and the United States.

Robinsohn's (1970, 1975) ambitious comparative project generated a number of country case studies of educational reform using a common framework (Federal Republic of Germany, German Democratic Republic, Soviet Union, England and Wales, France, Austria, and Sweden). However, the original plan for explicit comparative analysis of this rich material was ultimately abandoned due to analytical difficulties (Glowka, 1975: xxi-xxix).

Some of the more interesting theoretical and methodological ideas in the comparative study of educational reform have come out of the ongoing project on Educational Policymaking in Industrialized Countries (EPIC) at the University of Illinois (for example, Merritt and Coombs, 1977; Merritt, 1979; Coombs and Merritt, 1977), which has made a serious effort to live up to an exacting standard for rigorous scientific analysis in comparative work.

Meyer and his associates (1977) have analyzed comparatively aggregate national data, seeking to identify relationships among economic and political system characteristics and features of the educational system. Inkeles (1981) has undertaken a similar project. Methodologically, these studies satisfy the criteria of comparative study by systematically examining the covariance between a limited set of characteristics of national systems. However, the analysis of aggregate data tends to conceal variation within the unit of analysis and patterns of change over time. Nonetheless, this line of inquiry bears promise.

Although not directly addressed to questions of educational reform and innovation, the International Evaluation of Educational Achievement (IEA) study has had a remarkable impact on the scholarly and political debate. Based on achievement measures of national samples of students in different subject areas and in subsets of a total of 21 countries (for summary reports, see Passow et al., 1976; Peaker, 1975; Walker, 1976; also Husén, 1979; Inkeles, 1977), the study also yielded a wide range of information about the educational systems. Its results have become a major data source for testing hypotheses about the relationship between certain characteristics of the educational system and outcomes of the learning process. Since the data can also, with some caution, be set into the context of more general aggregate characteristics of the countries studied, they provide an opportunity for further and more genuinely comparative research on some societal correlates of achievement patterns.

Research on the legal and constitutional context of educational policy in different countries is still relatively scarce. Constitutional norms and practices can only partially explain cross-national variations in policy processes and innovation. The comparison of some key jurisdictional provisions across different countries has, however, proved to be quite instructive, as a recent comparative study of "the authority of the state in education" in Australia, France, Great Britain, Canada, Austria, Switzerland, and the United States shows (Bothe et al., 1976).

Other studies transcend the framework of one national system and include single-country and sometimes single-issue studies undertaken from the perspective of another country and with that country's policy agenda and interests in mind. Educational innovation and reform in the United States has been studied from the vantage point of the West German educational scene by Herz (1973) and Richter (1975), among others. Others, including Merritt (1979) and Weiler (1973), have had occasion to look in the opposite direction.

This research has yielded insights into the problems, conditions, and outcomes of educational reform efforts in different countries. The extent to which it has, however, contributed to a theoretical progression toward a better understanding of the political conditions and contingencies of educational innovation is a matter which Merritt and Coombs (1977: 250–254; compare Robinsohn, 1970: ix) judge with justified skepticism.

Merritt and Coombs predicate their notion of what comparative studies ought to look like on the need for progressive generalization and theory formation. Naschold (1974: 109) argues for a similar type of study, but for the obverse reason: to protect the advocate of educational reforms from overly hasty generalizations. For him as well as for Merritt and Coombs, the key task is to identify "the empirical range of variation in educational systems as a function of specific conditioning factors" (Naschold, 1974: 109). It is in this sense that, some few examples to the contrary notwithstanding (see above), the comparative study of educational innovation is still very much in its infancy.

If it is true that the present state of international research in the field of educational innovation consists largely of descriptive rather than analytical case studies which fail systematically to formulate and test hypotheses about the fate of educational reform, then we need to identify significant issues for comparative research rather than pursue greater methodological sophistication. Hence we have two tasks: We must take stock of the existing findings of comparative educational innovation research, and then we must seek careful formulations of theoretical questions for further analysis. Our theoretical frame of reference must reflect the educational and political realities which have already been described and analyzed in the field of educational reform. The second part of this chapter addresses the scope and depth of educational reforms, including their practical value for policy change as well as an empirical basis for deriving theoretical propositions about the nature and determinants of educational innovation. The third part outlines a theoretical agenda and argues the need, promise, and possible shape of the accompanying comparative research.

The State of the Art:
Observations and Queries

Given the methodology of existing comparative studies, what has been the utility of looking beyond national boundaries into other countries' efforts to reform and change their educational systems? Are the dynamics of the relationship between education and politics in any given country so unique that the search for commonalities, patterns, and generalizations is futile? The first part of this section presents three uses of comparative studies of educational innovation. It then reviews a few of the many typologies and propositions which the study of educational innovation in different contexts has generated.

UTILITY OF COMPARATIVE STUDIES
IN EDUCATIONAL INNOVATION

Despite the skeptical comments above, comparative and/or cross-national work in the field of educational reform has been useful in at least three ways.

Heuristic Utility

Even short of any systematic generalization produced by testing specific hypotheses across national cases, the material that resulted from studies such as the Robinsohn, EPIC, and IEA projects (and the publicity they received) have produced a better sense of what is unique in a given national policy context and what a number of countries may have in common, even though the extent and intensity of this learning process vary a great deal across countries. Both the policymaker (who tends to overestimate the uniqueness of whatever policy problem he or she faces) and the analyst of policy (who is more prone to look for generalizations) have gained from the corrective effect of exposure to concrete evidence on what is and is not unique in the reform policies of different countries (see Naschold, 1974: 109).

Second, the heuristic yield of comparative innovation analysis now consists of a set of preliminary, plausible, and reasonably promising propositions for further and more systematic study. Efforts at formulating more coherent research agendas (Merritt and Coombs, 1977; Weiler, 1973; Naschold, 1974: 59) will be reviewed later in this chapter.

Lastly, at least some of this material has alerted us to a number of important methodological issues, caveats, and problems which, if carefully reviewed, should help in the design of future comparative studies. The methodological lessons learned from the IEA study (Inkeles, 1977; Husén, 1979), or from the difficulties which the Robinsohn project faced, are cases in point.

Political Utility

The comparison of reform initiatives, difficulties, and results with other countries has loomed large in policy discussions on educational reform in a number of countries (Glowka, 1975: xxi-xxii). In fact, the degree to which such comparisons have played a role in the political debate in different countries would itself be an interesting subject for comparative study. Some of the particularly conspicuous examples include:

—the utilization of the results of the IEA projects in a number of countries to advocate different (and sometimes contradictory) educational reforms (see Husén, 1979: 379–380);

—The political effects and utilization of the reviews of educational systems in various countries conducted by OECD (for example, for the Federal Republic of Germany, see OECD, 1972a, 1972b), which are at least implicitly comparative, and to which most of the international "examiners" of a national educational system bring a heavily comparative perspective; and

—the commissioning of a comparative study of educational decision making in some Western countries by the West German Federal Ministry of Education (Bothe et al., 1976) and the utilization of some of its results in the federal government's *Strukturbericht* in 1978 (Bundesminister, 1978: 65–66 and 130–168).

Theoretical Utility

Comparative investigations into the politics of educational reform have generated a number of important theoretical "themes" which should be helpful for both the further development of theory and empirical cross-national work. These include the relationship of innovation, knowledge, and research; the issue of legitimacy in educational innovation; and different interpretations of the conflictual nature of educational reform. While each theme is intrinsically interesting, cross-national variations in the way they manifest themselves in different societies have contributed to their salience and interest as areas of further theoretical reflection and empirical work.

Work (and not only comparative work) on educational reform and related issues has also served as an important field of application for a number of significant theoretical developments. These include:

—the development of "convergence theory" on the gradual progression of industrialized societies toward a common social structure and thus to common patterns of education and educational change (Inkeles, 1981); and

—the ever-widening discussion on the role of different theories of the state in the analysis of educational policies (for example, Carnoy, 1984; Offe, 1975; Naschold, 1974: 9–14; Lenhardt, 1977; Lindberg et al., 1975; Daedalus, 1979), which is probably one of the seminal theoretical perspectives in the study of the politics of educational innovation.

Typologies and Generalizations: A Selected Review

The rest of this chapter could easily be filled with an inventory of the multitude of typologies, propositions, and hypotheses which the study of educational innovation—comparative and otherwise—has generated over the years (see, for example, Havelock, 1973; Pincus, 1974; Huberman, 1973; Morrish, 1976; Zaltman et al., 1977). It seems more appropriate to provide a broad categorization of various typologies and propositions, and to illustrate each category by a selected number of propositions which have *prima facie* utility for further comparative studies.

Among the propositions discussed here, we distinguish among three different kinds: (a) those dealing with the nature of the innovation itself; (b) those associated with the nature, composition, and characteristics of the organization or system that is to adopt the innovation (on the "symmetry" of [a] and [b], see Downs and Mohr, 1976: 701);

and (c) those that deal with characteristics of the process by which innovations are considered, adopted, and so forth. This allows us to look beyond the usual distinction between different "models" of innovation such as the R&D model, the social interaction model, and the problem-solving model (Havelock, 1973: 155–168).

Nature of the Innovation

Characteristics of innovations in education that seem to predict their eventual chances of success are cost, complexity, and conformity.

Cost. The cost of an innovation is a major determinant of its feasibility and tends to favor the more affluent elements of the political system (Downs and Mohr, 1976: 702–704; Orlich, 1979: 6–7; Peterson, 1973: 176–177). "Cost" in this context refers not only to fiscal, monetary resources, but also—and in many instances more importantly—to nonmonetary costs incurred through friction in the organization, alienation of clients, and other consequences of reform, including "adjustment costs" (Heidenheimer, 1974: 405).

Complexity. Just how simple or complex a given innovation is will affect not only its chances of success but also the kinds of groups on whose cooperation it will depend. In addition, as Downs and Mohr argue (1976: 702–704), the complexity of an innovation is strongly and inversely related to its communicability.

Conformity. Pincus (1974: 118–121) notes the importance of "bureaucratic safety," that is, the degree to which the nature and thrust of an innovation are compatible with and favorable to the current state of the bureaucracy which is to administer its adoption. Schools, according to this argument, are more likely to adopt innovations that promote bureaucratic and social stability. While this is originally a "micro" argument, its basic logic clearly applies to the question of whether or not certain educational reforms are compatible with the existing set of economic and political interests in a given country. Thus Orlich (1979: 6), after reviewing a host of innovation studies, concludes that "curriculum and instructionally related innovations are easier to implement than those requiring changes in organization or administration."

Characteristics of the Organization

The largest share of work on the determinants of innovation has focused on characteristics of the organization into which a given innovation is to be introduced. Much of this literature is derived from work at the micro level and is only taken into account here where it is relevant to a broader national or subnational policy context.

Resources. The mirror image of the cost of innovations, the amount and nature of resources available to the organization, looms large in many studies of educational innovation (Pincus, 1974: 119–120). Just as the issue of resources has played an important role in research, so it has in the political debate on educational innovations, from providing handy arguments against innovations deemed too costly (but in reality opposed on other grounds) to a whole range of ideas and initiatives on changing the resource structure of educational systems though finance reforms, voucher systems, and the like (Coons and Sugarman, 1978; Levin, 1979; Pincus, 1974: 134–138).

Organizational norms and attitudes. Among the strongest predictors of innovation are the prevailing norms and values of an organization (for a summary of the evidence on this point, see Pincus, 1974: 120–121). In the broader political realm, the value structure of both administrative and educational elites has been one of the more serious obstacles in the attempt to reform the educational system of countries like France and the Federal Republic of Germany (see Van de Graaff, 1976; Van de Graaff and Furth, 1978; Heidenheimer, 1974: 403–404; Merritt and Coombs, 1977: 267–268).

Organizational structure: centralization versus decentralization. Heidenheimer (1974: 403; also see Paulston, 1968; Weiler, 1973: 40–45), in comparing educational reform efforts in Sweden and West Germany, attributes a good portion of the variance to the relatively more centralized decision-making power in the hands of the National Board of Education in Sweden. Peterson (1973: 179) compares the decentralized mode of educational financing in the United States with the "centralized, focused character . . . of the partisan politics of educational reform in Britain."

Client relationships. Educational systems are, in Pincus's words, "the captive servant of a captive clientele" (1974: 115). By and large, they cannot select their clients, and their clients have little choice but to accept their services, except in systems with sizable and reasonably accessible private school systems. In the absence of competition, the relationship between the educational system and its clients is thus mainly determined by different degrees of client involvement in the system's decision-making processes. From what little evidence we have, parental and/or student involvement can work both ways as far as the success of reforms is concerned. For instance, parental initiative has been quite instrumental in both facilitating and hindering the development of *Gesamtschulen* in Germany (Weiler, 1973). A number of first attempts to come to terms with the issue of just how client participation works in the political context of educational reform on a comparative basis now exist (see especially Coombs and Merritt, 1977; Wilhelmi, 1974; for a comprehensive and carefully annotated bibliography on citizen participation in the United States, see Davies and Zerchykov, 1978).

Process Characteristics

Research on the characteristics of the process of educational change reflects an increasing preoccupation with adoption and implementation (Pressman and Wildavsky, 1979: 163-194; Pincus, 1974: 134). Rogers's (1962) pioneering work on the diffusion of innovations has shown how different kinds of processes affect both the initial adoption of an idea and its subsequent implementation. Few if any of these suggested relationships have been made the subject of comparative work, even though Merritt and Coombs's (1977: 260–264) discussion of "models for the analysis of educational reform," which remains curiously incomplete by omitting models in the Marxist tradition, leans heavily toward processual aspects of reform.

Planning. While planning is an ingredient in virtually all innovation and reform processes, approaches and effects vary widely. The relationship between educational reform and planning has received much attention (Weiler, 1978, 1980; Straumann, 1974; Levin, 1980a), although more conventional planning paradigms have inhibited rather than facilitated major educational reform (Weiler, 1980). Among the important efforts to rethink the notion of educational planning and to overcome these limitations are Raschert's (1974: 28) "pragmatist model of political planning," Offe's (1975: 82–100) discussion of "political steering mechanisms" in his "general topography of reform initiatives," Weiler's (1980) discussion of "educational planning and social change," and Naschold's (1974: 95–111) critical review of the analytical capacity of educational planning by the state. These advances notwithstanding, a wide field awaits the comparative analyst interested in pursuing the relationship between planning and reform in education.

External intervention. The relationship among different decision levels in a system is another source of processual variation which affects significantly the course of innovative action in education. The rich literature on federal initiatives in educational reform in the United States (for example, Berman and McLaughlin, 1978; Richter, 1975; Pincus, 1974: 123–124, 126–128; House, 1974: 204–248) and other federal states (Bothe et al., 1976; Weiler, 1973) documents the importance of the extent and nature of intergovernmental relations in determining the outcome of educational innovation. The role of incentives (Pincus, 1974) and the emergence and political salience of coalitions which gain access to effective levels of decision making are important factors (see Peterson, 1973: 178–179, on the effects of the civil rights coalition on federal educational policy), as is the increasing role of the courts (Kirp and Yudof, 1974; Kirp, 1977; Merritt, 1979; Duke University, 1975; Weiler, 1985).

Politics of Reform: Issues and Challenges

As mentioned earlier, the most important challenge to comparative analysis of educational innovation and reform lies not in the further development and perfection of comparative methodologies, but rather in the identification of both politically and theoretically significant issues. This section further develops and refines a theoretical agenda for comparative research on the politics of educational innovation. The question of how to proceed is informed not only by the excitement and frustration which research on a number of aspects of educational reform has generated, but also by that kind of reflection which translates normative assumptions about what is and is not important into theoretical priorities. This leads us to focus on the three interrelated themes of knowledge, legitimacy, and conflict.

INNOVATION AND KNOWLEDGE

Research and Reform: The Politics of Knowledge Utilization

The relationship between research and innovation in education touches on only one aspect of the relationship between knowledge and policy in contemporary societies. While there is an enormous literature on "knowledge utilization," its conceptual and theoretical structure is in a state of serious underdevelopment (as documented in the excellent effort by the Human Interaction Research Institute, 1976, to assess the state of the art of "Putting Knowledge to Use").

More specifically, our problem is to determine whether or not research affects what happens in educational systems. The assumption that it brings about educational change and, indeed, improvement has produced massive support for research and development in the United States and elsewhere. While many researchers and educators alike take this relationship for granted, the question has become the subject of considerable recent debate. In the United States the National Institute of Education commissioned the distinguished National Academy of Education to review whether and how educational research influences educational practice (Suppes, 1978). The result is a major volume of nine case studies, all of which, with somewhat varying degrees of conviction, conclude that research did indeed make a significant difference in one or another aspect of educational practice. In summarizing the evidence, Suppes admits that "all of us on occasion probably feel that there is little hope that research . . . will seriously affect practice," but goes on to note with satisfaction that "such pessimism is not historically supported by the evidence" (1978: xiii; for a critical review, see Levin, 1980b).

In an eloquent brief on the pivotal function of certain kinds of research for initiating reform processes, Becker (1971: 11–14) singles out the work of Edding in West Germany, Husén and Svennson in Sweden, and Basil Bernstein in England as prime examples. Becker and others (see Kuhlmann, 1970: I/139) have attributed a good deal of the initial momentum in the early 1970s for educational reform in West Germany to the impressive evidence on the determinants of learning outcomes gathered in Roth's book, *Begabung und Lernen* (1969). Husén makes a similar case in his discussion of the Swedish school reform (Suppes, 1978: 523-579).

In attempting to understand and assess the contribution of education to improving the "life chances" of youths from low-income and minority backgrounds, Levin (1976: 89) sounds a much more skeptical note. He asserts that "the social sciences cannot produce conclusive results that would support a particular educational strategy for improving the life attainments of students from low-income and minority families," and that "the evidence that does enter the courts or the policy arena is considered and utilized on the basis of factors other than its scientific 'validity.'" Such observations, and those made by Light and Glass (1979: 14) and House (1974: 305 and passim), cast doubt on some key assumptions underlying the cluster of typologies and propositions called the "research and development" or the "research and development and diffusion" model of innovation in education (Havelock, 1973: 161–164).

Even though Pincus (1974: 129) recognizes some of the major challenges to the R&D model, he maintains that the innovation process in education "may best be viewed both as a stimulus to social change and as a socially approved process of testing society's readiness for change." He proceeds to suggest an incentive-oriented notion of educational R&D that would be capable of making the most of the fact that, in his view, the educational system is still—the reservations of Bowles, Gintis, Jencks, and others notwithstanding—"the principal vehicle for policy reform" (Pincus, 1974: 128).

Despite these and other attempts to rescue the R&D model, the relationship between research and innovation, and hence the theoretical basis for the R&D model, remain tenuous. Research findings in this area are inconclusive and unstable in important regards (Downs and Mohr, 1976; Levin, 1976), and have been unable to move beyond accounting for a very modest portion of the variance on such key issues as educational effects (Light and Glass, 1979). Moreover, since the researchers are strongly indebted to the established order of epistemological, institutional, and social values (Levin, 1976: 86–87), they are unlikely to become a source of major educational change beyond the sometimes fancy yet ultimately rather insignificant modifications often referred to as "innovations" (see, for West Germany, the discussion in Kuhlmann, 1980: I/126). Furthermore, it is quite possible that certain changes in education are by their very nature likely to be decisively affected by forces much more powerful than even the most conclusive research results (for example, the changes brought about in Chinese education by the cultural revolution or the transformation or nontransformation of socially stratified systems of postelementary education in Great Britain and West Germany). At the same time, the evidentiary needs for advocacy and opposition may be beyond the capabilities of "normal" scientific research (as in the case of comparatively evaluating educational systems with different sets of goals).

Against the background of this dilemma, there are a number of ways to reconceptualize the relationship between research and the policy or reform process. Rivlin (1973), in reviewing Jencks's 1972 book, makes a case for a "forensic social science," which adopts an adversarial mode for weighing the pros and cons of a given policy issue. Levin (1976: 92–93), after discussing inadequacies in conventional attempts to use the social sciences to lay the groundwork for policy decisions, accords them what he calls a "heuristic" rather than a "deterministic" role—that is, he uses them "to frame the issues and their consequences rather than to obtain conclusive evidence on what is right and what is to be done." Kuhlmann, in his review of educational reform in West Germany, concludes that the main role of research has been to "shake up" some prevailing typologies of talent which leaned heavily toward models of "natural" ability (1970: I/139). Haller and Lenzen (1977: 9–10) see a threefold role for educational research: legitimation, to justify decisions originally taken for "extrascientific" reasons; optimization, to provide know-how for increasing the effectiveness of reform programs; and evaluation, to assess innovative experiments.

Experimental Paradigm of Reform

It seems almost too good to be true: "Reforms as Experiments"—the classical paradigm of scientific methodology transplanted into the realities of public policy. There emerged the prospect of being able to say, with the conviction of true scientists, that one social program was better than another, that advocates of a given innovation were "right" and their opponents "wrong." The notion was attractive enough, and some early social experiments, such as the Manhattan bail bond experiment (Riecken and Boruch, 1974: 1–2) and Campbell's (1969) pioneering work on the utilization of experimental designs in social policy situations, were studied with interest by policymakers and policy analysts.

In an attempt to substantiate the notion that "systematic experimental trials of proposed social programs have certain important advantages over other ways of learning what programs (or program elements) are effective under what circumstances and at what cost" (Riecken and Boruch, 1974: 3), the U.S. Social Science Research Council's Committee on Social Experimentation devoted a major effort in the early 1970s to elaborate "a method for planning and evaluating social intervention" (Riecken and Boruch, 1974; compare Boruch and Riecken, 1975). Experimental programs, including educational television in the United States and abroad, vocational education and counseling programs, curriculum development, and early childhood education (Riecken and Boruch, 1974: 308), loomed large in this early phase of developing and improving the concept and practice of experimentation. Major federal programs (Head Start, Follow Through, Titles I, III, VII, and VIII of the Elementary and

Secondary Education Act [ESEA], and others) went through rather large-scale experimental phases before being fully adopted or abandoned (Pincus, 1974: 129-131).

The United States was not alone in these efforts. When Sweden introduced a comprehensive system of secondary schooling in the 1950s and early 1960s, experimental studies of a number of proposed elements of the new system played a significant role in reinforcing the arguments of the advocates of reform (Heidenheimer, 1978: 22–25), even though some of the findings were later challenged on the basis of a reanalysis of the data (Heidenheimer, 1974: 404). In 1969 the West German *Bildungsrat* (Deutscher Bildungsrat, 1969) established a major experimental program of Gesamtschulen. This program was ostensibly predicated on the classical experimental conception of assessing the differential impact of two "treatments" (school types) on essentially similar student populations. A host of other experiments followed, and a survey conducted at the end of 1977 by the *Bund-Länder-Kommission* (1978) lists 611 experiments either completed or ongoing in precollegiate education alone.

All this represented a major effort to make the process of educational reform and innovation more "rational" and provide, through experimental innovation, an effective and transparent link between educational research and educational reform. Raschert (1974: 28), with reference to Habermas, sees the *Gesamtschule* experiment as an example of a "pragmatist model of political planning." It has three principal functions: articulation and reflection of needs; invention of practical models of action; and scientific evaluation and prognosis. In his view, the experiment provides a vehicle for progressive, step-by-step development as well as the simultaneous correction of political goals and scientifically established means. This represents an interesting and important variation on Campbell's original experimental paradigm. As it turns out, however, most educational experiments remain rather closely tied to the basic logic of the original experimental paradigm, which specifies in advance both the objective ("criterion") to be accomplished (for example, to increase achievement) and the alternative means or "treatments" through which it is to be accomplished.

The heavy emphasis on experimentation as a strategy for reform carried with it the hope that research practice, as well as researchers and practitioners, could be brought together in a mutually useful way. In both respects the experimental strategy has encountered major limitations and difficulties. While they do not eliminate the basic hope, they do suggest that the effectiveness of this device (a) is contingent upon a number of conditions external to the experimental situation and program, and (b) may consist of results that have very little to do with the comparative assessment and evaluation of different treatments, but a great deal to do with the issues of legitimacy and conflict in educational reform. A more systematic cross-national look at both of these possibilities would seem to be in order.

Before pursuing these issues further, however, let us look at some of the shortcomings of the experimental approach to educational reform. When I reviewed for the National Academy of Education in 1973 the developments surrounding the Gesamtschule in West Germany, I concluded that "from the point of view of generating 'objective' evidence on the relative performance of two different systems of education, the experimental (Gesamtschule) program was a failure virtually from its beginning" (Weiler, 1973: 51). I, as well as others, had reached that conclusion not so much because of the tremendous methodological problems inherent in such a massive comparison, but mainly because of the profoundly different normative and political connotations of each of the two different types of schooling. These different connotations caused a basic lack of agreement as to "the very criterion variables on which the performance of each system is to be tested" (Weiler, 1973: 47). Similarly, Raschert (1974: 204-207) saw both the "political" and "scientific" limitations of the program, which tend to draw rather narrow boundaries around the possibility for "rationalizing decisions by experimenting with institutional alternatives" (1974: 205).

We find related criticism of experimental approaches to major educational innovations in the United States. Pincus (1974: 129–130) concludes that these are either so small that they tend to "disappear from view" or, if they are larger, "have in general not been designed or evaluated in ways that would allow anyone to assess the reasons for their success and failure in the real-life setting of the school." He adds a point which is often overlooked in the more enthusiastic advocacy of experimentation, namely, that any substantial intervention in an existing social system is very likely to have important unintended effects. Since almost every major experiment in educational reform bears out this observation, it has important implications for any further research in this area, especially in terms of extending the scope of outcome phenomena which we would study in connection with any major experimental reform.

On similar grounds, and on the basis of studying the different assumptions about the ways in which education affects life chances, Levin (1976: 74–76) concludes that, for issues of this magnitude and complexity, an experimental approach is "politically and practically infeasible." Brise et al. (1973: 174 and passim), after reviewing the extensive experimental program of educational reform in the West German state of Baden-Württemberg, disqualify the entire program as a "democratic playground in social capitalism" and suspect, probably not without reason, that the program reflects an ideological utilization of science and research as an instrument of manipulation in the hands of a status-quo-oriented educational bureaucracy.

Whether or not these various observations on experimental programs are correct, they do raise a number of important questions for both further theoretical reflection and comparative policy analysis. Assumptions that would particularly benefit from such an effort include the notion that

(1) the relative political salience and controversiality of a given set of educational reforms is an important negative predictor of the effectiveness of an experimental design for initiating and evaluating the reform;

(2) reform through experimentation has a certain ideological quality which is deliberately used by dominant economic and political groups in the society to facilitate "pseudo-reforms" and oppose those reforms which might effectively alter the status quo;

(3) experimentation in the context of educational reform does not provide scientific information on the advantages and disadvantages of alternative educational arrangements, but rather legitimates existing processes of educational decision making and/or the management of social conflict in the design and implementation of reforms (compare Kuhlmann, 1970: 105; Haller and Lenzen, 1977: 1–102; Weiler, 1983a).

Innovation and Legitimacy

Legitimacy as an Issue

Recent scholarship in the social sciences in general, and in political science in particular, has paid increasing attention to the question of legitimacy of political regimes. While the notion of legitimacy itself has a long and distinguished history in social and political thought, the rather intense preoccupation with the legitimacy of the modern state as a *problem* is a rather recent and striking phenomenon (Kopp and Müller, 1980)—engaging as diverse a group of people as the authors of the Trilateral Commission's "Report on the Governability of Democracies" (Crozier et al., 1975), the entire 1975 convention of the West German Political Science Association (Kielmannsegg, 1976; Ebbighausen, 1976), critics like Ralf Dahrendorf (1979) and Sheldon Wolin (1980), and a wide range of scholars within and outside the Marxist tradition on both sides of the Atlantic (for example, Offe, 1972, 1976; Habermas, 1973; Lindberg et al., 1975; Rothschild, 1977; Wolfe, 1977; Freedman, 1978; Vidich and Glassman, 1979).

The argument that lies at the heart of this preoccupation postulates, on a variety of grounds, a rather serious problem of credibility and acceptability on the part of the modern state in its relationship to its society and its citizens: "Authority hath been broken into pieces," as Schaar (1969: 276) lets a seventeenth-century gentleman from *The Whitehall Debates* define the issue in its most general terms. More specific conceptualizations of the issue range from Rose's (1980) and Kavanagh's (1980) emphasis on the trade-off between regime effectiveness and civic consent, to Offe's view of the problem of legitimacy both as a threat to the state's "monopoly of politics" and as the tendency, based on the very nature of the capitalist state, toward an increasing "loss of state" *(Entstaatlichung)* in politics (1976: 98–99). Common to most conceptions of the legitimacy issue is the notion that, as the range and scope of the state's activities increase, there is a corresponding or, indeed, disproportionate increase in the need for legitimation (Habermas, 1973: 71)—a need that the state tends to satisfy by even further expanding its activities, thus perpetuating the spiral of increasing legitimacy needs which are forever harder to satisfy.

Even defining the nature of the issue is, of course, a way of hypothesizing about its origins and causes. Where the emphasis in conceptualizing the problem of legitimacy is, as in the case of Mayntz (1975) and others, on limitations in the political system's "directive capacity," the search for the roots of the problem leads right to the issue of "the increased load of tasks undertaken by modern capitalist governments" (Lindberg et al., 1975: x), and to the phenomenon of "overloaded politics" (Rose, 1980). Where, on the other hand, the problem of the legitimacy deficit of the modern state is seen in terms of shortcomings of existing modes of representation, the explanatory effort tends to concentrate on the loss of credibility and functioning of the party system, and on the concomitant erosion of party identification (compare Kaase, 1980; Berger, 1979) or, more broadly, on the costs of the "competitive democratic form of legitimation" (Habermas, 1973: 74) altogether. In Offe's (1976: 93) more probing perspective on the legitimacy issue, the modern capitalist state, as a result of the contradictions in its own "directive imperatives" *(kontradiktorische Steuerungsimperative)*, has lost the ability to legitimate itself on normative grounds, and is thus left with the alternative strategies for "legitimating" its continued existence through either material gratification or coercive repression—each of which, Offe argues, tends only to exacerbate rather than solve the real legitimacy problem (1976: 95–103).

It is clear to Offe and other Marxian theorists of the modern state that at the very heart of its legitimacy problems lies the class structure of capitalist society. Habermas (1973: 96) argues: "Because the reproduction of class societies is based on the privileged appropriation of socially produced wealth, all such societies must resolve the problem of distributing the surplus social product inequitably and yet legitimately." He sees the inherent difficulty of accomplishing this task as a main source of the state's legitimacy deficit (see Habermas, 1973: 73). Similarly, Wolfe (1977: 329) predicates his analysis of the legitimacy issue on the "inherent tensions between liberalism and democracy" under conditions of capitalism, and sees the crisis emerge as the late capitalist state, having exhausted solutions to these tensions, becomes a victim of its own contradictions in that it is "called on to solve problems at the same time that its ability to solve them is undermined" (1977: 10).

Legitimacy and Educational Reform

The most critical issues in the politics of educational reform stem from the question of legitimacy. Cross-national variations in the interpretation of the legitimacy issue should be a particularly interesting variable in studying the politics of education in general, and educational reform and innovation in particular.

At the most general level, since the state is involved in all decisions affecting education, it is in the state's interest to maintain the credibility of its own authority in educational matters. This is especially true in the case of innovations and reforms that demand a greater degree of compliance and thus a higher level of legitimacy than does the routine continuation of the status quo. The state's educational decisions, which involve such critical issues as socialization and status allocation, are most likely to raise questions about the legitimacy of the state's authority. Two educational issues have been particularly prone to raise such questions: measures to provide for greater equality in and through education (as in the case of comprehensive schools), and changes in curricular objectives and guidelines (Weiler, 1983b).

The contemporary debate on the legitimacy of the modern state suggests a number of different ways for dealing with the relationship between legitimacy and educational reform (for a more extensive review of the issue, see Weiler and Gonzalez, 1981, and Weiler, 1983a).

Legitimation and procedure. Reflecting Weberian traditions and the considerable influence the work of Luhmann (1969, 1975) has had on the contemporary legitimacy discussion in West Germany, one major set of propositions on the legitimacy of the modern state and its policy actions centers on the notion of "legitimation by procedure" *(Legitimation durch Verfahren)*. Its basic argument is that the state acquires legitimacy for its actions by virtue of following a particular set of presumably "rational" and generally accepted procedures; the prodecural quality thus becomes the basis for the legitimacy of a decision. Planning processes serve as a particularly appropriate test for the procedural legitimacy of policy decisions: A policy is legitimate to the extent that it results from a careful, rational planning process (Luhmann, 1975; Schatz, 1976; Scharpf, 1973).

While this notion of legitimation by procedure has been heavily criticized on the grounds that it lacks "material content" (Offe, 1976: 87; 1975: 249), it has been important in discussions on the nature and politics of educational reform. This is particularly true for the discussion of the legitimacy of curricular decisions (Baumert et al., 1978: 20–22; see also below), and for the rather intensive debate on the legalization of educational reform decisions (Oppermann, 1976; Richter, 1976; Gruschka and Rüdell, 1979; Weiler, 1981). Clearly, the rationale for stressing educational planning is derived from a procedural paradigm of policy legitimation (Weiler, 1978, 1980).

Legitimation by expertise. Policy decisions can also gain in legitimacy as a result of having been informed by scientific research. For example, experimental programs serve an important legitimating function—almost regardless of their results—as long as they confer the dignity and prestige of the scientific enterprise on a particular innovation or reform. Haller and Lenzen (1977: 12; compare Raschert, 1974) raise a number of important questions about the "current legitimatizing quality of educational research," but, with the possible exception of the area of curriculum development and reform, there have so far been few answers. Comparative inquiry in this area would be especially useful for gaining a better understanding of the possibilities and limitations of this particular notion of legitimating educational innovation.

Legitimation by symbols. Another important contribution to the discussion of the legitimacy of political authority stems from Edelman's work on the role of symbolism in politics (1964, 1975). Edelman contends that certain symbols evoke beliefs that are supportive of the state and its actions. Such beliefs "are not necessarily false, but it is social cues rather than their factual accuracy of demonstrability that brings them into being" (1975: 310). He cites the designation of "enemies" and "threats," the "reassuring" role of certain laws beyond their actual legal effect, and the use of official language as typical political symbols. His discussion of the use of tests or other devices of classification for the "symbolic evocation of merit" (Edelman, 1975: 315–316) could add another important dimension to the discussion of the legitimation of educational reform. In many countries the politics of educational reform have been strongly affected by the use of symbols—from the positive symbolic value of the term "innovation" itself all the way to the symbolic baggage carried by such concepts as equality, experimentation, and participation (see Naschold, 1974: 21–22). Edelman (1975: 319) also suggests conducting a "comparison of political symbolism and its consequences in different countries and cultures" for the special case of the politics of educational reform.

Legitimation by Participation

The issue of participation has been talked and written about in recent years for a variety of reasons and in many different contexts, and nowhere perhaps as ubiquitously as in education. For the United States alone, a careful bibliography on citizen participation in education lists over 800 titles (Davies and Zerchykov, 1978). Coombs and Merritt (1977) provide a useful comparative typology of various forms of "the public's role in educational policymaking," and a joint German-Swedish commission has prepared what is certainly the most thorough and comprehensive comparative study in this field to date, dealing with democratization and participation in schools and universities in the two countries (see summary volume by Wilhelmi, 1974).

Particularly interesting here is the relationship of participation to the issue of legitimacy. Participation is increasingly seen as a crucial source of legitimacy for policy decisions, especially in educational policy, but not only there (see Alemann, 1975; Rodenstein, 1978; Matthöfer, 1977). The basic argument is that if those most likely to be affected by its results are involved in the policymaking process, the legitimacy of the process and its results will be enhanced. However, both the justification and interpretation of this notion vary widely from one ideological frame of reference to another. Offe (1972: 153–168; compare 127–134), in his discussion of citizen initiatives, explains why Marxist scholars are skeptical of the ambivalent nature of participation: It can serve as an instrument for either the ruler or the ruled (see Baumert et al., 1978: 32). Those who accept participation as an important source of legitimation in educational policy and reform tend to see it not only as a relatively abstract principle of individual emancipation and self-determination, but also as an increasingly necessary complement and corrective for the inadequacies of decision processes in parliamentary systems of government (Baumert et al., 1978: 29–30) or, indeed, as a deliberate strategy to preempt and replace those processes (Büchner, 1972).

Curriculum Reform and Legitimacy

Few areas of educational innovation have been quite so controversial in terms of legitimacy as the field of curriculum development. An earlier analysis of curricular policymaking in the United States concluded that "the determination of the public school curriculum is not just influenced by political events; it is a political process in important ways" (Kirst and Walker, 1971: 480). The study suggests various political factors bearing on the curriculum development process but does not explicitly raise the question of legitimacy. By contrast, recent European writing on curriculum reform deals almost exclusively with the question of how curricular decisions, especially those dealing with the objectives of the learning process, acquire legitimacy given:

—the development of increasingly divergent theoretical and methodological paradigms in the disciplines on which curricular subjects depend (history, linguistics, and so on);

—increasing doubts about conventional notions of the learning abilities and learning needs of children at different age levels; and

—the competitive claims on children's attention by educational factors outside of family and school, notably in the media (Baumert et al., 1978: 18–19).

Curriculum development, therefore, will depend increasingly on new answers to the question of legitimacy, especially when there is a major political conflict over curriculum changes as in the case of the *Rahmenrichtlinien* in the West German state of Hesse. Raschert (1977: 24), in reviewing the history of curricular decisions, found numerous other examples of intensely politicized disputes over the legitimacy of particular changes and reforms.

The study of curriculum development has raised several issues worth further consideration (see also Frey et al., 1975):

—the legal quality of curricular objectives, as well as the opportunities and limits of their legitimation through parliamentary or other decision processes (Baumert et al., 1978: 22–23; on the limits of the legal dimension of curricular legitimacy, see Künzli, 1976: 201–202);

—the importance and limitations of educational research as a basis for legitimating curriculum decisions (Hameyer et al., 1976: 291–339; Baumert et al., 1978: 25–28);

—the conditions for and effect of the participation of teachers, students, and parents in the process of curriculum reform (Frey and Santini, 1976; Hesse, 1975; Baumert et al., 1978; Becker and Jungblut, 1972).

Our ongoing comparative study of "compensatory legitimation" in educational policy in the United States and the Federal Republic of Germany has begun to shed further light on these and a number of related questions (Weiler, 1983a).

INNOVATION AND CONFLICT

In education as elsewhere, innovation and conflict are close neighbors. Major educational reforms tend to be accompanied by considerable degrees of conflict. How are the two related? An understanding of that relationship presents yet another important challenge to the future study of the politics of educational reform, and like our earlier challenges it too stands to benefit from a comparative perspective.

Most importantly, we need to find out more about both the nature and the direction of the relationship between innovation and conflict. Does conflict lead to reform, or does reform lead to conflict? Do reforms typically come about as a result of conflict (for example, educational reforms as a result of student protest), or is it more likely that reforms—because of their own shortcomings—create more dissatisfaction, frustration, and, ultimately, conflict? Theoretical and empirical answers to these questions will form an important part of any theory about the relationship between the state and education.

At this point, the theoretical discussion on this issue tends to be bimodal. According to liberal conflict theorists such as Coser (1956), Dahrendorf (1958), and others, conflict precedes reform and is a necessary condition for it; in fact, one argument for the necessity and functionality of conflict in societies is that, without conflict, societies stagnate and fail to adjust, through social reform, to changing conditions and demands. A number of studies, notably Baldridge (1971), have applied this framework or variants of it to the study of change in educational organizations, and have found that the assumption of continuing conflict in organizations does not explain certain patterns of change and innovation (see Dill and Friedman, 1979: 417–418).

Arguing from a different theoretical position, Naschold (1974: 28–29) suggests that certain kinds of conflict conditions within the educational system contribute to the potential for change: mobilization of internal conflict within schools through politicized groups of students and teachers in the direction of a limited "syndicalist counter-force"; "horizontalization" of educational conflict by intertwining educational problems with those of other areas of reproduction (vocational training, urban development, and so on) into a wider "frontier of conflict"; and "verticalization" of educational problems by connecting them with the world of work and trade unions.

Perhaps tensions, cleavages, and conflicts existing in societies can generate momentum which may lead to reform and change (or, as in the case of the measures taken by the French government after the events of May, 1968, to pseudo-reforms). At the same time, there is a good deal of evidence suggesting that reforms result in conflict, sometimes even in more intense conflict than what preceded them. Raschert (1974: 204–205) points out that several essential aspects of the West German Gesamtschule were bound to lead to all kinds of conflict given the inherent logic of planning processes and perceived needs for stability in the entire educational system (for analogous observations from the United States, see House, 1974: 301–306). Drawing on examples from the policy areas of housing, traffic, education, and environmental protection, Offe (1972: 124–126) maintains that the modal pattern for the capitalist state is one where conflict does not cause reform but is caused by it. This is because the rhetoric of reform generates expectations which, given the highly limited capacity of the capitalist state for change, reforms are unable to meet, often leading to a situation that is worse than before.

In a particularly interesting and penetrating analysis of comprehensive secondary school reforms in Western Europe, Levin (1978) describes the dilemma they face in living up to their putative egalitarian intentions while at the same time contributing to the reproduction of wage labor for the capitalist system in which they operate. Since these reproduction needs require highly unequal educational outcomes, they are fundamentally at variance with the egalitarian claims that accompanied the introduction of comprehensive schools. Levin argues that, since comprehensive secondary schools cannot perform the task of stratification as well as their vertically structured predecessors, the role of stratification is now increasingly being taken over by institutions of postsecondary education through such devices as numerus clausus, permitting overcrowding, and higher dropout rates. Whatever higher education cannot accomplish, the labor market compensates for through rising rates of unemployment and underemployment among university graduates. If Levin's analysis is correct, such reforms may generate a substantial potential for conflict:

> These frustrations and feelings of dissatisfaction with both the educational system and the labor market will lead to increasing manifestations of class conflict and struggle. . . . These conflicts will place pressure on the state, capitalist enterprises, and the universities to seek a solution to the plight of an overeducated and underemployed proletariat. . . . The ultimate result of the reforms is the rapid formation of a new and highly conscious class with great potential for forcing social change" (Levin, 1978: 450).

All this suggests that educational reforms and their consequences are likely to confront the capitalist state—as well as the state in other societies, although for different reasons—with even greater problems as it strives for minimal consensus and legitimacy. In this confrontation, the state will use whatever legitimation strategies it can mobilize. In the field of education, the symbolic use of the notion of "reform" itself is tied to the belief that new also means more. Reforms mean additional resources, but the power of this particular legitimation device may be on the decline as Western societies approach "steady state" conditions. At the same time, research and knowledge as a legitimation strategy may also have limitations, even though the device of experimentation has served quite well temporarily to contain and manage reform-generated conflict (Weiler, 1973: 51; Kuhlmann, 1970: I/105).

Conclusion

Our review of the state of the art in the comparative study of educational innovation has first tried to identify the major ways in which research in this area has been useful. These utility functions may not always be what the authors of the studies intended them to be, but they have nonetheless played a major role in both the politics of educational reform and in advancing—however slowly—our theoretical understanding of the dynamics of reform and innovation. The balance sheet on this score is sufficiently favorable to encourage vigorous further pursuits in the comparative field, especially if they are guided by a careful perusal of such theoretical insights as we have gained so far.

Among these insights, the relationship between reform and legitimacy is particularly intriguing. A "map" of the potential territory for promising future research on the politics of educational reform and innovation has been presented. Since legitimacy, for whatever reason, is becoming an ever more precarious commodity in the modern state, reform policies are relevant for legitimacy at two levels. Generally, the very adoption of reform policies identifies an existing regime as forward-looking, flexible, and responsive to the changes of modern society, and thus enhances its credibility and legitimacy. Reforms, or at least a verbal commitment to reforms, become putative sources of added legitimacy. Second, however, one may well interpret from a legitimacy perspective some of the specific ways and strategies for making and implementing reform decisions. It is here that our observations on the perceived legitimizing potential of expertise and research, experimentation, participation, and so on should provide further guidance. It is possible to look at reform policies, in education as well as other policy areas, as strategies of "compensatory legitimation," that is, as ways to maximize the gains in legitimacy which the state, faced as it is with the erosion of its own legitimacy, may derive from the ways in which it goes about making and implementing policies of reform (Weiler, 1983a). Whether such "compensatory" strategies, however, will ultimately be adequate to halt or reverse the erosion of the modern state's legitimacy remains an open and troublesome question.

REFERENCES

ADAMS, R. S. (1978) Educational Planning: Towards a Qualitative Perspective. Paris: Unesco Press.
ALEMANN, U. von [ed.] (1975) Partizipation-Demokratisierung-Mitbestimmung. Opladen: Westdeutscher Verlag.
ASHFORD, D. E. (1978) Comparing Public Policies: New Concepts and Methods. Beverly Hills, CA: Sage.

BALDRIDGE, J. V. (1971) Power and Conflict in the University. New York: John Wiley.

BAUMERT, J., J. RASCHERT, et al. (1978) Vom Experiment zur Regelschule. Stuttgart: Klett-Cotta.

BECKER, E. and G. JUNGBLUT (1972) Strategien der Bildungsproduktion. Frankfurt: Suhrkamp Verlag.

BECKER, H. (1971) Bildungsforschung und Bildungsplanung. Frankfurt: Suhrkamp Verlag.

——— et al. (1976) Die Bildungsreform: Eine Bilanz. Stuttgart: Klett.

BERGER, S. (1979) "Politics and antipolitics in Western Europe in the seventies." Daedalus 108 (Winter): 27–50.

BERMAN, P. and M. W. McLAUGHLIN (1978) Rethinking the Federal Role in Education. Santa Monica, CA: Rand Corporation.

BLANC, E. and E. EGGER (1978) Educational Innovations in Switzerland: Traits and Trends. Paris: Unesco Press.

BORUCH, R. F. and H. W. RIECKEN [eds.] (1975) Experimental Testing of Public Policy. Boulder, CO: Westview Press.

BOTHE, M. et al. (1976) Die Befugnisse des Gesamtstaates im Bildungswesen: Rechtsvergleichender Bericht. Bonn: Bundesminister für Bildung und Wissenschaft.

BOURDIEU, P. and J. C. PASSERON (1977) Reproduction in Education, Society and Culture. London: Sage.

BRISE, V. et al. (1973) Grenzen kapitalistischer Bildungspolitik. Frankfurt: Athenäum Verlag.

BÜCHNER, P. (1972) Schulreform durch Bürgerinitiative. München: List.

Bundesminister für Bildung und Wissenschaft (1978) Bericht der Bundesregierung über die strukturellen Probleme des föderativen Bildungssystems. Bonn: Bundesminister für Bildung und Wissenschaft.

Bund-Länder-Kommission für Bildungsplanung und Forschungsförderung (1978) Informationsschrift 1978 über Modellversuche im Bildungswesen. Bonn: Bund-Länder-Kommission.

CAMPBELL, D. T. (1969) "Reforms as experiments." American Psychologist 24 (April): 409–429.

CARNOY, M. (1984) The State and Political Theory. Princeton, NJ: Princeton University Press.

——— and H. M. LEVIN (1976) The Limits of Educational Reform. New York: David McKay Company.

COOMBS, F. S. and R. L. MERRITT (1977) "The public's role in educational policymaking." Education and Urban Society 9 (February): 167–196.

COONS, J. E. and S. D. SUGARMAN (1978) Education by Choice: The Case for Family Control. Berkeley: University of California Press.

COSER, L. (1956) The Functions of Social Conflict. New York: Free Press.

CROZIER, M. J., S. P. HUNTINGTON, and J. WATANUKI (1975) The Crisis of Democracy: Report on the Governability of Democracies to the Trilateral Commission. New York: New York University Press.

Daedalus (1979) "The state." 108 (Fall): 1–174.

DAHRENDORF, R. (1979) Lebenschancen: Anläufe zur sozialen und politischen Theorie. Frankfurt: Suhrkamp Verlag. (Life Chances: Approaches to Social and Political Theory. Chicago: University of Chicago Press, 1979.)

——— (1976) "Bildung bleibt Bürgerrecht," pp. 63–71 in H. Becker et al., Die Bildungsreform: Eine Bilanz. Stuttgart: Klett-Verlag.

_____ (1958) "Toward a theory of social conflict." Journal of Conflict Resolution 2 (June): 170–183.

DAVIES, D. and R. ZERCHYKOV (1978) Citizen Participation in Education: Annotated Bibliography. Boston, MA: Institute for Responsive Education.

Deutscher Bildungsrat (1969) Einrichtung von Schulversuchen mit Gesamtschulen. Stuttgart: Klett-Verlag.

DIEZ-HOCHLEITNER, R. et al. (1978) The Spanish Educational Reform and Lifelong Education. Paris: Unesco Press.

DILL, D. H. and C. P. FRIEDMAN (1979) "An analysis of frameworks for research on innovation and change in higher education." Review of Educational Research 49 (Summer): 411–435.

DOWNS, G. W., Jr. and L. B. MOHR (1976) "Conceptual issues in the study of innovation." Administrative Science Quarterly 21 (December): 700–714.

Duke University School of Law (1975) "The courts, social science and school desegregation." Law and Contemporary Problems 39 (Winter): 1–216.

EBBIGHAUSEN, R. [ed.] (1976) Bürgerlicher Staat und politische Legitimation. Frankfurt: Suhrkamp Verlag.

EDELMAN, M. (1975) "Symbolism in politics," pp. 309–320 in L. N. Lindberg et al. (eds.), Stress and Contradiction in Modern Capitalism. Lexington, MA: D. C. Heath.

_____ (1964) The Symbolic Uses of Politics. Urbana: University of Illinois Press.

FREEDMAN, J. O. (1978) Crisis and Legitimacy. Cambridge: Cambridge University Press.

FREY, K. et al. [eds.] (1975) Curriculum-Handbuch (3 vols.). München: R. Piper.

FREY, K. and B. SANTINI (1976) "Legitimation von Innovationszielen im Innovationsprojckt Weiterbildungsschule Zug," pp. 222–234 in U. Hameyer et al. (eds.), Bedingungen und Modelle der Curriculuminnovation. Weinheim: Beltz-Verlag.

GALTUNG, J. (1980) "Schooling and future society," pp. 179–207 in H. N. Weiler (ed.), Educational Planning and Social Change. Paris: Unesco Press.

GLOWKA, P. (1975) "Einführung," pp. v-xxix in S. B. Robinsohn (ed.) Schulreform im gesellschaftlichen Vergleich, Vol. II. Stuttgart: Klett-Verlag.

GROSS, N. et al. (1971) Implementing Organizational Innovations: A Sociological Analysis of Planned Educational Change. New York: Basic Books.

GRUSCHKA, A. and G. RÜDELL (1979) "Bekommen Reformen nur Recht, wenn sie Recht haben?" Neue Sammlung 19 (March/April): 155–171.

HABERMAS, J. (1973) Legitimationsprobleme im Spätkapitalismus. Frankfurt: Suhrkamp-Verlag. (Legitimation Crisis. Boston: Beacon Press, 1975)

HALLER, H. D. and D. LENZEN [eds.] (1977) Wissenschaft im Reformprozess: Aufklärung oder Alibi? (Jahrbuch für Erziehungswissenschaft 1977/78). Stuttgart: Klett-Cotta.

HAMEYER, U. et al. [eds.] (1976) Bedingungen und Modelle der Curriculuminnovation. Weinheim: Beltz-Verlag.

HAVELOCK, R. G. (1973) The Change Agent's Guide to Innovation in Education. Englewood Cliffs, NJ: Educational Technology.

HECLO, H. (1974) Modern Social Politics in Britain and Sweden: From Relief to Income Maintenance. New Haven, CT: Yale University Press.

HEIDENHEIMER, A. J. (1978) Major Reforms of the Swedish Education System: 1950–1975. Washington, DC: The World Bank

———— (1974) "The politics of educational reform: Explaining different outcomes of school comprehensivization in Sweden and West Germany." Comparative Education Review 18 (October): 388–410.

———— et al. (1975) Comparative Public Policy: The Politics of Social Choice in Europe and America. New York: St. Martin's.

HENTIG, H. von (1979) Systemzwang und Selbstbestimmung: Über die Bedingungen der Gesamtschule in der Industriegesellschaft. Stuttgart: Klett-Verlag.

HERZ, J. (1978) "Legitimacy: can we retrieve it?" Comparative Politics 10 (April): 317-343.

HERZ, O. (1973) "Ansätze und Beispiele für Innovationsstrategien in den USA." Zeitschrift für Pädagogik 19 (August): 583–601.

HESSE, H. A. (1975) "Basisorientierte Modelle der Curriculumreform." pp. 270–278 in K. Frey et al. (eds.), Curriculum Handbuch, vol. I. München: R. Piper.

HOUSE, E. R. (1974) The Politics of Educational Innovation. Berkeley, CA: McCutchan.

HUBERMAN, A. M. (1973) Understanding Change in Education: An Introduction. Paris: Unesco Press.

Human Interaction Research Institute (1976) Putting Knowledge to Use. Los Angeles, CA: Human Interaction Research Institute.

HUSÉN, T. (1979) "An international research venture in retrospect: the IEA surveys." Comparative Education Review 23 (October): 371–385.

———— (1974) The Learning Society. London: Methuen.

INKELES, A. (1981) "Convergence and divergence in industrial societies," pp. 3–38 in M. O. Attir et al. (eds.), Directions of Change: Essays on Modernization Theory, Research, and Realities. Boulder, CO: Westview Press.

———— (1977) "The international evaluation of educational achievement." Proceedings of the National Academy of Education 4: 139–200.

JENKS, C. (1972) Inequality: A Reassessment of the Effect of Family and Schooling in America. New York: Basic Books.

KAASE, M. (1980) "The crisis of authority: myth and reality," pp. 175–198 in R. Rose (ed.), Challenge to Governance. Beverly Hills, CA: Sage.

KATZ, M. B. (1975) Class, Bureaucracy, and Schools: The Illusion of Educational Change in America (exp. ed.). New York: Praeger.

KAVANAGH, D. (1980) "Political leadership: the labours of Sisyphus," pp. 215–235 in R. Rose (ed.), Challenge to Governance. Beverly Hills, CA: Sage.

KIELMANNSEGG, P. Graf [ed.] (1976) Legitimationsprobleme politischer Systeme. Politische Vierteljahresschrift, Sonderheft 7/1976. Opladen: Westdeutscher Verlag.

KIRP, D. L. (1977) "Law, politics and equal educational opportunity: the limits of judicial involvement." Harvard Educational Review 47 (May): 117–137.

———— and M. G. YUDOF (1974) Educational Policy and the Law. Berkeley, CA: McCutchan.

KIRST, M. W. and D. F. WALKER (1971) "An analysis of curriculum policy-making." Review of Educational Research 41 (December): 479-509.

KOPP, M. and H. P. MÜLLER (1980) Herrschaft und Legitimität in modernen Industriegesellschaften: Eine Untersuchung der Ansätze von Max Weber, Niklas Luhmann, Claus Offe, Jürgen Habermas. München: Tuduv.

KUHLMANN, C. (1970) "Schulreform und Gesellschaft in der Bundesrepublik Deutschland 1946–1966," pp. 1/1-1/206 in S. B. Robinsohn (ed.) Schulreform im gesellschaftlichen Prozess, vol. I. Stuttgart: Klett-Verlag.

KÜNZLI, R. (1976) "Legitimation von Innovationszielen," pp. 197-213 in U. Hameyer et al. (eds.) Bedingungen und Modelle der Curriculuminnovation. Weinheim: Beltz-Verlag.

LENHARDT, G. (1977) "Bildungspolitik und privatwirtschaftliche Rationalität: Marxistische Perspektiven zur Bildungsreform," pp. 179–199 in J. Derbolav (ed.), Grundlagen und Probleme der Bildungspolitik. München: R. Piper.

LEVIN, H. M. (1980a) "The limits of educational planning," pp. 15–47 in H. N. Weiler (ed.) Educational Planning and Social Change. Paris: Unesco Press.

———— (1980b) "Review of Patrick Suppes (ed.), *Impact of Research on Education.*" Prospects 10: 513–515.

———— (1979) Educational Vouchers and Social Policy. Stanford, CA: Institute for Research in Educational Finance and Governance, IFG Program Report 79/B 12.

———— (1978) "The dilemma of comprehensive secondary school reforms in Western Europe." Comparative Education Review 22 (October): 434–451.

———— (1976) "Education, life chances, and the courts: the role of social science evidence," pp. 73–100 in N. F. Ashline et al. (eds.) Education, Inequality, and National Policy. Lexington, MA: D. C. Heath.

LIGHT, R. J. and G. V. GLASS (1979) "Capitalizing on variation: how conflicting research findings can be helpful for policy; policy for the unpredictable (uncertainty research and policy)." Educational Researcher 8 (October): 7–14.

LINDBERG, L. N. et al. [eds.] (1975) Stress and Contradiction in Modern Capitalism. Lexington, MA: D. C. Heath.

LISKE, C. et al. [eds.] (1975) Comparative Public Policy: Issues, Theories, and Methods. New York: John Wiley.

LUHMANN, N. (1975) Politische Planung. Opladen: Westdeutscher Verlag.

———— (1969) Legitimation durch Verfahren. Neuwied: Luchterhand Verlag.

MATTHÖFER, H. [ed.] (1977) Bürgerbeteiligung und Bürgerinitiativen: Legitimation und Partizipation in der Demokratie angesichts gesellschaftlicher Konfliktsituationen. Villingen: Neckar Verlag.

MAYNTZ, R. (1975) "Legitimacy and the directive capacity of the political system," pp. 261–274 in L. N. Lindberg et al. (eds.) Stress and Contradiction in Modern Capitalism. Lexington, MA: D. C. Heath.

MERRITT, R. L. (1979) "The courts, the universities and the right of admission in the Federal German Republic." Minerva 17 (Spring): 1–32.

———— and F. S. COOMBS (1977) "Politics and educational reform." Comparative Education Review 21 (June/October): 247–273.

MEYER, J. W. et al. (1977) "The world educational revolution, 1950–1970." Sociology of Education 50 (October): 242–258.

MORRISH, I. (1976) Aspects of Educational Change. New York: John Wiley.

NASCHOLD, F. (1974) Schulreform als Gesellschaftskonflikt. Frankfurt: Athenäum Verlag.

OECD (1972a) Educational Policy and Planning: Germany. Paris: OECD.

———— (1972b) Reviews of National Policies for Education: Germany. Paris: OECD.

———— (1971) The Management of Innovation in Education. Paris: OECD.

OFFE, C. (1976) "Überlegungen und Hypothesen zum Problem politischer Legitimation," pp. 80–105 in R. Ebbighausen (ed.) Bürgerlicher Staat und politische Legitimation. Frankfurt: Suhrkamp Verlag.

———— (1975) Berufsbildungsreform: Eine Fallstudie über Reformpolitik. Frankfurt: Suhrkamp Verlag.

———— (1972) Strukturprobleme des kaptialistischen Staates. Frankfurt: Suhrkamp Verlag.

OPPERMANN, T. (1976) "Nach welchen rechtlichen Grundsätzen sind das öffentliche Schulwesen und die Stellung der an ihm Beteiligten zu ordnen?" pp. C5–C108 in Verhandlungen des einundfünfzigsten Deutschen Juristentages, Band I, Teil C. München: Verlag C. H. Beck.

ORLICH, D. C. (1979) "Federal educational policy: the paradox of innovation and centralization." Educational Researcher 8 (July/August): 4–9.

OWENS, R. G. and C. R. STEINHOFF (1976) Administering Change in Schools. Englewood Cliffs, NJ: Prentice-Hall.

PASSOW, A. H. et al. (1976) The National Case Study: An Empirical Comparative Study of Twenty-One Educational Systems. Stockholm: Almqvist and Wiksell.

PAULSTON, R. G. (1968) Educational Change in Sweden: Planning and Accepting the Comprehensive School Reforms. New York: Teachers College Press.

PEAKER, G. F. (1975) An Empirical Study of Education in Twenty-One Countries: A Technical Report. Stockholm: Almqvist and Wiksell.

PETERSON, P. E. (1973) "The politics of educational reform in England and the United States." Comparative Education Review 17 (June): 160–179.

PINCUS, J. (1974) "Incentives for innovation in the public schools." Review of Educational Research 44 (Winter): 113–143.

PRESSMAN, J. L. and A. WILDAVSKY (1979) Implementation. Berkeley: University of California Press.

RASCHERT, J. (1977) "Probleme der Legitimation von Lehrplänen und Richtinien," pp. 21–37 in H. D. Haller and D. Lenzen (eds.) Wissenschaft im Reformprozess. Stuttgart: Klett-Cotta.

———— (1974) Gesamtschule: Ein gesellschaftliches Experiment. Stuttgart: Klett-Verlag.

RICHTER, I. (1976) "Nach welchen rechtlichen Grundsätzen sind das öffentliche Schulwesen und die Stellung der an ihm Beteiligten zu ordnen?" (Referat auf dem 51. Deutschen Juristentag, 1976). Berlin: Max-Planck-Institut für Bildungsforschung (mimeo)

———— (1975) Die unorganisierbare Bildungsreform: Innovations-, Legitimations- und Relevanzprobleme im amerikanischen Bildungswesen. München: R. Piper.

RIECKEN, H. W. and R. F. BORUCH (1974) Social Experimentation: A Method for Planning and Evaluating Social Intervention. New York: Academic Press.

RIVLIN, A. M. (1973) "Forensic social science." Harvard Educational Review 43 (February): 61–75.

ROBINSOHN, S. B. (1975) Schulreform im gesellschaftlichen Vergleich, Vol. II. Stuttgart: Klett-Verlag.

———— (1970) Schulreform im gesellschaftlichen Prozess, Vol. I. Stuttgart: Klett-Verlag.

RODENSTEIN, M. (1978) Bürgerinitiativen und politisches System: Eine Auseinandersetzung mit soziologischen Legitimationstheorien. Giessen: Focus-Verlag.

ROGERS, D. (1977) An Inventory of Educational Improvement Efforts in the New York City Public Schools. New York: Teachers College Press.

ROGERS, E. M. (1962) Diffusion of Innovations. New York: Free Press.

ROGOWSKI, R. (1974) Rational Legitimacy: A Theory of Political Support. Princeton NJ: Princeton University Press.

ROSE, R. [ed.] (1980) Challenge to Governance: Studies in Overloaded Politics. Beverly Hills, CA: Sage.

ROTH, H. [ed.] (1969) Begabung und Lernen. Stuttgart: Klett-Verlag.

ROTHSCHILD, J. (1977) "Observations on political legitimacy in contemporary Europe." Political Science Quarterly 92 (Fall): 487–501.

SCHAAR, J. H. (1969) "Legitimacy in the modern state," pp. 276–327 in P. Green and S. Levinson (eds.) Power and Community: Dissenting Essays in Political Science. New York: Pantheon.

SCHARPF, F. W. (1973) Planung als politischer Prozess: Aufsätze zur Theorie der planenden Demokratie. Frankfurt: Suhrkamp Verlag.

SCHATZ, H. (1976) "The development of political planning in the Federal Republic of Germany," pp. 41–68 in Klaus von Beyme et al. (eds.) German Political Systems: Theory and Practice in the Two Germanies. Beverly Hills, CA: Sage.

SCRIBNER, J. D. [ed.] (1977) The Politics of Education. 76th Yearbook of the National Society for the Study of Education. Chicago: University of Chicago Press.

STRAUMANN, P. R. (1974) Neue Konzepte der Bildungsplanung. Reinbek bei Hamburg: Rowohlt Taschenbuch Verlag.

SUPPES, P. [ed.] (1978) Impact of Research on Education: Some Case Studies. Washington, DC: National Academy of Education.

VAN DE GRAAFF, J. H. (1976) "The politics of innovation in French higher education: the university insitutes of technology." Higher Education 5 (May): 189–210.

_____ and D. FURTH (1978) "France," pp. 49–66 in J. H. van de Graaff et al. (eds.) Academic Power: Patterns of Authority in Seven National Systems of Higher Education. New York: Praeger.

VIDICH, A. J. and R. M. GLASSMAN [eds.] (1979) Conflict and Control: Challenge to Legitimacy of Modern Governments. Beverly Hills, CA: Sage.

WALKER, D. A. (1976) The IEA Six-Subject Survey: An Empirical Study of Education in Twenty-One Countries. Stockholm: Almqvist and Wiksell.

WEILER, H. N. (1983a) "Legalization, expertise, and participation: strategies of compensatory legitimation in educational policy." Comparative Education Review 27 (June): 259–277.

_____ (1983b) "West Germany: educational policy as compensatory legitimation," pp. 33-54 in M. Thomas (ed.) Politics and Education: Cases from Eleven Nations. Oxford: Pergamon Press.

_____ (1981) Equal Protection, Legitimacy, and the Legalization of Education: The Role of the Federal Constitutional Court in West Germany. Stanford, CA: Stanford University, Institute for Research in Educational Finance and Governance.

_____ [ed.] (1980) Educational Planning and Social Change. Paris: Unesco Press.

_____ (1978) "Towards a political economy of educational planning." Prospects 8 (3): 247–267.

_____ (1973) The Politics of Educational Innovation: Recent Developments in West German School Reform. Stanford, CA: Stanford University, School of Education (mimeo).

_____ and H. V. GONZALEZ II (1981) Education and Legitimacy: A Preliminary Review of Literature and Issues. Stanford, CA: Stanford University, Institute for Research on Educational Finance and Government.

WILHELMI, J. (1974) Demokratisierung und Mitwirkung in Schule und Hochschule (Kurzfassung des Kommissionberichtes). Braunschweig: Westermann-Verlag.

WOLFE, A. (1977) The Limits of Legitimacy: Political Contradictions of Contemporary Capitalism. New York: Free Press.

WOLIN, S. S. (1980) "Reagan country." The New York Review of Books 27 (December 18): 9–12.

ZALTMAN, G. et al. (1977) Dynamic Educational Change: Models, Strategies, Tactics, and Management. New York: Free Press.

DISCUSSION ON THE CHAPTER BY WEILER

D I E T R I C H   G O L D S C H M I D T
K A R L   W.   D E U T S C H
T H E O D O R   H A N F
H A N S   N.   W E I L E R

DIETRICH GOLDSCHMIDT

While I agree with the general concept presented by Professor Weiler, I should like to expand on it a bit through reference to comparative studies in which I have been involved.

First of all, comparative research in education must be formalized very carefully to ensure that the same things are being examined in the various countries. Social conflict in educational reform stands out as an obvious characteristic in all the Western countries we investigated. The more we got into details, however, the more apparent it became that each nation's unique history produces its own particular brand of conflict and educational reform. The competition in West Germany between the vertical system of education and the comprehensive school is a good illustration. Other countries with a long tradition of comprehensive schools do not have such a conflict. There the rivalry may be between private boarding schools and the public system, or between metropolitan and suburban schools. Another illustration, on which I know of no comparative research, concerns the effects of the migration of the well-to-do to the suburbs. Does shifting their children to private schools, as occurs in some countries, create stronger class conflict than does the Federal Republic's vertical system? Focusing on such individual differences does not make comparison less meaningful, but may serve to limit the generalizability of the conclusions.

A lack of concern with functional equivalence can also lead policymakers and researchers to ask the wrong questions. Some time ago, State Secretary Klaus von Dohnanyi of the West German Federal Ministry of Education and Science asked for research on participation in the public and higher-education systems of Sweden and West Germany. He wondered why the Federal Republic did not follow the Swedish system for participation in higher education rather than the "third-parity" system then being used in German universities. The phrase most characteristic of Swedish culture is "planning by consensus." It derives from the country's tradition of reform since the 1930s and the long rule of the Swedish Labor party, and generally creates a climate in which everyone is willing to come to some kind of consensus. In West Germany, by contrast, a country riddled by conflicts, it was clear that Sweden's mode of participation would be inappropriate and that, if we really wanted participation, we would have to look elsewhere for models.

A second point pertains to the length of time required to move from the invention of an idea to its implementation. Consider the changes in teacher-training programs after the publication in the early 1960s of Georg Picht's book, *Die Deutsche Bildungskatastrophe,* to which Weiler referred. Nothing in that book is truly original. Picht merely exploited data provided earlier by Friedrich Edding, as well as thinking by numerous scholars on the interaction among educational sociology, educational policy, and the educational system. The enormous publicity occasioned by the book's publication brought to fruition, at a stroke as it were, a process of rethinking that had been under way for quite some time.

The research needed for educational reform has generally lagged behind the point in time at which it was needed. This has meant that the research results were not produced quickly enough to give real legitimacy to the reform; and, by the time the results of a particular project were available, the situation that had originally required the research had changed. Referring again to my own research on participation, the German-Swedish comparison was commissioned in the spring of 1971 and the final report submitted in June 1973. By then, however, the question of participation was no longer relevant, and our results were ignored in policymaking. Such research, as well as that initiated by individuals to answer their own questions, may well have an important bearing on future educational development. Its practical, short-term effects may nonetheless be minimal. The political system simply develops too fast for researchers to keep abreast of it.

KARL W. DEUTSCH

I am delighted with the richness of material in Weiler's chapter. It raises four theoretical questions that I believe deserve attention. The first concerns a general tension in education between, on the one hand, the development of human *capacities,* both on a short-term basis—aptitudes achieved by the time a student leaves secondary school—and over an active lifetime, and, on the other hand, the allocation of *life chances,* which is primarily a short-term consideration. The latter asks whether or not the student will be admitted to a university, be able to study medicine, find appropriate employment, and so on. This West German or Western European concern focuses much more on questions of privilege and equality than what I see as the more important issue of developing human capacities. The danger is that if Western societies do not improve their abilities to produce and learn, quarrels about privilege will become quarrels about getting cabin spaces on a sinking ship.

An exclusive emphasis on equality frequently ingnores key dimensions of social mobility. For one thing, societies vary in the rigidity of their social structures. In Europe there is a stronger tradition of stratification, and in the United States a greater tradition of mobility. Similarly, the question of whether or not the current division of labor is accepted or defined as provisional finds different answers as one goes from country to country. Every society must find places for its young people within existing job structures, because changes in job structures do not occur as rapidly as graduating classes change. Yet job structures and the stratification that goes with them do change, and this fact has significant implications for our education systems.

Writers who stress the stratification of life chances rarely include social mobility matrices in their arguments. Yet some 50 percent of the people in most modern and highly industrialized countries do not belong to the social class of their fathers. This is very different from the situation in Europe at the time of Karl Marx, when perhaps less than one-fifth of the population was in a class other than that into which they or their fathers were born. Thus the question not only of actual social mobility, but also of *needed* social mobility—job structures needed over the next twenty, thirty, or forty years—seems to be neglected in the argument.

Second, there is in West Germany and to some extent in the United States a continual attempt to blame capitalism for any inequality in the distribution of life chances. But are life chances in noncapitalist societies necessarily better, more equal, or more freely available? The German Federal Republic is full of young people who have fled East Germany to escape its rigid allocation of life chances. Although it is true that life chances in communist states are allocated by different criteria than in the West, the fact is that the allocation there is rigid. We should rather undertake a systematic, comparative anal-

ysis of the characteristics of *all* industrial societies, for only then can
we see which specific problems are attributable to capitalism and
which are not. The questions of whether or not there are any systems
that are more successful in allocating life chances, how provisional
the allocation is, and what it is possible for individuals to do, are
essential ones.

Third, it would be useful to have a working definition of social
class, a term used frequently in Weiler's chapter. We are all familiar
with Karl Marx's conception of class. I would propose as a new
operational definition that subset of people in a society whose experiences of social learning, or whose probabilistic reinforcement
schedules (encountered by them in society), are highly consonant.
People who move out of the class of their parents, whose childhood
experiences are not reinforced by their experiences in adult life—
because of education, for instance—do not believe in the classic terms
of just one class.

One can, perhaps, berate these people for having a false consciousness, for being "vacillating intellectuals," "petit bourgeois," or,
in Professor Weiler's citation of Levin's beautifully chosen phrase,
an "overeducated and underemployed proletariat." But what we call
them does not change in the least their real situation, which involves
cross-pressures and dissonant experiences of social reinforcement.
Instead of trying to force late twentieth-century people into some
early nineteenth-century category, we might for instance explore how
the framework suggested by the sociologist, Frank Parkin, fits the
present situation. Such indicators as the ratios of pay for people with
medium or higher education and those with less education, the conditions of life for these people, their contact choices, and so on, can
be used to develop a different class concept.

The fourth theoretic point concerns the issue of legitimacy. Again,
an operational definition would be useful, and I propose the following: Legitimacy is a prediction of value compatibility. When I say to
a small child poking its finger into all sorts of unknown things, "It's
all right," I am telling him that he can satisfy his value of curiosity
without badly impairing some other value, such as health, safety, or
the avoidance of pain. If I say to him, "Uh-uh, you mustn't poke
your finger into the electrical outlet," I am telling him that this is not
legitimate. Legitimacy means that you can seek one value without
destroying another value that is also important to you. If we ask what
are the compatibilities of value expectations, and what are the compatibilities of the rewards that make these up, we can then return to
the questions of legitimacy that are implied in the previous chapter.

It has been asked whether conflicts cause reforms or reforms cause conflicts. That reminds me of the chicken and the egg. In other words, since we are dealing with feedback loops in sequences of feedback processes, mapping them into one-way causations is not very helpful. Clearly, if one wants chickens primarily for roasting, the breeder will select the chicks for their muscles and deal with the eggs the best he can. If one wants eggs for shipping, the breeder will concentrate on the thickness of the shell. That is, you pick the particular links in a feedback sequence that are operationally important for what you want to do.

It is not useful to deny the feedback sequence. We are dealing with conflicts, which produce pressures for reform, which in turn produce new conflicts, and what we should study is the nature of the whole sequence. Are the sequences converging toward a tolerably stable consensus, or are they diverging toward bigger and bigger deviations, bigger and bigger conflicts? There are amplifying feedbacks and negative feedbacks. There are feedbacks that are stable and unstable and those that become increasingly stable or increasingly unstable. There is a body of responsible researchers on education who have mapped their knowledge of the special problems they have studied onto an obsolete conceptual apparatus, an apparatus in which class, legitimacy, capacity, development, conflict, reform sequences, feedback sequences, and so on, are not used with the full power of modern political theory. Weiler's chapter brings this out very well, and I think we can make a little progress precisely because we are beginning to realize it.

The last point I want to make relates to Goldschmidt's claim that things work in Sweden because of consensus. It is widely believed, and there is some truth in it, that some societies have a higher traditional consensus than others. On the whole, social consensus increases with per capita income. Years ago, I published a paper that divided countries into five categories of states according to per capita income. In sixteen or so countries with the lowest incomes, there had been fifteen forcible overthrows of government; in another sixteen countries in the top category of per capita income, there had been only one governmental overthrow. That occurred in 1958 in France with de Gaulle's takeover and was accomplished with a minimum of bloodshed. That is, there is a fairly direct correlation. (The middle, transitional governments had the bloodiest revolutions.)

In addition, there are struggles for the preservation of class privilege, even in the richest and most conventional societies that have the longest traditions of consensus. One can note, for example, the backlash among the English middle classes when they elected Mrs. Thatcher, and vice versa in the waves of strikes in England that involved status as well as income; the fact that the German middle class is reacting against the comprehensive school; that the Social Democratic government in Sweden is not in office at the moment; and that the English Labour party is trying to abolish "public" (that is, private) schools. Clearly, we need more research on the ecology of consensus.

Social consensus and dissensus are themselves the results of learning processes. The Austrian middle class, which fought social reforms in the early 1930s and enthusiastically supported the civil war in February 1934, was by the 1970s prepared to live with the reform-minded Bruno Kreisky. The Spanish middle class, which supported Franco in the 1930s against a socialist mayor of Madrid, similarly accepts a socialist mayor of Madrid today. In other words, people can learn to accept what they previously considered intolerable.

Yet this is not always the case. Learning processes in a milieu may ultimately produce consensus, but the milieu itself will sometimes lash out against the results of that consensus. A threatened group will produce such backlash phenomena again and again. They typically spring up rapidly and then gradually subside. We might thus consider seriously the "half-life" of such backlash sentiments.

From this perspective we can return to the question of how life chances are distributed. If we understand upper-middle-class predilections in West Germany on policies that change the way in which life chances are distributed—their origins, their strengths, and probable duration—and the entire body of middle-class resentments—their strength, duration, and possible successes—we can begin to deal within one basic framework with possible changes deriving from such innovations as comprehensive schools. We know, too, that all societies must adjust a great deal to changing circumstances even if we do not know precisely what these circumstances will be. Most people stay in the work force for forty years, for instance, but technology will render half their jobs obsolete after twenty years. How will retraining be provided, and what will be its costs to society in both human and financial terms? How such matters are decided will directly affect citizens' life chances. We have the possibility here of moving from a rhetoric of conflict to an acceptance of conflict as an important part of a larger learning and adjustment process. I believe that it is this larger process that will turn out to be decisive.

THEODOR HANF

One historical aspect of the comprehensive school debate which has often been neglected is the postwar reaction to the *Deutsche Einheitsschule,* an incipient comprehensive school introduced in Germany during the Nazi period. The temper of the times, bolstered by an anti-Nazi sentiment, dictated a return to traditional German culture and humanistic, Christian education, such as had existed before 1933. Anti-Nazism, of course, and later—after the German Democratic Republic created its polytechnical schools—anticommunism, do not explain the entire phenomenon, but it is certainly part of the explanation of the intensity with which more traditional, formal schools were supported after 1945.

Turning to the question of educational innovation, I would add that a major factor in Western Europe and elsewhere has been the emergence of a category of people whom we might designate "education brokers." Such people collect bits and pieces of educational research and "trade" them to professional politicians, very often encouraging the latter to accept educational policies which they otherwise might never have considered. Education brokers have clearly played an aggressive and important role in the Federal Republic.

The problem is that educational goals, which have only a tenuous relationship with research results, keep changing. For example, early attempts to formulate an active educational policy in the Federal Republic were predicated on the argument that the educational system should be adapted to economic necessities, that we needed more graduates. Emphasis then shifted to the socializing benefits to be derived from education. People were encouraged to attend secondary schools because that was a good way to improve their life chances. This was followed by the argument that education is not a privilege, but rather an entitlement. And finally, when the first unemployed graduates began to appear on the market, it was argued that, "After all, education is a value in itself—why shouldn't a taxi driver be a specialist on Goethe?" These four arguments continue to be used today, and they have played a greater role in making policy than either the researchers or the politicians have admitted.

A second characteristic of these education brokers is that their typical approach is a heuristic one. It focuses on issues in a piecemeal fashion, just as research has been presented to the public in a highly selective way. For example, when we look at the comprehensive school, we do not examine the function of that type of school within the total educational system. Herein lies a partial answer to the question raised earlier in our discussion about what all this has to do with freedom. Very simply, freedom was the example which, for political reasons, many people wanted to emulate.

Third, discussion has very often focused more on what education *should* do that on what it *can* do, and alternatives about the possible functions of education have not been clarified in the public debate. There are the dual concerns of equality and curriculum. The former is essentially that of whether or not the educational system should play any role whatever in the allocation of life chances and, if so, what that role should be. We are familiar with the argument that an educational system which plays no role in allocation will not change the state of equality in a society. The radical position ignores the use of education for allocation in favor of strengthening its socializing power. Although these two goals have never really been viewed as being in conflict, it is true that the harder one pushes to use education for selection, the more difficulties one has with the socializing function, and vice versa.

Similar problems exist within the socializing function itself, which encompasses the formation and transmission of general capabilities as well as political socialization. Discussion in Western Europe has focused entirely too much on the latter issue, for politicians still believe in the efficacy of educational experiences in guiding future political behavior. Empirical studies on political socialization, however, show that this is a very tricky matter. Political socialization often produces unanticipated consequences; indeed, sometimes quite the opposite of what was intended.

The debate between political socialization on the one hand and the allocation of life chances on the other has produced intense bitterness in educational politics, particularly in West Germany, and the real issue of whether comprehensive schools have contributed more or less to improved capabilities than have other systems has largely disappeared from the arena. Instead, the debate has become an ideological one, completely overshadowed by the perception of education as an instrument for achieving goals that are in fact largely unattainable through education.

Those who would completely abolish the schools' allocative function are obviously aiming for a totally egalitarian society that doesn't exist. As Karl Deutsch has pointed out, even the educational system in socialist countries is highly selective and allocative. The questions, simply put, are: Is the school a good agency for allocation in our society? Is there any alternative agency for allocation? (So far, no reasonable alternative has been presented.) If education is to have an allocative function, how should it achieve this, and at what level? Should allocation be done mainly through orientation, or should it be done by selection, through some kind of academic culture? Research to date suggests that the selective function should be postponed as long as possible, that it is better to have it occur at the secondary level than at the primary, and better at the tertiary level than at the secondary. It is at this point that the real debate should begin.

The conclusion I would draw is that we should lower our expectations of education as an agent of political socialization and an instrument for producing social equality. Education is far less efficient in these respects than it can be in developing children's capabilities. In a pluralistic society, where there is little consensus on values, it is unreasonable to suppose, even on the normative level, that education should usurp the parliament's right to set values for the society.

HANS N. WEILER

The notion of education brokers is an interesting one that could be applied to institutions as well as individuals. The entire field of educational reforms, at least in the countries with which I am familiar, is characterized by a rather peculiar type of brokerage institution. The West German *Bildungsrat,* for example, straddles the domains of scholarship and politics, providing a kind of linkage between them. Similar institutions exist in the R&D community in the United States.

I have a little difficulty, however, with Theodor Hanf's last point concerning educational goals. The facts of political life tell us that, whether we consider it right or wrong, schools continue to be viewed as instruments of socialization and mechanisms for allocating status. Those very perceptions fuel the conflict over educational reforms. They explain why educational finance reform in the United States is such a highly politicized issue, and why the *Rahmenrichtlinien* in the West German state of Hesse are so disputed. These perceptions may be faulty in terms of what schools do in reality, but a realization of their existence is essential for understanding the political momentum of and relationship between reform and conflict.

THEODOR HANF

A possible solution to this dilemma would be to publicize widely the results of research on the efficacy of schools as agents for political socialization. Policymakers might relax a bit when they realize that the school is actually a poor tool for political persuasion. If this can be accomplished, the other socializing tasks of education—developing capabilities, helping children to discover their own personalities, and preparing them for professional roles—would stand a better chance. That is, we can approach the question of what a good school should be by eliminating functions that schools cannot appropriately perform.

Permit me to return briefly to the issues of change, on the one hand, and innovation on the other. Over the course of the last two decades, the biggest changes in education in both industrialized Western Europe and developing countries in the Third World have been based on policies grounded in wrong assumptions or misguided theories. In the Third World, the most significant movements have rested on the assumption that education is the best investment for development. This notion stemmed from the correlation allegedly found between high educational input and a large gross national product. It is a statistical relationship that has never been proved to be entirely accurate. That fact notwithstanding, at a time when they could better use these funds for national development, Third World countries typically spend as much as a third of their budgets on a kind of education that is not very useful to them.

In Western Europe, too, changes in educational policy have sometimes been predicated on very shaky notions firmly held at high levels of government. The question of whether or not German industry needed more graduates, for instance, remains unresolved even today. Some analysts insist that the calculations that led to such a conclusion were basically faulty. As evidence, they point to the case of Switzerland. Although similar statistical calculations there had produced a similar result, Switzerland's relatively underdeveloped educational system could not implement change so rapidly; nevertheless, the country's economy is doing remarkably well today.

DIETRICH GOLDSCHMIDT

I want to add a few words about the situation in Germany after 1945. A particularly sad feature of the general circumstances was summed up in the words of a respected economics professor whom I interviewed in 1953 about the postwar era. "You know," he said, "under the dictatorship scholarly work was not possible—the desks were empty, that is, even those who were not Nazis but stayed on during the Nazi period were psychologically not in a position to be creative. Furthermore, by 1945 many members of the intelligentsia had left or were dead. Those who remained—no matter how active politically they had been during the Nazi era—had to prove that they had not been Nazis. Listening to their arguments, one gains the impression that Hitler had descended on Germany like a bolt of lightning and that, once the thunderstorm had moved on, it turned out that no one had participated in any of it. These people, as well as some of the few who really had not been committed to Nazism and nonetheless had managed to survive, naturally favored a return to the Germany that had existed before the war."

Intellectual and spiritual revival was set aside in favor of economic reconstruction. The social developments, such as opening up higher education to a broader spectrum of people, that were occurring in the United States, Sweden, and elsewhere did not take place in West Germany until the 1960s. They affected most directly the generation born around 1945, those who became conscious of the country's situation only when its reconstruction was half finished. These children, who had never experienced Nazism, war, or extreme poverty, could confront their parents: "You talk about education, you talk about democracy—where are the results of all this talk?" The student revolution of the 1960s was, to be sure, experienced all around the world in some form or another, but it was surely an important element in bringing the idea of reform to the awareness of the German people. Thereafter, of course, we went to the other extreme, with the effect that we are now up to the gills in reforms. It seems to be very difficult to find middle ground in these matters.

With reference to Hanf's remarks about education's function, I do not think it realistic to assume that the public will relinquish its traditional view that socialization to adult life is the main goal of education. However, we are not here to discuss education policy, but rather innovation in education. We should consider whether or not the time is ripe for the development of new methods of innovation. Here the relationship between the public and private domains intrudes again, for clearly the introduction by the state of new types of schools requires the support of the majority of the population. Attempts of this nature have largely failed in the Federal Republic. Accordingly, the development of new methods must now be shifted to the initiative of private groups and individuals.

KARL W. DEUTSCH

Professor Goldschmidt has neatly summarized the point of this conference. We can only seek innovation which is perceived to have a direct relationship with a specific set of values. It is easy to see what makes one mousetrap better than another; what makes a school superior is not so clear. An essential part of the innovation process is thus the perception, implicit or explicit, of some common values for at least part of, if not the whole, society. The shift of emphasis in education, from socialization and categorizing people for the job market to the development of the pupil's capacities and personality, would indicate an important reorientation in values. But irrespective of the values involved, there must be *some* values in order to judge whether the realization of an innovation will be for the better or not.

DIETRICH GOLDSCHMIDT

In analyzing further the innovative thrust in the mid-1960s, several other factors may be added to those already suggested. For one thing, there were demographic developments. The birthrate grew by nearly 50 percent from 1946 to 1964. This fact raised some obvious questions about the need to expand teaching facilities and staffs. Second, the social view of education was changing. The rebuilding of the social sciences, however slow this was in coming in postwar Germany, brought criticism by such people as Helmut Schelsky and Jürgen Habermas of the idealistic concept of education that contributed to its destruction.

Third, Sputnik and the technology it represented affected educational reform in West Germany by making it seem likely that the country's industry would have to continue growing even after reaching the stage of full reconstruction. On the one hand it was argued that growth in the "hard" sciences and technology was essential. On the other hand it was argued that growth in human capital would be even more beneficial to West German industry. Social critics like Ralf Dahrendorf claimed that education was a civil right. Such arguments made it clear that many things would have to be changed in German education.

Even before the crisis of 1967–1968, the two major parties in the Federal Republic joined together in the Grand Coalition because people could see that reforms were necessary which would require a two-thirds majority in parliament. Among the most prominent of them was the reform of the Basic Law, which gave limited rights to the federal government to reform the school and higher-education systems. That step paved the way for a rapid succession of reforms in the field of education.

CHAPTER 9

LEGAL CULTURE AND THE CHANCES FOR LEGAL INNOVATION

ERHARD BLANKENBURG

Law is usually expected more to stabilize than to change. Accordingly, lawyers are usually seen as members of a conservative profession. For both generalizations, however, there are many counterexamples. Law has been used to change social structure, and there are lawyers who promote such changes. Thus we must ask about the conditions in which members of the legal profession become agents for change. This chapter does so on the substantive issues involved in legal innovations by relating them to the structure of the legal profession in different countries.

Concept of "Legal Culture"

Since law is defined in the context of national systems, it is more deeply involved in cultural patterns than are other features of the social structure. To what extent, then, are the chances of innovativeness as a function of "legal culture"?

The concept of legal culture summarizes those features of legal institutions which differ even among Western industrial countries. Such institutional features are partly laid down by the law itself: the kinds of courts that exist and their competence; the degree of legalism, that is, the degree to which the activities of public administrations and private organizations are bound to precise legal regulations; and the extent to which such legalistic expectations reach into different areas of social relations. While such features do not go beyond the level of normative expectations, the concept of legal culture covers behavioral differences as well: the degree to which legal norms are actually mobilized, and the extent to which legal problems are actually implemented.

The explanatory linkage among legal expectations, enforcement, and behavioral compliance is complex. It depends partly on the institutions that implement law. Administrations, police, the law profession, and courts are shaped by the way they recruit and train their personnel. The realization of legal expectations thus depends on the structure and activity of legal professions and paraprofessions. Their size, recruitment, and careers all form part of what we call "legal culture."

With so many features involved simultaneously, legal culture becomes a descriptive concept. Since our units of analysis are countries, there are more variables in the concept of culture than there are cases to compare. This makes it difficult to operationalize our hypotheses in terms of quantitative comparisons. We need much more description and analysis of pertinent cases before we can design adequate quantitative indicators. In addition, many of our variables, which in legal theory are treated as nominal differences (for example, case law versus codified law), are differentiated in reality only in *gradual* terms (in other words, they are continuous variables).

Social Conditions of the "Access to Law" Movement

THE INNOVATIVE CASES

The discussion in the 1960s and 1970s of access to justice has been dominated by Anglo-American scholars.[1] Its driving force has been a pragmatic interest in innovating institutions, with the oldest and most far reaching one being the development in England of legal aid and neighborhood law centers (Zander, 1978); the most widely publicized being the legal services movement of the War on Poverty in the United States of the 1960s (Johnson, 1974); and the most diverse being continental European attempts to import legal aid schemes and neighborhood law shops, the most successful of which, in the Netherlands, has been imitated in Belgium, France, and even Switzerland (Schuyt et al., 1976; Revon, 1978).

An important factor in this movement has been the effect of scientific discussion and international imitation. The first wave was accompanied by research into legal problems which were not met by traditional counseling services. It aimed mainly at improving access to legal institutions for people in socially disadvantaged strata. A second wave of the movement extended more deeply into the middle classes. "Public interest law" in the United States took up such broad-gauged issues as consumer protection, environmental issues, and control of the professions. The third wave can be seen as a reaction to disappointment over the slow rate of progress in increasing the chances for access to law. Legal strategies often had frustrating results, what with courts being overcrowded and procedural formalities replacing substantive issues. Thus the same legal reformers who had recently been advocating increased access to law soon began looking for alternative institutions to handle social problems in a delegalized manner.

All three waves of reform had a very strong innovative impetus, and all three were fostered mainly by progressive elements in the legal profession. They were innovative in that (1) they invented new forms of services that enable socially weak and politically underrepresented groups to claim their rights in the legal arena; and (2) they contributed to substantive changes of law that gave new and more explicit rights to these groups and interests.

The "access to law" movement might be considered a response to some of the challenges of postindustrial Western countries. The most apparent challenge, if we look at the clientele of neighborhood law centers in London, Los Angeles, and Amsterdam, is the problem of urban slum populations. England, the United States, and the Netherlands, as well as the French-speaking countries on the European continent, experienced during the 1950s and 1960s a massive economic immigration. Immigration from Latin American countries to the United States, from former Asian colonies to Great Britain, from Indonesia to the Netherlands, and from North Africa to France and Belgium can be seen merely as the most recent consequence of an imperialistic past. Since the immigrants were largely unskilled, however, they had access only to poorly paid jobs; and since they migrated mainly to highly industrialized areas, they aggravated the problems of urban infrastructures which were already under pressure because of the native population's flight to suburbia. Bringing with them their own family structure and cultural ties, the predominantly non-Caucasian immigrants moved into quarters in the big cities that tended to become ghettos with massive problems of unemployment, high crime rates, and a widening gap of cultural and economic deprivation compared to the absorbing (or, rather, nonabsorbing) home population.

In the 1970s all these countries introduced stricter measures to control and prevent immigration, thus increasing the penetration of legal controls into society via the administration of employment policy and immigration. Legal controls, already present in regulating social welfare, increased with growing numbers and kinds of landlord-tenant problems and with racial tensions in the emerging slums. It is no wonder, then, that the counterpart of such increasing legalistic control has been the development of legal aid institutions trying by legal means to defend the poor against the controlling institutions.

Immigration problems, however, are not the only ones explaining the first wave of new legal aid institutions. They account for some specific forms of legal aid, such as neighborhood law centers, but not for the growth of legal aid schemes in England or "Judicare" in some of the more rural parts of the United States. Legal aid has been a broader movement answering to the latent needs of different sorts of people in different social environments.

Nevertheless, legal aid institutions have been imitated across social (and national) boundaries, and they have undergone a history from innovative beginnings to more stable activity of a day-to-day variety. The developmental cycle from early innovativeness to routinized institutionalization which the legal aid movement of the U.S. Office for Economic Opportunity (OEO) went through resembles what Max Weber, speaking of charismatic leadership, called the process of *Veralltäglichung*. When the Legal Services Corporation was founded in Washington in 1974, many of the former collaborators of the OEO's legal services saw it as the end of attempts within the framework of the War on Poverty to improve basically and by legal means the situation of the poor. But even if the enthusiastic expectations of the innovative years have waned, the Legal Services Corporation Act nonetheless signifies a stabilization of institutions that provide "legal assistance to those who would otherwise be unable to afford adequate legal counsel" (Legal Services Corporation, 1978). (In 1977 the LSC funded 320 legal services programs operating in about 700 neighborhood offices throughout the United States.) The bar had in principle accepted the need for specific forms of legal services aimed at specific legal needs—even though local bar associations in some places still feared any competition by federally subsidized lawyers.

Routinization of the legal aid movement went together with the broadened needs to which the Legal Services Corporation responds. We can characterize these as a general challenge to postindustrial societies: Informal ways of insuring against life risks are increasingly replaced by formal ones. With a loss of the economic functions of the family, the individual depends increasingly on social institutions such as old-age pensions, health insurance, and unemployment benefits. Lower socioeconomic strata, especially, encounter difficulties in obtaining their rights from public administration, big employers, or housing corporations. Civil courts are traditionally institutions used to enforce claims of big organizations against individuals rather than to defend the rights of individuals. Whereas most lawyers, having been traditionally preoccupied with the legal problems of the propertied middle classes, are ill prepared to advise the poor of their needs, neighborhood law centers have appeared to provide such services and taken up issues that might not pay well enough for a business-minded lawyer. Subsidized legal services have developed areas of legal activity which subsequently could become the object of regular lawyer services as well. In short, rather than competing with traditional lawyers, public service lawyers fulfill the function of exploring new markets for legal services.

Similar arguments can be deduced with respect to the development of legal aid in the United Kingdom, the Netherlands, and Sweden. Today, about half the forensic income of barristers in England stems from legal aid clients. Their business has not replaced a formerly private clientele but is largely additional income to a barrister's office. The same holds true of the second wave of the American access-to-law movement. Public interest issues considerably extended the scope of lawyers' activities. The self-interest of the profession in developing new markets for their services must therefore be considered as one reason, among others, for the expansion of such movements.

Any explanation of changes in the infrastructure of legal services requires us to see the changes both as a *response* to social problems and demands for legal help, as well as a *supply* of services which are possible because the legal profession is interested in offering them. Accordingly, the rise of the legal aid movement and its routinization can be explained by two social conditions: (1) the increasing demand for defensive legal action in a world that is increasingly regulated by big organizations, administration, and consequently legal regulations; and (2) the (objective) interest of a growing legal profession in finding additional areas of competence into which it can introduce its services (even though such an interest is not subjectively perceived by many established lawyers).

A CONSERVATIVE CASE: THE FEDERAL REPUBLIC OF GERMANY

Both social conditions hold true for all the Western postindustrial countries. Although some led in developing legal aid, others, such as the Federal Republic of Germany, have been very conservative. Can it be that the social conditions that led to the legal aid devel-

opment in Anglo-Saxon countries is absent in West Germany, or are
there other reasons which prevent institutional innovation in providing access to the law?

The inactivity of West German legal policy with respect to legal
aid is legitimized by lawyers through reference to traditional institutions. They point to the *Armenrecht,* a provision of the Civil Procedures Code of 1877 (§§114–127) which allows the courts to cover
courtroom costs and lawyers' fees of any party that cannot afford
them, provided that a case has some likelihood of success in court.
In 1972 lawyers, who had long complained that their remuneration
in such cases was lower than in ordinary cases, obtained changes in
fee schedules that adapted their Armenrecht fees to the normal rates
(Cappelletti and Garth, 1978: 21). This could hardly be called an
access-to-law reform, however, since it leaves out any attempt to
improve the availability of pretrial counseling and ignores the institutional conditions for mobilizing law for cases in which the party
does not yet know whether or not it has any rights, and, if so, how
to use them. Armenrecht is accessible only after a lawsuit has been
filed. Since using it requires legal information, it presupposes legal
counsel rather than encouraging it. Consequently, it has been used
rarely and even then—except in Hamburg, where the ÖRA provides
its clients with information and access to the Armenrecht in cases of
several other types (Falke et al., 1978)—mainly in divorce cases where
the parties are compelled to use the law and have legal counsel.

Though the prevailing consensus in West German discussion has
accepted as satisfactory the modest and inefficient subsidization of
court cases through the Armenrecht (Baumgärtel, 1976; Grunsky and
Trocker, 1976), it has been critical of any more far-reaching access-
to-law policy (Arbeitsgemeinschaft, 1974: 98). Some lawyers, especially those in the Social Democratic party, have proposed setting up
more public legal counseling offices in line with Hamburg's ÖRA
model (Falke et al., 1978; Falke, 1978; and, on West Berlin's long-
standing legal counseling scheme, Reifner, 1978). The *Anwaltsverein,*
a voluntary bar association, reinforced its pro bono work at special
hours in the lower district courts, and some of the *Länder* (most
widely publicized in Bavaria and the Saarland) offer counseling services in their courts as well. The federal government used these model
experiments as a basis for the "Law on Legal Aid" which is currently
before parliament, albeit with little chance of being enacted.

All in all, however, these attempts to reform the conditions of
access to law are directed exclusively at lowering the cost barrier for
people with moderate financial means. They do not address any of
the informational and social barriers hindering access to the law, but

rather increase them by devising bureaucratic procedures to check on a party's entitlement to public legal assistance. The discussion among West German lawyers has not taken notice of the differences in social problems which legal aid schemes in other countries have brought to light, nor has it reflected any perception of the need to offer a different kind of institution, starting with the physical location and layout of offices, which like the neighborhood law centers can lower the barriers of access for the economically disadvantaged.

Trying the explain this difference in problem awareness brings us back to the historical conditions that initiated the charismatic phase of legal services in the United States, England, and the Netherlands. Some of the social problems of these countries are by far less serious than those in the Federal Republic of Germany. In the latter there was no comparable urban immigration to speed up local innovations. West Germany, free of any significant colonial past, drew its immigrant labor force from Eastern Europe throughout the nineteenth and twentieth centuries. Post-1945 Germans experienced a forced reimmigration, followed by a twenty-year period of slow economic and political migration from east to west. The Federal Republic consequently was very late in encouraging immigration from Mediterranean countries.

The fact that urban poverty and immigrant slums pose less severe social problems than in other countries does not by itself explain the absence of a West German legal aid movement. It would be an oversimplification to attribute the access-to-law movement elsewhere wholly to the urban problems caused by immigration (even though this might have been its most dramatic cause). Legal aid in England started at the same time as the local Citizens' Advice Bureaus, which were originally designed after 1945 to help reintegrate returning soldiers, and most of the second wave—efforts to represent diffuse interests by legal means—responded to social problems of the indigenous population, largely its middle classes. Public interest law in the United States is not restricted to large metropolitan areas, nor does it take up the problems of the country's immigrant population. It treats problems raised by consumers, clients of government offices, and those who are subject to total institutions such as mental hospitals or homes for the aged. It does not take up cudgels on behalf of underprivileged groups such as worker clients and tenants. Moreover, it extends to such diffuse interests as consumer problems and environmental concerns.

Although such diffuse-interest issues are universal in all postindustrial countries (and not only those in the West), the specific form they find in public interest law conforms to the American legal tra-

dition. It is a movement that needs lawyer elites (or, rather, coun-
terelites) as protagonists, and it has developed around such legal
institutions as adversarial litigation and case-law traditions, as well
as such specific instruments as class-action suits and plea bargaining.
Public interest law firms have been promoted by liberals in the law
schools and major foundations. They are embedded in the uniquely
American framework of lobbying institutions which fulfill some of
the functions that the party system does on the European continent.

Legal as well as political institutions thus explain why similar interests are represented in different forms in various countries. Lawyers take part in public interest campaigns in the Federal Republic
as well, but they are neither prominent in them nor are their means
predominantly legal, as they are in the public-interest law movement.
Especially environmentalists and those objecting to town planning,
nuclear energy, or industrial investment in Germany organize around
spontaneous action groups (*Bürgerinitiativen*), which use political
pressure inside and outside established party organizations, as well
as the legal means of administrative complaints and procedures. Litigation, especially going before administrative courts, is only one of
their techniques, and usually a last-ditch attempt to prolong decision
procedures and hence make them more costly. Consequently, public
interest issues in West Germany are seen as endangering the political
parties, not as a movement for changing patterns of access to law
(Ansay and Gessner, 1974; Spies, 1982).

Similarly, what Cappelletti calls the "third wave of the access-to-
law" discussion in the United States refers to problems specific to the
American legal tradition. Even though Germans complain about the
length of time it takes to settle lawsuits before their courts (Baumgärtel and Mes, 1971; Baumgärtel and Hohmann, 1972; Bundesrechtsanwaltskammer, 1975: i; in the United States, Zeisel et al.,
1959; in Italy, Castellano et al., 1965), a comparison with American
courts makes those in the Federal Republic look like models of spee-
diness and efficiency (Bundesrechtsanwaltskammer, 1975: ii). Institutional innovation such as the "Stuttgart model" for handling the
Civil Procedural Code has been effective in reducing the orientation
of German judges to the written case files, involving the parties more
in oral proceedings, speeding up still further the resolution of lawsuits,
and encouraging a judge to reach settlements rather than go all the
way to final judgment (Bender, 1978). Such a step is within the scope
of procedural discretion, just as the delegation of powers to para-
professionals (such as the *Rechtspfleger*) is a step toward treating
routine cases in a bureaucraticized way (Bender and Eckert, 1978).

The West Germany default action (*Mahnverfahren*) is a bureaucratic means for providing creditors with a legal title to collect debts—an automatic legal stamp without substantive control should the respondent reject the claim and thereby initiate a lawsuit to clarify the case. It is a precourt procedure to enforce small (and big) claims rather than an encouragement for respondents to contest the claims.

Much of the activity of West German courts is thus part of an institutional setup that leaves the individual with no choice but defense through legal means—if that individual knows how to go about it and from whom to seek legal assistance. It is speedier and more efficient than the judiciary in many other countries, and it employs many more judges and considerably fewer attorneys than do the English or American legal systems. Comparative indicators show that its output-organization is much more, and its input-organization much less developed than that of other Western legal systems (Johnson et al., 1977).

The statistics of the West German and American legal professions provide a clear-cut indicator of the differences between the two legal cultures. Both countries have roughly the same number of legally trained people per 10,000 population. In the United States, however, three-quarters of all jurists are practicing lawyers. In the Federal Republic the legal profession has traditionally consisted of four groups of about equal size: judges, lawyers, civil servants, and private employees. Every fifth member of the profession is a judge; every fourth works as a civil servant in public administration. The group of jurists employed in private firms has traditionally been as large as that of practicing lawyers (Rüschemeyer, 1973), but in recent years admissions to the bar have risen (a fact that has led to fears that increasing competition might threaten the norms of conduct of practicing lawyers). Only recently have practicing lawyers, now composing about one-third of the legal profession, outnumbered each of the three other groups.

Legal training centers on the role of the judge, whose tenured career begins as soon as he or she has finished legal studies. The emphasis on the judge's role is reflected in some of the features of procedural law. West German court procedures are dominated by the judge, whose role is more active than that of his or her counterpart in the American adversary system. In civil as well as criminal courts, the West German judge is obliged to investigate all the facts pertaining to the case. In this investigation, the judge does not rely on the arguments presented by either of the concerned parties or their legal counsel, but prepares cases and especially oral proceedings on

222

Innovation in the Public Sector

the basis of well-documented files and briefs. Observations of courts show a range of behavior from the authoritarian to the patriarchal pattern, but they rarely show a judge allowing the parties or legal counsel to dominate the course of the oral proceedings (Blankenburg et al., 1979).

The combination of these characteristics explains why the American legal system must look for alternatives to litigation in court. The large number of lawyers, their relative freedom to advertise (legalized by the Supreme Court), and the possibility to arrange for contingency fees all make the input-organization of the litigation system very strong. Similarly, the limited personnel capacity of the courts leads to delays which act as a barrier against filing cases for litigation.

Without such delays in and high costs of court cases, the pressure in West Germany to look for alternatives to conflict resolution is much lower than in the United States. Even among businessmen, settlements can be cheaper and more expedient if a judge is the mediator (with possible continuation up to a judicial decision; Kohler, 1967). The gradual atrophy of institutions for mediation (such as the *Schiedsmann*), which are given legal status in the Civil Procedural Code, indicates that the demand for extra-court alternatives is in fact low. Geared mainly to private penal prosecutions and interpersonal conflicts over charges of insult, the Schiedsmann lost clients as rules of status faded away, and with them the need to "save face" and defend one's honor by legal means (Bierbrauer et al., 1978). Alternative forms of conflict resolution are not considered an urgent need in the West German legal discussion, because the country's courts successfully act as a mediatory institution where settlements can be reached with the help of a judge (Röhn, 1983).

A functional relationship exists between the dominance of lawyers in the American legal profession and the fact that the scope of their activities extends beyond that of German lawyers. Some of the functions American lawyers exercise in registering real estate or building contracts are partly administrative, partly court responsibilities in the Federal Republic. German lawyers do not have any authority to question witnesses in cases that they represent before the court, and they rarely enter into extensive investigations, as American lawyers sometimes do when they both search for cases and organize ways in which to present their clients' interests. German lawyers restrict their efforts more to handling legal matters, not providing all-around services for their clients. Again, we may argue that there is a correspondence between the comparatively small number of lawyers in the Federal Republic, the limited authority given them by the procedural code, and the restricted interpretation they have of their functions. These factors can explain why public-interest lawyers are nonexistent, and why legal possibilities to bring before courts diffuse interest cases such as American class-action suits are unknown in West German law.

Summary: Ideal Types of Two Legal Cultures

Part of the answer to the question of why the West German legal profession has not adopted the innovative role that American lawyers did in the 1960s and 1970s is that some of the social problems that American lawyers tackled do not exist to the same degree in West Germany. This explanation emphasizes the demand side: The two countries do not face the same pressure for innovation. A second answer is on the supply side of innovative capacities. Some patterns in German legal culture are more resistant to change, while some characteristics of American legal culture promote innovation.

Comparative jurists would start describing the differences between the two legal cultures by explaining the consequences of having case law on the one hand, and codified law on the other. These differences, however, are most relevant in traditional legal fields such as civil or penal law. They are of diminishing importance in new and quickly developing legal fields, including public law and economic and social regulation. In these legal fields, codified law is continually being revised and adapted by amendments, while in the American legal system administrative rulemaking is equally as rigid and thus the equivalent of codified law.

More important than these modes of legal regulation are behavioral differences, such as may be found by asking, On whose initiative is law usually formulated? If new law is initiated on a case-by-case basis, there is a greater chance that legal innovations will be initiated from many different sources, and thus that law will be more responsive to new social problems. Technically, such a case-by-case mobilization of new legal issues is possible in both legal systems. It is nevertheless more likely in a system where the legal profession is dominated by lawyers, as in the United States, than in one which is oriented toward the role of the judge and to a large degree incorporated in the civil service.

This difference between a lawyer-centered legal profession in the United States and a judge-oriented one in West Germany is reflected in and stabilized by the respective systems of legal education. The clue to understanding them lies in the institutions that administer the professional examinations. While in the United States state bar associations give the qualifying examinations for membership in the legal profession, a German jurist takes two state examinations, one certifying university learning and the other experience as an apprentice judge in juridical institutions. There is a multitude of law schools in many American states. Their highly diverse quality, however, produces an extremely stratified profession. By comparison, West German law faculties are still quite uniform (although an ideological cleavage between established and new faculties has developed in the last dozen years). They are equally dependent on the conditions which are set by the examining boards of the state ministries, and they are equally involved in defining consensus and dissensus on the interpretation of legal codifications.

This again hints at the basic difference in orientation between the two legal professions: American legal education is largely oriented toward teaching students the advocative task of using law in the interest of a client. West German university teaching, apart from starting with principles and abstractions, approaches law from the point of view of a neutral judge who tries to find out and define where "justice" lies.

A last element deserving mention fits into the pattern of an advocate-oriented legal culture on the one hand and one oriented to the judge and authority on the other. Procedural law in American courts is largely advocatory, that is, the lawyers of both sides determine how a case is presented while the judge listens to them rather passively. In West German courts, investigation by the judge predominates. The judge not only prepares a case carefully by collecting all relevant matters in a file, as suggested earlier, but also dominates the proceedings by leading the arguments and asking most of the questions. While the results of social-psychological studies, aimed at finding out which of the two modes gets nearer to the truth, are based mainly on evaluations of laboratory participants, one finding stands out: Advocatory investigations are more creative in bringing to light facts in favor of the disadvantaged party, and they counteract biases better on the part of decision-making judges (Thibaut and Walker, 1975: 28–51).

It must nonetheless be emphasized that the argument pertains only to a lack of innovativeness among *lawyers* in Germany. There are historical precedents in Germany for all three waves of the American access-to-law movement. Around the turn of the century, trade unions and communities developed an extensive system of legal aid bureaus, as many as 916 throughout the Reich in 1912 (Reichsarbeitsblatt,

1913). The mediatory institution of the Schiedsmann, mentioned earlier, is an example of what is now called the third wave in the United States. And for public-interest law there is a functional equivalent in the Federal Republic: the spread of political action groups (*Bürgerinitiativen*) which organize around specific issues, acting mainly in the political arena but usually using court action as one of their strategies.

The presence of these functional equivalents indicates that the main argument for the lack of innovativeness in German legal culture is on the demand side: The pressure of social problems in the course of rapid industrialization at the end of the nineteenth century led to innovative responses, but they came mainly from outside the legal profession. These legal aid as well as mediatory institutions began to die out after World War I, were misused by fascism's corporatist ideology (Reifner, 1978), and were ignored in the Federal Republic until the end of the 1970s. Only recently has the government proposed a law for legal aid out of court and for covering lawyers' fees in court for people with moderate financial means (Bundestag, 1979). Even this proposed legislation derives from arguments of imitation, such as the question, asked earlier, of why there has been no access-to-law movement in the Federal Republic of Germany as in the Anglo-Saxon countries. If our generalizations on the difference between the two legal cultures hold true, legislated legal aid will remain under the tight control of the judiciary and hence will be less innovative with respect to both new forms of legal services and substantive changes of law than has been the case in more lawyer-centered legal cultures.

What are the lessons to be drawn from this comparison of two cases for a general theory of innovation? First of all, *legal innovation comes from outside the legal system*. Pressing social problems must exist before the law and the legal profession will change. Second, *the existing institutionalized patterns of law and legal behavior* (integrated under the concept of "legal culture") *will make such a change more or less likely*. We singled out one commonality of all the variables that distinguish American and West German legal culture: *The more advocatory the legal institutions, the more they will facilitate innovative changes*.

Advocacy can be institutionalized in different ways. Plausibly, we would look for it among the lawyers. In a legal culture that is oriented mainly to the authority of the judge, however, advocacy is found in other institutions, either powerful solidary associations (such as trade unions) or spontaneous civic action groups. Both of these are actors in the political as well as the legal arena of interest representation.

Consequently, their advocacy is channeled more often through legislative action than court decisions—a relationship that corresponds
to the general differences between case law and codified law traditions. They lead to the following conclusion about the chances for
legal innovation. *A legal culture with an active lawyers' profession
and an advocacy orientation is more likely than others to (1) be sensitive
to needs and problems that can be met by legal means, (2) innovate
services that facilitate popular access to law, and (3) change substantive
law accordingly.* This hypothesis provides the basis for quantitative
testing across more countries than were examined here.

A greater likelihood of innovation in an advocacy culture may
nonetheless have a price. While there are many attempts by active
lawyers to establish new rights and "invent" new forms of legal claims,
each of them can be challenged by the next case that comes up in
court. Advocates are strong in inventing, but they are weak in dif-
fusing their inventions. Codified law does this by establishing norms;
it uses authoritative means to enforce them and thus transforms the
problem of diffusion into one of implementation. This distinction
between diffusion and implementation suggests a final generalization:
Advocacy leads to a legal market, encouraging inventions and leaving
it to diffusion mechanisms to generalize them, whereas *legalism in
the sense of formulating binding codes of law leads to a centralization
of legal authority.* In the latter case, once innovation gets through the
bottleneck of legislation, it has a great chance of being effective.[2]

NOTES

1. This becomes apparent in Cappelletti's attempts to document international
contributions to the access-to-law concept. I have adapted his very apt ordering of the
twenty-year history of American law reforms into three waves of an access-to-law
movement (Cappelletti and Garth, 1978).

2. The similarity of this argument to those raised by Ellwein (this volume) should
be noted.

REFERENCES

ANSAY, I., and V. GESSNER [eds.] (1974) Gastarbeiter in Gesellschaft und Recht.
    München: C. H. Beck'sche Verlagsbuchhandlung.
Arbeitsgemeinschaft Sozialdemokratischer Juristen (1974) Recht und Politik 10: 98ff.
BAUMGÄRTEL, G. (1976) Gleicher Zugang zum Recht für Alle: Ein Grundproblem
    des Rechtschutzes. Köln: Carl Heymanns Verlag.

_____ and P. MES [eds.] (1971) Rechtstatsachen zur Dauer des Zivilprozesses (erste Instanz): Modell einer Gesetzesvorbereitung mittels elektronischer Datenverarbeitungsanlagen. Köln: Carl Heymanns Verlag.

BAUMGÄRTEL, G. and G. HOHMANN [eds.] (1972) Rechstatsachen zur Dauer des Zivilprozesses (zweite Instanz): Modell einer Gesetzesvorbereitung mittels elektronischer Datenverarbeitungsanlagen. Köln: Carl Heymanns Verlag.

BENDER, R. (1978) "The Stuttgart model," pp. 431–475 in M. Cappelletti (ed.) Access to Justice (vol. 2). Milano: A. Giuffrè.

_____ and H. ECKERT (1978) "The Rechtspfleger in the FRG," pp. 478–487 in M. Cappelletti (ed.) Access to Justice (vol. 2). Milano: A. Giuffrè.

BIERBRAUER, G., J. FALKE, and K.-F. KOCH (1978) "Conflict and its settlement: legal basis, function and performance of the institution of the Schiedsmann," pp. 41–51 in M. Cappelletti (ed.) Access to Justice (vol. 2). Milano: A. Giuffrè.

BLANKENBURG, E. and W. KAUPEN [eds.] (1978) Rechtsbedürfnis und Rechtschilfe: Empirische Ansätze im internationalen Vergleich. Jahrbuch für Rechtssoziologie und Rechtstheorie (vol. 5). Opladen: Westdeutscher Verlag.

BLANKENBURG, E., R. ROGOWSKI, and S. SCHÖNHOLZ (1979) "Phenomena of legalization: observations in a German labour court," pp. 33–66 in European Yearbook in Law and Sociology 1978. The Hague: Martinus Nijhoff.

Bundesrechtsanwaltskammer [ed.] (1975) Tatsachen zur Reform der Zivilgerichtsbarkeit, vol. 1: Daten und Berechnungen. Tübingen: C. B. Mohr.

Bundestag (1979) Drucksachen 8/3311, 8/1713, 8/3695. Bonn: Bundesdruckerei.

CAPPELLETTI, M. and B. GARTH (1978) "Access to justice: the worldwide movement to make rights effective," pp. 3–124 in M. Cappelletti (ed.), Access to Justice, (vol. 1). Milano: A. Giuffrè.

CASTELLANO, C., C. PACE, and G. PALOMBA (1965) L'Effizienza della giustizia italiana e i suoi effetti economico-sociali. Bari: Laterza.

FALKE, J. (1978) "Zugang zum Recht: Fallstudie zur ÖRA in Hamburg," pp. 13–42 in E. Blankenburg and W. Kaupen (eds.) Rechtsbedürfnis und Rechtshilfe: Empirische Ansätze im internationalen Vergleich. Jahrbuch für Rechtssoziologie und Rechtstheorie (vol. 5). Opladen: Westdeutscher Verlag.

_____ G. BIERBRAUER, and K.-F. KOCH (1978) "Legal advice and the nonjudicial settlement of disputes," pp. 105–152 in M. Cappelletti (ed.) Access to Justice (vol. 2). Milano: A Giuffrè.

GRUNSKY, W. and N. TROCKER (1976) Empfehlen sich im Interesse einer effektiven Rechtsverwirklichung für alle Bürger Änderungen des Systems des Kosten- und Gebührenrechts? Gutachten A and B of the 51st Deutscher Juristentag. München: C. H. Beck'sche Verlagsbuchhandlung.

JOHNSON, E., Jr. (1974) Justice and Reform: The Formative Years of the OEO Legal Services Program. New York: Russell Sage Foundation.

_____ et al. (1977) "A comparative analysis of the justice system of seven industrial democracies." Los Angeles: University of Southern California. (unpublished)

KOHLER, K. (1967) Die moderne Praxis des Schiedsgerichtswesens in der Wirtschaft: Ergebnisse einer Untersuchung in Frankfurt-am-Main. Berlin: Duncker & Humblot.

Legal Services Corporation (1978) Annual Report 1977. Washington, DC: Legal Services Corporation.

Reichsarbeitsblatt (1913) Vol. 11, Beiheft 7 (July).

REIFNER, U. (1978) "Rechtsfürsorge und Rechtsbetreuung: Tendenzen der Entwicklung von Rechtshilfe und Anwaltschaft von 1904–1939." Berlin: Wissenschaftszentrum Berlin, International Institute of Management.

REVON, C. (1978) Boutiques de droit. Paris: Solin.

RÖHL, K. (1983) Der Vergleich im Zivilprozess. Opladen: Westdeutscher Verlag.

RÜSCHEMEYER, D. (1973) Lawyers and Their Society: A Comparative Study of the Legal Profession in Germany and in the United States. Cambridge, MA: Harvard University Press.

SCHUYT, K., K. GROENENDIJK, and B. SLOOT (1976) De Weg naar het Recht: Een rechtssociologisch ondersoek naar de samenhangen tussen maatschappelijke ongelijkheid en juridische hulpverlening. Deventer: Kluwer.

SPIES, U. (1982) "Rechtsberatung fur Ausländer." Ph.D. dissertation, Freie Universität Berlin.

THIBAUT, J. W. and L. WALKER (1975) Procedural Justice: A Psychological Analysis. Hillsdale, NJ: Erlbaum.

ZANDER, M. (1978) Legal Services for the Community. London: Maurice Temple Smith.

ZEISEL, H., H. KALVEN, and B. BUCHHOLZ (1959) Delay in the Court. Boston: Little, Brown.

CHAPTER 10

LARGE-SCALE POLICY INNOVATION IN EAST AND WEST EUROPEAN AGRICULTURE

RONALD A. FRANCISCO

Agriculture occupies a disproportional amount of the attention of governments in developed societies. Almost everywhere, however, agriculture represents a relatively declining share of the total economy and an absolutely declining share of the population and labor force. At the same time, policymakers are accused of timidity in facing organized farm interests. Everywhere, agriculture is considered a "problem" (Wädekin, 1980: 312). Indeed, some even suggest that "the making of an agricultural policy is beyond question the most difficult of all tasks that confront a government" (Robinson, 1969: 28).

Few who have followed the wrangling in the European Community (EC) over the Common Agricultural Policy (CAP) would dispute these assertions. Nor are they invalid in the United States or in Eastern Europe, where the wrangling has been conducted less publicly but with at least as much frustration while trying to forge an effective farm and food policy. This chapter explores the impediments to rational policymaking in agriculture by focusing on the issue of innovation in large-scale agricultural public policy.

We will deal principally with the Common Agricultural Policy of the European Communities and with the large-scale policy innovations of the less integrated Eastern European CMEA (Council for Mutual Economic Assistance). We will also grapple with some of the different conceptual and methodological problems that plague research on innovation and diffusion as it moves across national boundaries and policymaking levels.

Indicators and Innovation Scores

The strong emphasis in innovation research on the sequence of adoption has been coupled with widespread use of powerful statistical tests, especially correlation and multiple regression. This tradition has been carried recently into the arena of public policy, especially as political scientists have drawn upon established measurement and analytic techniques.

However, public policy innovation and more simple material innovations differ on fundamental points. Policy innovations are likely to be much more complex, reflect much more variance in implementation, and produce a much larger standard deviation of "innovativeness" across several innovations. Therefore, standard statistical procedures demand more caution in their application to policy innovation, and in interpretation as well.

A growing body of research on innovativeness among American states indicates a number of these problems: Innovations change in character from adopter to adopter, scores on determinants of innovation change from innovation to innovation, and "innovativeness" is not a pervasive characteristic, but is issue- and time-specific at best (Gray, 1973; Downs, 1976). Although relatively little cross-national research has been published in the policy realm, it is likely that higher levels of system interference will magnify these problems as research moves across national boundaries.

If we are interested in anything more substantial than the pattern of diffusion, we confront inherent methodological problems. This is underscored in any examination of innovation in agricultural policy, particularly beyond the single-nation case. For example, it is critical that groups relevant to the policymaking process be considered in any policy research. Sensitive governments make food and agricultural policy by balancing conflicting consumer and producer demands. Yet measuring this influence in any quantitative sense is very difficult (Downs, 1976: 27). Nor have standard quantitative techniques accounted successfully for variance in any policy innovation research that involved complex interaction and system interference. Variance is generally better explained by more conventional means (Downs, 1976: 120–131). The same is true even in multiple-innovation research (Downs and Mohr, 1976: 707).

This chapter, then, attempts to explain variations across European nations and across policymaking levels by examining the dynamics of the decision-making process, rather than by assigning dubious innovativeness scores. This approach developed also from the inherent obstacles to systematic measurement of the implementation of either European agricultural policy innovation. The West European Mansholt plan involves budget expenditures, but intensity of implementation does not necessarily correlate with expenditure. Nor is the reduction in the farm population, a basic goal of the Mansholt plan, a very effective indicator. The farm population is declining almost everywhere, and there is no way to distinguish the market from the age-related and policy causes. The CMEA does not provide very complete information about the extent of agroindustrial integration. Nor do national governments uniformly publish more than simple data on the number and type of enterprises. Hence it is difficult to determine quantitatively the extent and kind of integration (that is, either horizontal or vertical) from these data.

Theoretic Aspects of Innovation in Agricultural Policy

There is a long-standing tradition of research on the determinants and diffusion of innovations. Yet one reason that researchers on policy innovation have encountered conceptual and methodological difficulty is that they are exploring two relatively neglected types of innovation: collective and authority innovation decisions (Rogers with Shoemaker, 1971). Moving beyond the micro level, the individual adopter, introduces many complications. Therefore, our reservoir of ready propositions is more meager in this type of research, but already a good basis for theoretic development is being established.

NEED: THE NEGLECTED DETERMINANT

The growing body of policy research on innovations in political science focuses on the U.S. state level. Several competing explanatory models have emerged that provide the basis for a theory of diffusion of innovations among state governments. Yet these explanations curiously neglect one obvious factor—the relative need for the innovation. This is particularly true in the case of collective innovation decisions, such as those requiring legislative adoption. As Eyestone (1977: 441) has pointed out:

> Unless we are willing to assume very powerful state bureaucracies, it must be expected that any innovation requiring legislative action would become law only if the legislature saw a need for it, over and above the suggestions of policy professionals in the state executive branch.

> Or let us suppose that . . . legislators . . . feel a clear need to act. In this instance they may emulate the policy of another state not because of expert pressure, but because the other state provides a *timely model* which may be seen as the solution to a vexing local political problem.

Although some researchers have sought to include the aspect of need in their models, usually in the form of a "performance gap," they do not treat this as an independent variable and do not measure it systematically. We will examine the proposition that need influenced national variations in support for the Mansholt plan in the EC and for agroindustrial integration in the CMEA.

RISKS AND COSTS

Logically the counterpart of need, but again a theoretically neglected factor, is the risk or cost associated with a particular innovation. Deutsch (1971: 30–31) has discussed the role of risk in the propensity of traditional cultures to distrust agricultural innovation; he also proposed the assumption of some potential risk by the public sector. Yet there is surprisingly little appreciation of the importance of this variable in other innovation research. To some extent, this concern is subsumed in the "trial stage" or "trialability" components of many diffusion models (Rogers, 1962: 84–85). But risk and the related factor of cost are seldom fundamental concerns, perhaps because they vary from adopter to adopter in many innovations (Downs and Mohr, 1976: 703). Nonetheless, we shall be testing the validity for large-scale agricultural policy innovation of Mohr's (1969) contention that motivation and resources are the two necessary conditions for adoption.

COLLECTIVE INNOVATION DECISIONS: THE EC

The European Community's adoption of the Mansholt plan (to reform the Common Agricultural Policy) was a drawn-out process that conforms to the criteria for "collective innovation-decisions." Rogers and Shoemaker (1971: 277–90) set out several tentative propositions about this form of innovation, based on the limited research that had appeared by 1971 (most of it in case-study form). We shall examine the Mansholt adoption with respect to seven of these:

(1) Stimulators of collective innovation decisions are more cosmopolite than other members of the social system.

(2) Initiators of collective innovation decisions in a social system are unlikely to be the same individuals as the legitimizers.

(3) The rate of adoption of a collective innovation is positively related to the degree to which the social system's legitimizers are involved in the decision.

(4) Legitimizers of collective innovation decisions possess higher social status than other members of the social system.

(5) The rate of adoption of collective innovations is positively related to the degree of power concentration in a system.

(6) Satisfaction with a collective innovation decision is positively related to the degree of power concentration in a system.

(7) Member acceptance of collective innovation decisions is positively related to member cohesion within the social system.

THE CMEA: PATTERNS OF DIFFUSION

The collective innovation model is inappropriate as an analytic device for the case of the East European CMEA. Ironically, the CMEA states that internally practice democratic centralism retain more sovereignty than EC states vis-à-vis internal policy reforms. Especially in the area of agriculture, the Soviet Union often seeks to encourage, but frequently does not require, emulation of its practices in all CMEA countries (Jaehne, 1980). Hence, the CMEA environment is much more equivalent to the American federal-state relationship than to the EC's consensus decision making and centralization. The theoretical questions raised in the case of state-level innovations are therefore relevant to the CMEA: What are the demographic and socioeconomic characteristics of adopters, and of laggards? Is the diffusion of the point-source variety, or does it resemble the imitation-emulation model? How much complex interaction among system actors exists, and how does it affect the adoption decision?

THE POWER ELITE PERSPECTIVE

Rogers and Shoemaker posit the existence of an upper stratum, a power elite, in every social system. They hypothesize that "the power elite in a social system screen out potentially restructuring innovations while allowing the introduction of innovations that mainly affect the functioning of the system" (1971: 341). In addition, "the power elite . . . encourage the introduction of innovations whose consequences not only raise average levels of Good, but also lead to a less equal distribution of Good" (1971: 342). The pervasiveness of this line of argumentation in the literature suggests that it would be useful to examine the Mansholt plan and agroindustrial integration in terms of their "restructuring" character and their effect on the distribution of resources within each system.

THE EFFECT OF SUPRANATIONAL INTEGRATION

There has been almost no research on innovation and diffusion at the supranational level. However, the published literature in the field of regional integration is strongly imbued with a positive evaluation of supranational policymaking. Therefore, we shall exploit an opportunity to assess the impact of the degree of integration on innovativeness, and on the speed and pattern of diffusion. The EC represents an integrated system, the CMEA a loose confederation.

The EC and the Mansholt Plan

Even as the EC struggled to implement its newly forged Common Agricultural Policy in the mid-1960s, EC Commissioner for Agriculture Sicco Mansholt prepared the groundwork for a major and controversial policy innovation. He correctly understood that the price-support system of the CAP implied rapidly escalating costs for the community, yet did not correct the fundamental problems of agricultural production and farm income.

Mansholt argued for structural reforms: increasing farm size and eliminating noncontiguous strip farming, reducing the agricultural labor force, educating the farm population, providing technical assistance, and so forth. These reforms were designed to create a climate for the diffusion of technical innovations and generally improve the economic viability of the European family farm—a unit that lagged far behind its counterpart in the industrial and service sectors.

THE INNOVATION

By December 1968, Mansholt was ready. The European Commission presented to the Council of Ministers a plan drafted by Mansholt and dubbed "Agriculture 1980" (European Commission, 1968).

The plan proposed a radical restructuring of farming in the European Community:

(1) a reduction in the emphasis on market and price policies, and priority for the removal of economic and legislative barriers which made it difficult to increase the size of farms and to improve the mobility of labor;

(2) a reduction in the acreage of farmland with the EC; and

(3) encouragement and acceleration of the existing drift of workers from the land to the towns, so that the total agricultural labor force would be reduced from 14 to 6 percent of the working population (the figure had been 28 percent in 1950 and 21 in 1960 for the EC of the Six).

The plan also called for extensive improvement in agricultural education, since income disparities due to education could never be eliminated fully through price policy (see Josling, 1973: 268).

While Mansholt urged a de-emphasis of price-support policy, he did not eliminate it or even suggest phasing it out gradually. To do so would have been politically untenable (Marsh, 1976: 6). Yet Mansholt clearly sought to reflect the prevailing opinion among economists that price supports do not foster efficiency and actually impede adaptation (see Robinson, 1969; Marsh, 1977; Johnson, 1973). But even this veiled suggestion provoked virulent opposition. After a bitter two-year struggle, the Mansholt plan failed. It was replaced on January 1, 1971, with a mild alternative drafted by West German Agricultural Minister Josef Ertl. Directives did not become effective until 1973, and even now the program remains basically a national one, unevenly and poorly implemented (see Averyt, 1977: 111).

Nearly two decades after the fundamental Mansholt innovations had become entrenched public policy in Eastern Europe, Western Europe continues to debate. The basic reasons for this laggard behavior lie in the production context of the EC, in the complex decision-making structure, and most of all in the goal hierarchy of the community.

PREINNOVATION CONTEXT

A few central facts define the basic condition of the agricultural sector in the EC. Whereas U.S. farms average 200 hectares (ha.), farms in the European Community are much smaller, about 18 ha. The worker/land ratio in the EC is barely one to ten, while in the United States only one worker typically cares for 136 ha. In the late

1960s, although the EC had only 21 percent as much arable land as the United States, four times as many people depended on agriculture for their livelihood. Agricultural incomes in Western Europe lagged far behind industrial wages, and the gap was not reduced in the first years of the CAP. Yet EC producer prices for agricultural commodities uniformly range from 50 to 100 percent higher than world market prices.

This was the context that Mansholt surveyed as vice president of the European Commission in the 1960s. Reform was urgently needed. The alternative (which, alas, has come to pass) was ever larger subsidies to European farmers without concomitant improvement in basic farm efficiency. "Market pressures" could not be counted on in the future, since mechanization, the first and easiest reform, was virtually complete given the small size of EC farms.

The need for innovative structural policy was obvious. This was underscored by a survey of European farmers during 1966-1967 that showed that many, especially in poorer regions, did not believe they could help themselves, nor that anyone else could or would help them (Raup, 1970: 149). Nonetheless, the EC had traditionally opposed mandatory structural reform, and to suggest it required "political courage" (Averyt, 1977: 92).

Mansholt had two basic factors in his favor. First, the primary outcome of the bitter EC controversy over agricultural funding in 1965-1966 was an enhanced role for the European Commission (Poullet and Deprez, 1977: 188–189). Mansholt was a key figure in the commission and was well positioned to determine the EC's agenda. Second, demographic evidence showed that any structural reform would likely yield dramatic results by 1980. During 1966–1967, 64 percent of EC farmers were over fifty years old. In all, 73 percent had no direct successor, and this was 47 percent of the total farming community. Further, farms with successors were generally larger and more economically viable than others—sixteen ha. against an average of seven ha. Thus, natural attrition would free hundreds of thousands of hectares, and the EC would need only simple consolidation authority to gain large increases in average farm size (see OECD, 1973: 15).

GOALS OF THE EC

What Mansholt did not fully appreciate was the disparity between his perception of the EC's goals and needs and the community's own view. From Mansholt's perspective, there was clearly a sufficient level of "need" in the agricultural sector to foster thorough policy innovation. Yet adoption was postponed and resisted by major actors in the EC. What went wrong?

The Treaty of Rome established only general policy objectives for agriculture in the EC. These included maintaining a balance in supply and demand, providing farmers with a fair income, protecting farmers from price speculations, and ensuring equitable supplies to consumers at fair prices. In practice, the goal structure of the EC is much less balanced.

First, the EC pursues above all else the goal of a fair income for farmers. This is achieved through price supports and makes European food very expensive by world standards. Yet there is little concern for the "fair consumer price" mandate of the Treaty of Rome. Incomes have not kept pace under the CAP, but this goal is deeply entrenched, and performance has been good enough to create substantial fears among farmers of any abandonment of the essential pricing system as the basic guarantee of their income.

Second, productivity is clearly a goal, but a secondary one. EC productivity has grown impressively, but all too often in the wrong commodities. The community is faced with embarrassing surpluses of wine, milk, butter, beef, sugar, and soft wheat while it still imports massive quantities of small and large grains. Again, the pricing policy, designed foremost for income maintenance, distorts the normal market mechanisms (see Marsh, 1977: 612).

Third, the EC pays lip service to the problem of world hunger, but it does little actively to ameliorate the condition of the poor. It drives a very hard bargain in commodity trade with Third World nations, often refuses to discuss freer trade in key commodities, and provides "food aid" largely as a mechanism for disposing of its most troublesome surpluses (see Zartmann, 1971; OECD, 1973: 84–85). Indeed, the EC draws such massive quantities of basic grains from the world market that it actually drives prices up and weakens the Third World's ability to compete for needed supplies.[1] In addition, the community frequently alienates its philanthropic constituency by refusing free disbursement of many surpluses in order to secure token prices in arranged bulk sales, often with the CMEA.

What is clear from the EC goal hierarchy is that it is most salient to the farmers themselves, and that they control the political power to maintain a goal structure similar to their own vision. Mansholt did not appreciate this sufficiently. The "need" he perceived as a community citizen was not perceived by community farmers (see Cairncross et al., 1974: 91–115).

THE DECISION-MAKING STRUCTURE

Agriculture's voracious appetite for the time of the European Commission and the budget of the community is offset by one major factor: It is the key that binds the community together, and it is one of very few success stories in transnational (or supranational) policymaking (see Lindberg and Scheingold, 1970). Yet it is important to note that EC policy is not the product of a supranational organization, but of an interorganizational system (see Busch and Puchala, 1976).

In terms of legal structure, the EC appears to function as a simple supranational organization. The European Commission proposes policy, the Council of Ministers acts on it with the aid and advice of the Committee of Permanent Representatives. Nonetheless, the view is misleading for several reasons.

First, the European Commission, the key "supranational" institution in the EC framework, has no autonomous popular legitimacy. This fact seriously impairs its leadership and policy guidance role (see Caporaso, 1974: 97). As a consequence, the commission seeks to deal with a complex of interest groups during all phases of policyhmaking in order to generate support for its decisions. Officially, the commission deals only with so-called Eurogroups, or supranational umbrella organizations of national interest groups. Foremost among these in agriculture is COPA, the Eurogroup with the broadest constituency and the organization most concerned with cereals policy and structural reforms (see Nielson, 1972). In practice, however, the commission is forced to deal behind the scenes with dissident national groups and attempt to mediate controversies over policy among rival national interest groups, such as those in France. Hence, there is a great deal more national-level input in commission policymaking than is generally assumed. The institution that is supposed to function above petty national interests and systematically determine the "best" policy for the EC is in fact a highly politicized organ accountable not only to the council, but to a variety of groups as well.

Second, the Council of Ministers is bound by formal and informal requirements for consensus decision making. Article 149 of the Treaty of Rome requires council unanimity when acting on proposals from the commission. Further, national veto claims were established during the period of French intransigence in the deGaulle era. This accounts for the council's famous marathon sessions and its desperate search for compromise on critical issues. Indeed, Alting von Geusau (1969: 59) has described this decision-making system as "permanent crisis"—

the need for unanimity under the pressure of deadlines and the demands of competing groups.

Therefore, EC policy is the product of a complex set of interactions among subnational groups, national groups, competing Eurogroups, governments, the council, the commission, the various agencies that supplement the community's administration, and more recently the directly elected European Parliament. Although the council is the sovereign decision maker of the EC with no need to heed other bodies, it regularly considers the perspectives and demands of all these diverse interests. The EC functions under this arrangement, but it is plainly cumbersome, and it has not been a fertile ground for policy innovation.

THE ADOPTION DECISION

The Mansholt plan was presented to the Council of Ministers in December 1968. It was adopted, in greatly diluted form in March 1971. In the interim, it "caused more controversy in the European Community than any other program in its history" (Rosenthal, 1975: 79). The struggle that Mansholt's plan precipitated has been widely studied as a key model of EC decision making (see Rosenthal, 1975: 79-100). Our interest, however, lies less in the detailed battles over the plan than in the interpretation of these deliberations as a collective innovation decision.

Busch and Puchala (1976: 251) have emphasized that success in the EC depends most on transnational bargaining capabilities. Mansholt understood this. He carefully assessed the distribution of opinion throughout the community before he introduced his innovation package. As opinion leader, he sought to short-circuit established opposition groups such as COPA and maintained active formal and informal consultation at all levels throughout the decision (Averyt, 1977: 83; Nielson, 1972: 231). Yet even the "Mansholt mystique" (Rosenthal, 1975) was powerless to overcome the formidable opposition that confronted the plan on many levels.

Large farmers did not need structural reform, since they already operated at an efficient scale. Yet they enjoyed the high guaranteed prices that the EC maintained in order to sustain marginal farm incomes. These large-scale farmers dominated COPA's leadership. Small farmers were suspicious of structural reform. They saw it as a threat to their traditional way of life and to their family holdings. Some feared, legitimately, that they would be forced to abandon farming. The French and Italian governments favored structural reform, since they stood to gain most from it. The German government, citing its burdensome share of the cost, dissented. German farmers were virulent in their opposition. Many feared that the Mansholt plan would lead to "collectivization" on the scale that Ulbricht had forced on East Germany in 1960 (see Rosenthal, 1975: 87). The Dutch, already the most efficient producers, stood to gain little and showed little enthusiasm.

Although Mansholt exploited all of his policy network contacts and was doubtless the most effective available change agent, the plan began to falter. Mansholt admitted that the proposals needed amendment (see Muth, 1970). By June 1969, the German government was under such intense domestic political pressure that it prepared an alternative plan. Mansholt displayed open anger toward the German government but eventually relented. In May 1970 the commission offered a second Mansholt plan, dubbed the "Mini-Mansholt plan," that addressed most of the German objections. The Germans remained dissatisfied. Tension grew and by February 1971, the commission had virtually issued an ultimatum: any country desiring price increases must support structural reform (Rosenthal, 1975: 84).

This attitude provoked fear and anger among farmers throughout the community. As the council met on March 22 to decide the future of the community's argricultural policy, emotions ran high. The next day, 80,000 irate farmers stormed Brussels. The protest reached riot proportions, with one death and more than 140 injured. Similar protests were staged throughout the community. COPA organized a meeting of 1200 agricultural leaders on the same day and issued the ultimate threat: If no way could be found out of the community's immobility, agricultural policy would revert to the national level (Rosenthal, 1975: 93). Since the EC was effectively integrated only in agriculture, this suggestion amounted to a willingness to undo the entire European framework. Finally, on March 25, after 45 hours of fierce argument, the council emerged with an agreement. The farmers got their price increases. Mansholt got very little structural reform.

The commission issued directives that specified structural goals, but not means. Implementation was left to individual nations. Deadlines for implementation were pushed back several times, finally to 1973. To date, very little has been spent on structural reform. Italy and Greece receive the bulk of the funds, but this amounts to little money in the aggregate, and structural reform funds are often diverted to cover deficits in the price guarantee sector (see Andrews, 1973: 84). Reform plans differ considerably across national lines, and most emphasize farm income rather than efficient economies of scale (see Marsh, 1976: 46). Pressure for reform built again in 1980 and 1981. Financial need was the impetus once more, fueled by British and later German objections to their disproportionately large net contributions to the EC. As reform forces began to develop momentum, however, a set of unusual world financial circumstances reduced the growth in agricultural subsidies for the first time, and reform would now be technical, not structural (Bremer, 1981). Mansholt's innovation has, in effect, been rejected.

The CMEA: Agroindustrial Integration

The Council for Mutual Economic Assistance (CMEA) arose in response to the creation of the EC. It has long emulated the EC's organizational form, although the CMEA maintains no supranational authority equivalent to the European commission and issues almost no supranational policy. There is no question, of course, that the Soviet Union is the dominant member of the association. Yet the Soviets do not impose specific policies on member nations as long as no country steps outside the well-established parameters of social, political, and economic policy. For example, Poland remains largely uncollectivized in its agricultural sector, despite Soviet desires to achieve fully collectivized agriculture throughout Eastern Europe. Yet any nation that has already adopted collectivization may assume that a recision of this policy is not acceptable to the Soviets.

THE INNOVATION

Agroindustrial integration takes two primary forms. First, horizontal integration implies increased coordination among farms in their production, financing, and product specialization. Second, vertical integration involves a step beyond interfarm coordination toward genuine joint planning and coordination with the industrial and food processing sector. The final outcome of this process is a giant production chain from raw inputs to final processed outputs, with agriculture only one branch of the food industry.

Although this organizational form is an innovation in Eastern Europe, it is by no means a genuinely new or untried idea. Agroindustrial integration is well advanced in the United States and in parts of Western Europe (see Hoos, 1969). It is also an established concept in Marxist-Leninist theory, particularly in Lenin's stress on the need to adopt industrial procedures in the agricultural sector (see Komlo, 1969).

THE PREINNOVATION CONTEXT

Most agricultural production in Eastern Europe had been collectivized by the early 1960s. Since then, growth rates have been maintained at an impressive level. Yet this is misleading, because the Eastern Europe rates started from a much lower initial base than that in the West. As a consequence, CMEA agricultural yields are significantly lower than their West European equivalents, and most of East-Central Europe, once a food exporting center, cannot achieve agricultural self-sufficiency. This was not a particularly difficult problem until the early 1970s. The Soviet Union had supplied most of its allies with the extra grain they required to meet the needs of their livestock sectors. This policy came to a rather abrupt halt in 1972 as the Soviet Union itself became a net grain importer. The allies were instructed to find other sources of grain and were encouraged to develop their own productive capacities.

The incentive to produce more is great, because the only available sources for grain imports require the expenditure of precious hard foreign currency. Hence, the East European states have pursued the goal of agricultural modernization with zeal since 1972. Investment levels have been very high, and the production of things like fertilizer and better machinery has increased dramatically. Yet these policies have not produced the same ratio of benefit to cost that is maintained in Western Europe, and this has led CMEA governments to search for policy and organizational improvements.

GOALS AND NEEDS

The primary goal for agriculture throughout Eastern Europe is increased productivity and self-sufficiency. Indeed, this is a genuine national priority in most countries, since they are rapidly being drained of their currency reserves, are deeply in debt to the West, and depend in no small measure on adequate food supplies for political legitimacy. Farm income is also a consideration in the CMEA, and some nations, notably East Germany and Czechoslovakia, have actually equalized farm and industrial wages. But this is done less as a social welfare measure (as in the EC) than as an incentive to increase productivity. Consumer food prices are kept low through subsidies. This policy has become politically necessary, and its cost can only be reduced through more efficient agricultural production.

Yet the only proven means to augment farm productivity is missing from the available arsenal of methods in the CMEA. Collectivized agriculture has surpassed private agriculture in productivity in only one nation: Israel. In other cases, there is a statistically significant difference in the efficiency of production between collective and private farming (U.S. Congress, 1974). But decollectivization is not a viable policy alternative in the CMEA, although some nations (such as Hungary) have flirted with incentive schemes. As a consequence, policymakers have eagerly sought innovative solutions to rather dire, if seemingly inherent, needs.

THE DECISION-MAKING STRUCTURE

The CMEA does not maintain a supranational policymaking authority. It has adopted grand schemes of coordination and cooperation in agriculture, but they are far from realization. There is, in contrast to the EC, almost no common agricultural financing, division of production, or structural reform (see Jaehne, 1980). Hence, decision making remains firmly at the national level.

This is not to say that important linkages do not exist among nations. In fact, cross-fertilization of public policy is widespread. Since all CMEA countries are ostensibly socialist in the Soviet sense (Wädekin, 1980), any policy adopted in a single nation is presumably suited to any other nation, despite enormous diversity in agricultural policies. Of course, the principal model for all other nations is the Soviet Union. The Soviets conducted extensive testing of the agroindustrial integration model in the early 1970s and issued strong, positive evaluations of its effectiveness (Schoonover, 1977: 88). Bulgaria, one of the most orthodox CMEA members, also gave glowing reports of its extensive plan of horizontal integration (Wiedemann, 1980). These two announcements gave strong impetus to a remarkably swift diffusion of the innovation along the lines of the emulation model.

THE ADOPTION DECISION

Bulgaria led the entire CMEA in its aggressive adoption and implementation of agroindustrial horizontal integration. Analyses have demonstrated rather clearly that this has not been a particularly helpful decision for raising productivity (see Wiedemann, 1980). Yet it was quickly copied in the Soviet Union, Romania, East Germany, Hungary, and partially in Czechoslovakia (see Jacobs, 1980; Bajaja, 1980; and Csizmadia, 1977). The East Germans, Bulgarians, and Romanians have the most advanced systems. Others are moving rather slowly.

Vertical integration is best developed in East Germany. Bulgaria has also established a strong program, and Hungary's is proving to be the most effective in achieving greater production flexibility. Romania and Czechoslovakia are committed to vertical integration programs, but they have made almost no progress toward implementation (see Jacobs, 1980).

Past experience with integration schemes in Eastern Europe has not been very positive. The recent wave of innovation in this sector has not yet been implemented long enough to draw firm conclusions about the impact of the agroindustrial model. Yet Hungary is very satisfied with its programs, and it is going ahead rapidly with their development. The same is true in the German Democratic Republic, where the commitment to this policy is massive in terms of investments and manpower.

Supranational Policy Innovation: Theoretic Implications

We have explored two rather different innovation decisions in two dissimilar supranational environments. In spite of the conceptual and measurement problems that were anticipated at the outset in systematically analyzing multilevel, cross-national innovations, it is possible to draw some preliminary conclusions about the nature of innovation at this elevated plane of public policy.

NEED, RISK, AND COST

There is little question that need is the variable that accounts best for the failure of the Mansholt plan and the success of agroindustrial integration. The EC certainly needs structural reform, but it is the perceived need of the salient decision makers that appears to count, not the objective need of the potential adopter. The perceived need of EC agricultural interests is in improved farm income, not better economies of scale. The CMEA, however, has both an objective and a perceived need for better productivity. Whether agroindustrial integration is the proper policy to achieve this objective is doubtful, but it is certainly the rationale behind the adoption of this innovation.

Need does not, however, affect innovation decisions independently. Obviously, levels of risk and cost must be considered as well. The need of the EC simply did not approach the level of perceived cost and risk for the implementation of the original Mansholt plan. Farmers felt the risk was too great, and opposing governments, especially Germany, balked at the level of expenditure that would be required. The need for augmented productivity in Eastern Europe is sufficiently large, however, to justify fairly great risks and relatively high costs. Hence, agroindustrial integration, both a risky and high-cost policy, is justified in terms of its potential to fulfill the CMEA nations' needs.

COLLECTIVE INNOVATION: THE EC

The formation of agricultural policy in the EC conforms closely to the Rogers and Shoemaker model of collective innovation decisions. No decision on adoption can be made without full consensus of all governments and most affected interest groups. The Mansholt deliberations were without question an attempt at collective innovation. Not all of Rogers and Shoemaker's propositions, however, are testable in the context of the Mansholt decision.

The first proposition is quite clearly confirmed. Stimulators of the structural reform movement in the EC were indeed more cosmopolite than other members of the system. They were largely intellectuals, especially economists and high-level Eurocrats, like Mansholt himself. The lack of initiative at any more pedestrian level clearly reduced the credibility of the program.

Initiators of the Mansholt plan and its legitimizers were different individuals, although this is not entirely clear. Legitimizers tended to be individual, usually dissident, interest groups and a few governments. These legitimizers were involved in the adoption decisions, but adoption did not proceed any more quickly because of their presence. This is basically because legitimizers were not more important or higher-status members of the social system.

The proposition with the greatest support from the Mansholt evidence maintains that the rate of adoption is positively related to the degree of power concentration in a system. The EC is an almost completely decentralized system. It functions through a process of consensus-building and moves very slowly toward adoption of new ideas. Similarly, the lack of satisfaction with Mansholt's plan and the very low degree of member acceptance can be explained by the decentralization and low level of member cohesion in the decision-making system of the EC.

THE CMEA: DIFFUSION PATTERNS AND ADOPTER CHARACTERISTICS

The diffusion of the agroindustrial integration plan seems more strongly consistent with the emulation than the point-source model. Yet Soviet support for the concept, especially its very prominent support, plainly gave impetus to the rate and breadth of diffusion in the CMEA.

The question of the characteristics of the adopters is more muddled. It seems that recent American doubts about earlier explanations of state innovativeness as a function of wealth and industrialization are valid for the CMEA as well. The wealthiest and most industrialized CMEA state, East Germany, did adopt agroindustrial integration quickly and fully, but so did poor and rural Bulgaria and Romania. Czechoslovakia, only slightly less developed than East Germany, has done very little in this area.

Rogers and Shoemaker's concept of the power elite does not seem applicable to the EC but is valid for the CMEA. Here, the genuine restructuring innovation of decollectivization is proscribed. Policies such as agroindustrial integration, affecting only the functioning of the system, are approved. It appears that there is also a bias toward innovations that raise the average level of public good and that benefit the higher policymaking strata as well.

THE IMPACT OF SUPRANATIONAL INTEGRATION

One could easily claim that the Mansholt plan failed precisely because the EC is integrated politically in the agricultural sector, while agroindustrial integration succeeded in the CMEA because of the absence of supranational authority. There is no doubt that the EC is more cumbersome because of its level of integration and that it is considerably less innovative than individual, national governments. Yet this might be explained by the lack of a legitimate center in the EC. The Commission has no basis of popular legitimacy. Nor is there any other institution in the European Community that has stimulated a shift in citizen allegiance from the national to the supranational level. Perhaps if this were accomplished, as in the United States, innovation would not prove as difficult as it appears to be in the EC today, even though it probably would not be accelerated either.

NOTE

1. The EC exports its high-priced surplus grain through a system of subsidies. However, it must still purchase large quantities of hard wheat (for baking) and feed grains from the world market. In the mid-1970s these purchases were in the range of 40 million metric tons annually. They have subsequently declined, but the EC remains second only to the USSR in total grain imports.

REFERENCES

ALTING VON GEUSAU, F.A.M. (1969) Beyond the European Community. Leyden: A. W. Sijthoff.

ANDREWS, S. (1973) Agriculture and the Common Market. Ames: Iowa State University Press.

AVERYT, W.F., Jr. (1977) Agropolitics in the European Community. New York: Praeger.

BAJAJA, V. (1980) "Concentration and specialization in Czechoslovak and East German farming," pp. 263–293 in R.A. Francisco et al. (eds.), Agricultural Policies in the USSR and Eastern Europe. Boulder, CO: Westview Press.

BREMER, H.-H. (1981) "Die Pleite wird vertagt." Die Zeit, 13 November: 11.

BUSCH, P. and D. PUCHALA (1976) "Interests, influence, integration: political structure in the European Communities." Comparative Political Studies 9 (October): 235–254.

CAIRNCROSS, A. (1974) Economic Policy for the European Community. London: Macmillan.

CAPORASO, J. A. (1974) The Structure and Function of European Integration. Pacific Palisades, CA: Goodyear.

CSIZMADIA, E. (1977) Socialist Agriculture in Hungary. Budapest: Akademaiai Kiado.

DEUTSCH, K. W. (1971) "Developmental change: some political aspects," pp. 27–50 in J. P. Leagans and C. P. Loomis (eds.) Behavioral Change in Agriculture. Ithaca, NY: Cornell University Press.

DOWNS, G. W., Jr. (1976) Bureaucracy, Innovation, and Public Policy. Lexington, MA: D.C. Heath.

—— and L. B. MOHR (1976) "Conceptual issues in the study of innovation." Administrative Science Quarterly 21 (December): 700–714.

European Commission (1968) Memorandum on the Reform of Agriculture in the European Economic Community. Brussels.

EYESTONE, R. (1977) "Confusion, diffusion, and innovation." American Political Science Review 71 (June): 441–447.

FRANCISCO, R. A., B. A. LAIRD, and R. D. LAIRD [eds.] (1980) Agricultural Policies in the USSR and Eastern Europe. Boulder, CO: Westview Press.

—— [eds.] (1979) The Political Economy of Collectivized Agriculture. New York: Pergamon Press.

GARY, V. (1973) "Innovation in the states: a diffusion study." American Political Science Review 67 (December): 1174–1186.

HOOS, S. (1969) "Joint decision-making processes in present-day agriculture," pp. 379-388 in U. Papi and C. Nunn (eds.) Economic Problems of Agriculture in Industrial Societies. London: Macmillan.

JACOBS, E. M. (1980) "The impact of agro-industrial integration programs on East European agriculture," pp. 237–262 in R. A. Francisco et al. (eds.) Agricultural Policies in the USSR and Eastern Europe. Boulder, CO: Westview Press.

JAEHNE, G. (1980) "Problems of agricultural integration within the CMEA," pp. 221–235 in R. A. Francisco et al. (eds.) Agricultural Policies in the USSR and Eastern Europe. Boulder, CO: Westview Press.

JOHNSON, D. G. (1973) World Agriculture in Disarray. London: Macmillan.

JOSLING, T. (1973) "The common agricultural policy of the EEC," pp. 267–296 in M. B. Krauss (ed.) The Economics of Integration. London: George Allen & Unwin.

KOMLO, L. (1969) "The problems of vertical integration in agriculture," pp. 365–376 in U. Papi and C. Nunn (eds.) Economic Problems of Agriculture in Industrial Societies. London: Macmillan.

LINDBERG, L. and S. A. SCHEINGOLD (1970) Europe's Would-Be Polity. Englewood Cliffs, NJ: Prentice-Hall.

MARSH, J. S. (1977) "Europe's agriculture: reform of the CAP." International Affairs 53 (October): 604–614.

—— (1976) "European agriculture in an uncertain world," pp. 3–64 in J. S. Marsh et al. (eds.) European Economic Issues. New York: Praeger.

MECKSTROTH, T.W. (1975) "'Most different systems' and 'most similar systems': a study in the logic of comparative inquiry." Comparative Political Studies 8 (July): 132-157.

MOHR, L. B. (1969) "Determinants of innovations in organizations. " American Political Science Review 63 (March): 111–126.

MUTH, H. P. (1970) French Agriculture and the Political Integration of Western Europe. Leyden: A.W. Sijthoff.

NIELSON, T. T. (1972) "European groups and the Common Agricultural Policy," pp. 215–234 in G. Ionescu (ed.) The New Politics of European Integration. London: Macmillan.

OECD (1973) The State of Agriculture in the EED. Paris: OECD.

PAPI, U. and C. NUNN [eds.] (1969) Economic Problems of Agriculture in Industrial Societies. London: Macmillan.

POULLET, E. and G. DEPREZ (1977) "The place of the commission within the institutional system," pp. 229–242 in C. Sasse et al. (eds.) Decision-Making in the European Community. New York: Praeger.

RAUP, P. M. (1970) "Constraints and potentials in agriculture," pp. 126–170 in R. H. Beck et al. (eds.) The Changing Structure of Europe. Minneapolis: University of Minnesota Press.

ROBINSON, E.A.G. (1969) "The desirable level of agriculture in the advanced industrial economies," pp. 26–44 in U. Papi and C. Nunn (eds.) Economic Problems of Agriculture in Industrial Societies. London: Macmillan.

ROGERS, E. with F. F. SHOEMAKER (1971) Communication of Innovations: A Cross-Cultural Approach. New York: Free Press.

ROSENTHAL, G. G. (1975) The Men Behind the Decisions. Lexington, MA: D. C. Heath.

SCHOONOVER, D. M. (1977) "Soviet agriculture in the 1976–1980 plan," pp. 79–84 in R. Laird et al. (eds.) The Future of Agriculture in the Soviet Union and Eastern Europe. Boulder, CO: Westview Press.

U.S. Congress, Joint Economic Committee (1974) Agricultural Output and Productivity in Eastern Europe and some Comparisons with the USSR and the USA. Washington, DC: Government Printing Office.

WÄDEKIN, K. E. (1980) "Conclusion," pp. 311–327 in R. A. Francisco et al. (eds.) Agricultural Policies in the USSR and Eastern Europe. Boulder, CO: Westview Press.

WALKER, J. (1969) "Diffusion of innovations among the American states." American Political Science Review 63 (September): 880–899.

WIEDEMANN, P. (1980) "The origins and development of agro-industrial development in Bulgaria," pp. 97–135 in R. A. Francisco et al. (eds.) Agricultural Policies in the USSR and Eastern Europe. Boulder, CO: Westview Press.

ZARTMANN, I. W. (1971) The Politics of Trade Negotiations Between Africa and the European Economic Community. Princeton NJ: Princeton University Press.

PART IV

Prospects for Innovation in the Public Sector

CHAPTER 11

TRENDS AND PERSPECTIVES IN INNOVATION POLICIES

G E R H A R D   O.   M E N S C H

> "Forewarned, forearmed."
> (Cervantes, 1615)

Compared to the rapid political-economic developments and sudden jumps in technology taking place in the 1980s, the changes during the 1960s and 1970s may appear to have occurred at a snail's pace. The gradual changes of those two decades allowed policymakers substantial breathing room for preparing their decisions and implementing them. In the coming years, the economies of Western industrialized countries are headed toward two major discontinuities: a shake-out in many mature industries, which are in a state of disequilibrium, and the breakthrough of "basic innovations" at "punctuated equilibrium" segments. Thus we should expect that:

(1) A cluster of major factor-saving innovations in many mature industries will occur now and throughout the decade. These will boost productivity and profitability of leading companies in many branches of existing industry, but the advances will have contractive side effects, occurring at the expense of less competitive rivals, and reductions in employment and income that the radical innovations will squeeze out of the subcontractor networks.

(2) Subsequently, a cluster of basic product innovations will occur, creating new and revolutionizing certain old branches of industry and infrastructure. These basic innovations are demand-augmenting; the expansive effects of these innovations will generate new employment and income opportunities that will offset partly the contractive effects mentioned above. The expansive and contractive effects will not bal-

ance out, however, neither in the short run nor in the long, neither in sectors nor in regions.

(3) Hence, policymakers responsible for innovation will soon be faced with unfamiliar situations which beg for an immediate response under conditions of great urgency and painful uncertainty. There will be too little time available for developing an unconstrained, optimal response. Rather, policymakers will have to resort to the pool of technical and managerial knowledge then available, however inadequate it may be for doing a first-rate job.

A large pool of unutilized knowledge has become available by now because of the efforts of scientists, innovators, and policymakers ten, twenty, or even fifty years ago. No matter how large it is, however, the pool will be small compared to the vast need; it will be muddied by proprietary rights, and the transfer of knowledge and resources will lag.

This chapter, aimed at policymakers who will be charged with the task of innovating to meet such foreseeable contingencies, has two goals: to forewarn them of the discontinuities that lie ahead; and to alert them to the pragmatic redirection that will attend the shift in emphasis from "government by objectives" to "government by exception." This pragmatic redirection will make life exciting for anyone in the driver's seat, but also more risky for everyone. The following theory of discontinuity, which draws from the post-Schumpeterian theory of innovation combined with neoclassical economic theory, suggests means to find the better options among the second-best and to retain a sense of direction amid times of turbulence.

A Theory of Discontinuity

The theory outlined here relies on both inductive and deductive reasoning, on the logical principles of both Bacon and Descartes. It proceeds inductively by way of partial generalizations in the tradition of *clinical* research (Roethlisberger, 1977) and pursues a strategy of data-guided abstraction consistent with that described by Glaser and Strauss in *The Discovery of Grounded Theory* (1967). At the same time, this search for order is guided by deductive reasoning; within the framework of neoclassical *analytic* theory, it axiomatizes political-economic and sociotechnical change as a Schumpeterian process of creative destruction (Schumpeter, 1942).

Of particular relevance here are some notions deduced from this body of general theory about economic motion: the ambivalence of technological progress and the simultaneity of creative and destructive effects; imbalances between these effects (for example, in employment), biases, and sharp or gradual reversals (for example, in investment); discontinuous developments and phase transitions (e.g., in interest, debt, deficits, savings, and credit; Mensch, Kaasch, et al., 1980; Mensch, Weidlich, et al., 1985; Mensch, 1981). These concepts will be used for classifying and relating various types of observations on innovation, the management of innovation, and policies of innovation, and for putting them in perspective in a theoretically meaningful and scientifically defensible manner.

Since most innovation research done up to this day is clinical and somewhat casuistic, the innovation policymaker suffers from imperfect feedback. Since clinical research statements are mostly right but sometimes wrong, innovation research provides insufficient guidance for project selection and program choices. Therefore, the entrepreneurial element and uncertainty involved in any innovation will have to be shared by innovation policymakers. Can their risk be reduced?

REVERSAL IN RISK-TAKING AND THE PROPENSITY TO INNOVATE

Our field research in 64 small and medium-sized industrial corporations (Mensch, 1982) revealed that the financial strength of a firm, measured in terms of profitability, permits the firm to support in-house research and development, and to bear greater risks. This does not, however, guarantee a successful innovation in the end. We found that just as many firms experiencing financial difficulties succeed in innovation as do profitable firms. In the innovation stage, people who cannot afford to fail make doubly sure they do not overlook some risk of failure, whereas people in profitable companies may not guard as carefully against Murphy's Law. People working with public money on a corporate innovation project are not likely to be more effective than they would be with corporate funds. Hence, there is the danger that public co-financing of private sector innovation may appear to be ineffective.

Innovation policymakers have indeed become somewhat defensive about the risk of failure in publicly co-financed projects and have sometimes turned overly prudent. Consequently, based on past experience valid only for a previous phase which has changed, two factors would seem to work in favor of the innovation policymaker in the future phase:

(1) A better understanding of the complicated relationship between public support and private project performance will increase measurably the effectiveness of innovation policies.

(2) Analytic innovation theory suggests that the era in which private investors are reluctant to undertake risky investments in basic innovations (Mensch, 1971, 1972) may soon give way to a period of high propensity, bringing about a dramatic improvement in the conditions for success of publicly supported basic invention and innovation.

LIMITS TO INNOVATION POLICY: PICKING WINNERS

One important limit, of which innovation policymakers usually are well aware, is the inability of innovation research to predict the success or failure of individual innovation projects. This restriction has very important ramifications for practical policymaking. In all Western countries, innovation policy is considered part of a more general investment policy, which in turn is part of sectoral policy (sometimes abbreviated as "industrial policy"). In 1984, the policy question became a presidential campaign issue. Nearly all industrialized countries have produced position papers on industrial policy, all of which describe a general need for some form of "positive adjustment policy." At the same time, all governments express concern that such a policy will probably do more harm than good. Since industrial policy choices are public decisions made under conditions of uncertainty, the core issue is: Who carries the almost certain losses (destructive effects) associated with the uncertain social and private gains (creative effects)? Who takes the blame for failures? Does the peril of being blamed generate drag?

This difficulty has long been recognized by both policymakers and recipients. At the ministerial meeting in 1978 of the Organization for Economic Cooperation and Development, for example, participants drafted a list of cautions for the design of goals for positive adjustment policies. The report put out by President Carter's Commission for a National Agenda for the Eighties stated:

> Not only are efforts by government to designate "winners" and "losers" likely to be fraught with difficulty, as indicated by the experiences of countries that have tried this approach, but they are very likely to foster divisiveness and politicization, rather than consensus and cohesion (President's Commission, 1980: 70).

"BOTTOM-UP" APPROACH TO INNOVATION POLICYMAKING

Recognizing the predicament of federal industrial policy, the overly stringent requirement of picking winners and losers, local and state-level authorities have begun to focus on regional innovation strategies. The so-called "bottom-up" approach may turn out to be an alternative to the "top-down" approach of federal industrial policy-making; it may work in the problem areas where the federal government moves too slowly or too broadly to do well.

Can these bottom-up initiatives be less controversial than the top-down industrial policy initiated at the national level? The President's commission (1980: 70) specified the dimensions of the goal conflicts and alternative choices available for designing policies:

> There are two broad approaches to the consideration of policy options: (1) the creation of a favorable general economic environment that rewards innovation and increases productivity, and (2) industry- or sector-specific policies. The second approach encompasses two contradictory strategies: "picking the winners" and reindustrialization. Advocates of "picking the winners" argue that the government should attempt to anticipate future developments and concentrate its resources and incentives on the probable growth sectors of the economy. Advocates of reindustrialization argue, on the other hand, that government policies should be directed at achieving a long-term rebuilding of America's traditional industry base.

Clearly, these issues would be controversial in all locations where resource allocations have to be made. The "bottom-up" approach has the advantages of spreading the risk of failure and of widening the set of emerging successes due to the mobilization of competitive forces.

Structural Readiness for Innovation

Analytic innovation research as a special subdiscipline of mathematical economics may be too unspecific as yet for determining the odds for an individual innovation but specific enough for determining the structural readiness for certain types of innovations. This would be of great value in setting priorities. This section will summarize some recent advances in this branch of mathematical economics (punctuated equilibrium theory), so that they may be related to a body of observations with which the experienced innovation policy-maker is likely to be familiar. Both types of knowledge will also be related to socioeconomic developments expected to take place over the next few years.

THEORY OF ECONOMIC MOTION

From the general theory of economic motion may be derived a special stage theory of discontinuous economic development which incorporates such notions as "strategic windows" or "structural readiness" for certain types of innovations. We will start with the notion of an abstract economy, in the neoclassical tradition, and conceptualize the evolution of the economic system through three variables (x, y, and z) and by the appropriate equation of motion:

$$dx/dt = f_1(x,y,z)$$
$$dy/dt = f_2(x,y,z)$$
$$dz/dt = f_3(x,y,z)$$

The variables exhibit the short-term, medium-term, and long-term behavior of the economic system, respectively, so that x may change rapidly in any discrete interval of time, whereas y may change only slowly, with significant changes accumulating only over intermediate periods. Hence, y's are considered parameters in short-term analysis. The z's are constant in short-term and in medium-term analysis, but may gradually change over the long haul, or change abruptly at critical junctures (punctuated equilibrium states) in the course of economic development. The z variables are thus called *constitutive*.

Mathemetical economics has thus far not been able to integrate the clinical results of empirical research on innovation. There is nevertheless one line of established neoclassical theory which is directly applicable to this line of theorizing, namely, the two-sector analysis of Uzawa (1961, 1963), Solow (1961), and Inada (1963). Over twenty years ago, these authors ruled out the occurrence of multiple equilibria by the so-called "Inada condition." However, their modeling allows for a generalization which then permits the occurrence of phase transitions and discontinuities or switches between alternative states, and of sudden reversals in the propensity to invest and innovate. These concepts are of great concern to innovation policymakers in government agencies and industrial corporations.

The above equations of economic motion imply that there exist at least two types of discontinuities in the aggregate economic process: Some discontinuities shift the y parameters (only) and may be associated with an incremental structural change in the economy. Other discontinuities modify certain basic characteristics of the economic system (constitutive change) by shifting the z values of the aspects that are constant except in periods of phase transition. In fact, both the medium-range and long-range phases in economic development begin and end in phase transitions (discontinuities) that coincide, or are identical with, the turns of the business cycles and secular movements, respectively. I call them Type Y and Type Z discontinuities. It should be noted that this theoretical proposition has little in com-

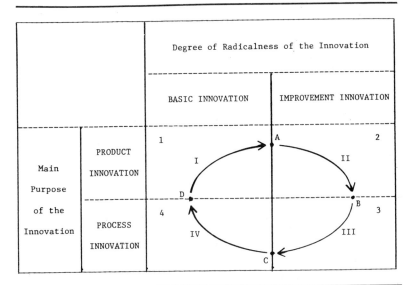

FIGURE 11.1: Phase Transition Scheme

mon with the notion of long waves (Kondratieff cycles), although there is some superficial similarity in a few of the phenomenological terms used.

PHASE-TRANSITION THEORY

We can now connect the deductive and inductive parts of the theory. This is done by relating the two types of discontinuities deduced from the general theory of motion to the two types of innovation I first inferred in the 1970s from clinical research (Mensch, 1971, 1972), that is, basic innovations and improvement innovations. This distinction is now widely accepted, along with the traditional distinction made between product innovations and process innovations. The general theory shows us the correct way to use the two classifications jointly, thus obtaining a phase-transition theory grounded in empirical observations and clinical innovation research (Figure 11.1).

The phase-transition scheme pictured in Figure 11.1 requires a purpose-oriented definition of product and process innovations. *Product* innovations extend to the innovating firm the demand in the markets that lie further downstream (with "downstream" defined in the tradition of the Austrian and Swedish school, which sees the system of production as a multiple-stage, staggered process). Basic and intermediate goods flow from upstream to the consumer. *Process* innovations, then, are intensifications in the use of the factors of production, which the innovating firm purchases in the labor market and capital market, and from supplier industries further upstream in the staggered production process. Hence, in the aggregate, product innovations extensify the scale and scope of the process of staggered production, whereas process innovations intensify the process, thereby putting additional stress and strain on physical and human resources, and squeezing out obsolete factors.

This is classical economics. In Ricardo's terms, product and process innovations are economic motions at the extensive and intensive "best-practice" frontiers. We may equate product innovations with exten-sifying investments and with "expansionary" macroeconomic effects (Keynes), and we may equate process innovations with intensifying investments and with "contractionary" aggregate effects (Wicksell). This assumption is called the classical investment assumption as an analogy to the classical savings assumption: All workers spend all their income, whereas all capitalists save all their gains. On the basis of the classical investment and savings assumptions, we can then integrate clinical innovation research with mathematical growth and stability theory.

To construct the 2×2 matrix in Figure 11.1, we must also dif-ferentiate the innovations by degree of radicalness: Basic innovations either diversify and add to (extensify) the productive sector, or strain and squeeze out (intentisfy) productive factors, and they do this in a more radical and fundamentally new (revolutionary) fashion. Im-provement innovations do this more gradually (evolutionary).

These four types of innovations, which belong to the four fields (1, 2, 3, and 4) in Figure 11.1, conform to empirical findings suggesting that the four types tend to cluster in certain phases of the macro-economic process if viewed from the long-range perspective of four or five decades. These phases, denoted by I, II, III, and IV, happen to correspond exactly to the types just described. The four points (A, B, C, and D) in Figure 11.1 represent phase transitions. As will be noted, this cycle also happens to come full circle along with the four phase transitions, which in turn correspond to periods when the economic system becomes structurally ready for a Type Z discontinuity.

VERIFYING THE MODEL

Our general theory of economic motion thus states that innovators move the extensive and intensive boundaries of the economic system by introducing product and process innovations. These movements (progress) are energized by "Schumpeterian competition": While innovators move the best-practice frontiers, imitators press on and move the average-practice frontiers of the business area. The expansionary and contractionary effects of this movement are measurable on the macro level of the economy as major and minor cycles. If we include socioeconomic side effects, we obtain a constructive specification of the Schumpeterian process of creative destruction.[1]

Let us now verify the schematic model of discontinuities and clusters of types of innovations by going full circle in Figure 11.1. First we look at the motion of the economy between points A and C. Starting point A is the phase transition from (I) "recovery" after World War II to (II) "prosperity" in the postwar period. In West Germany this transition is called the *Wirtschaftswunder*. Point C, at the other end of the semi-circle, is the phase transition from (III) "recession" to (IV) "depression," an interlude which I call "stalemate in technology" (Mensch, 1975/1979). It is this transitional phase which we seem to be entering or are in now.[2]

The main proposition states which phase (I to IV) is dominated by which type of innovation (1 to 4): Phase I by basic product innovations (1); Phase II by product improvement innovations (2); Phase III by process improvement innovations (3); and Phase IV by basic process innovations (4). For example, at point A, Phase I becomes Phase II and industrial progress is dominated by sequences of product improvements as they occurred after 1945 in many new industries such as air transportation, television, and plastics manufacturing. During the 1950s a number of macroeconomists in the equilibrium tradition argued that the product-affective effects of those years were just temporary disequilibria. These would disappear, they said, as the economy approached the path of equilibrium growth. In our scheme, the transitional period of equilibrium growth corresponds to Point B. In the Harrod-Robinson tradition of classifying inventions and investment biases, if the expansionary forces and the contractionary forces balance out, and if they maintain a Golden-Rule proportion as envisioned by the neoclassical synthesis of Samuelson, Solow, and other eminent economists, then stable growth results. In terms of the more general discontinuity theory of motion, however, the state of equilibrium at Point B is a transient one, in fact a phase tradition (Type Z discontinuity). This explains why economic growth during the 1960s and the 1970s did not conform to the expectations of equilibrium growth theorists.

In the late 1960s economists came to realize that the economy had entered a state in which product innovation was crowded out by process innovation. During Phase II the Type 3 innovation became the most frequent and effective one. A number of scholarly articles (for example, Diamond, 1965; Frey, 1969) discussed the impossibility of sustained growth if process innovation overshadows product innovation.

Although analytic growth theory could not provide conclusive proof of the conjectured disequilibrium, evidence for it came from clinical innovation research inspired by Abernathy (see Utterback and Abernathy, 1975; Hill and Utterback, 1979). Their model of product and process innovation validated the existence of cross-overs in the frequencies of product versus process innovations in a variety of industries during the mid-1960s. Since then there has been a rationalization bias (Mensch, 1978) that grew stronger as the mix of innovative investments became more biased toward process innovations.

BASIC-PROCESS VERSUS IMPROVEMENT-PROCESS INNOVATIONS: WHERE WE STAND

Thus we appear to stand midway between Points B and D in Figure 11.1, in the lower semi-circle. Point C, representing the phase transition from recession (III) to depression (IV), is a passage during which the majority of industrial corporations that serve stagnating or even declining markets can survive only by further intensifying the factor squeeze in response to the profit squeeze. This factor-saving pressure reinforces the contractive effects when firms advance from undertaking moderate improvement-process innovations toward radical basic-process innovations, passing the productivity thresholds they approached in Phase III.

For an illustration of the difference between basic-process and improvement-process innovations, and the discontinuity effect (of Type Z) that the cross-over to the more radical type entails, consider the creation of a so-called "knee" in the experience curve of some branch of manufacturing, such as machine-tool making. A knee is a spectacular reduction in per-unit cost achieved by a firm through the introduction of some radical method for saving factors of production and avoiding waste. During the 1960s and 1970s, this branch of manufacturing experienced a sequence of process-improvement innovations (Type 3), or, in other words, even better ways to make machine tools with machines—first the introduction of numerically controlled machines, then computerized numerically controlled machines, and so on—which resulted in a gradual decrease in the per-unit costs in real terms. This is depicted in Figure 11.2, which describes the best-practice frontier movements of and along this "intensive margin" (as

Per Unit Cost

(real terms)

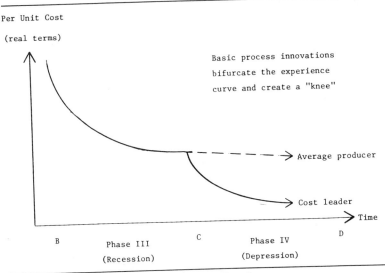

Basic process innovations bifurcate the experience curve and create a "knee"

→ Average producer

→ Cost leader

→ Time

B   Phase III   C   Phase IV   D
                    (Recession)   (Depression)

FIGURE 11.2:   Shift of the Best-Practice Frontier

defined by Ricardo) and the separation of the best- and average-practice frontier by a knee.

The technologies with which the machine-tool industry is currently experimenting (as are many other branches of industry) are basic-process innovations such as industrial robots, computer-assisted design, vertically integrated batch processing, whole "flexible" manufacturing systems, and the automated factory. If more of these basic-process innovations (of Type 4) advance from the experimental to the truly effective stage, then the leading corporations producing investment goods will have to undertake a quantum jump in capital intensity. At the same time, leading users of this new technology will obtain a great competitive edge over their market rivals, who face a widespread shake-out. By and large, the contractionary aggregate effects of this intensification should be expected to outweigh temporarily the gains from higher productivity during Phase IV.

MATHEMATICAL ECONOMIC ANALYSIS OF CLINICAL FINDINGS: WHAT'S UP?

We have now reached the point where we can integrate clinical innovation research findings with mathematical economic analysis and venture an outlook into the future. Neoclassical equilibrium theory—

derived by Uzawa (1961) in his two-sector model and subsequently clarified by Solow (1961) and Inada (1963)—shows that economic systems become structurally unstable if the capital intensity of the sector producing investment goods jumps ahead of capital intensity in the consumer goods sector. This is known as the "neoclassical capital intensity condition" for economic stability. If this condition is disturbed, the unequal pace of technological advance can seriously distort the staggered production process. Goods and services cannot move from the factory to the consumers as rapidly as the intermediate products stack up at the door of the factory; even so, these goods and services keep on flowing downstream faster than they can pass through the final stages. The result: excess supply. In consequence of this flow disequilibrium, concentrated manufacturers of consumer goods experience market congestion, which forces them to balance the reduction in purchases with cuts in their work force. Since downstream companies do not soak up the excess flow coming from upstream, the bankruptcy rate among producers of investment goods will increase so long as capital costs do not drop. Many of the hardhit firms are small and highly specialized companies that employ the most versatile and talented workers.

Whereas neoclassical theory suggests that Phase IV is a period of structural instability, I postulate that structural instability means readiness for basic-product innovations: Phase IV, the depression, ends when at Point D the predominant innovation activity shifts again from mostly basic-process innovations (Type 4) to mostly basic-product innovations (Type 1). This recovery can be depicted as a cross-over in the respective frequencies of basic innovations of Type 1 and Type 4 (that is, by the ratio of expansionary to rationalizing innovations, or E/R ratio). Figure 11.3 shows steep increases of the E/R ratio at points D around 1825, 1886, and 1929. These years have dreadful names among economic historians: the time of distress (in Great Britain) and pauperism (on the Continent), the great depression of the 1880s, and the world economic crisis of the 1930s.

Our mathematical theory of discontinuity, combined with longitudinal data from clinical innovation research, does not suggest specific predictions but yields at least one plausible scenario. We are approaching another Point D phase transition, with a rapid increase in the propensity for basic-product innovations. As in similar historical periods, we may expect a new cluster of radical innovations.

E/R Ratio

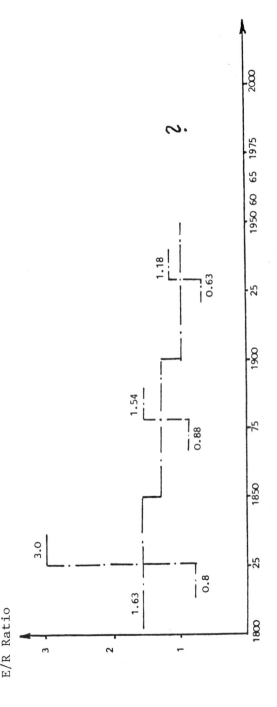

SOURCE: I am grateful to a team of colleagues at the International Institute of Management, Science Center Berlin, for classifying all basic innovations listed in Mensch (1975/1959) into E types or R types.

NOTE: The E/R ratio indicates the relative frequency of either type of basic innovation in Phase III as compared to Phase I (that is, before versus after the phase transition D in Figure 11.1), where E is the unweighted frequency of basic-product innovations in some period ("expansionary"), and R is the unweighted frequency of basic process innovations in some time period ("rationalizing").

FIGURE 11.3: Reversal of the E/R Ratio in History

Issues for Policymakers

Two issues of governance follow directly from the need for innovation policy geared to phases (that is, variant over time): internal reform in response to the environmental turbulence, and optimal adaptation to exogenous developments.

Timing innovation policies to transitions in phases, which would provide for greater flexibility, is possible only if the extent of general regulation of policy missions and programs is relaxed and policymakers are permitted more room for improvisation, discretionary action, and entrepreneurship. In these circumstances, we may see even more government by exception and less government by objectives than in the past. This implies decreased control over performance in the system of government by delegation, certainly in the innovation policy domain. This is a major challenge to the democratic system.

Another issue of governance concerns the optimal adaptation of innovation policy to exogenous developments, foreign competition, and change in the World Economic Order. Here we enter terra incognita. The optimal adaptation of innovation policy is bounded by irrational relationships within and among various layers of the relevant environment.

One set of irrational relationships interconnect the internal policy fields, such as income and employment policy, investment policy, social policy, and defense policy. There are several "econo-muddled" trade-off barriers to optimal innovation policy, all of which, however, may rapidly shift as the temporary economic (dis)equilibrium is punctuated in some sectors.

Another set of irrational relationships interconnects the external policy fields, such as foreign policy and defense policy. These relationships will also become more fuzzy in the 1980s as the nuclear equilibrium established in the 1970s between the superpowers (Kissinger's principle of "essential equivalence") is punctuated; defense spending in NATO countries will affect both NATO's military posture and economic competition among the allies in conventional fields of high technology (including computers, robots, and airplanes) and low technology (including steel, chickens, and textiles).

For the innovator, who in any event carries a heavy burden struggling with a project's intrinsic uncertainties (for example, technology, financing, and market risk), the added external uncertainty will make innovating very hard indeed. The contradictions across the policy layers that surround the innovator make it almost impossible to calculate the costs and benefits of innovative investments. In such circumstances, innovation policy can make a substantial contribution by reestablishing a clear, trustworthy working environment for the basic innovator.

NOTES

1. The long-term modeling is described at greater length in Mensch (1981); the short-term fluctuations are represented and analyzed through our model of the Schumpeter Clock (Mensch, Weidlich, et al., 1984). Together, these elements contribute a theory of economic evolution which contains general and temporary equilibria, disequilibria, and punctuated equilibria as special cases and as building blocks in a more comprehensive body of knowledge.

2. Mensch (1975/1979) describes similar phase transitions in economic history: the 1820s, the 1880s, and the 1930s. I discoverd that there was an unusually high frequency of basic innovations around 1825, 1886, and 1935, and conjectured, *ceteris paribus*, the next surge of basic innovations to be distributed around 1989, +5 years standard deviation.

REFERENCES

DIAMOND, P. A. (1965) "Technical change and the measurement of capital and output." Review of Economic Studies 32 (October): 289–298.

DI TELLA, T. S. (1972) "The concept of polarized development in regional planning," pp. 65–99 in A. Kuklinski and R. Petrella (eds.) Growth Poles and Regional Policies: A Seminar. The Hague: Mouton.

FREUDENBERGER, H. and G. O. MENSCH (1975) Von der Provinzstadt zur Industrieregion (Brünn-Studie). Göttingen: Vanderhoeck & Ruprecht.

FREY, B. (1969) "Product and process innovations in economic growth." Zeitschrift für Nationalökonomie 29 (May): 29–38.

GLASER, B. G. and A. L. STRAUSS (1967) The Discovery of Grounded Theory. Chicago: Aldine.

HILL, C. T. and J. M. UTTERBACK [eds.] (1979) Technological Innovation for a Dynamic Economy. New York: Pergamon Press.

INADA, K. (1963) "On a two-sector model of economic growth: comments and a generalization." Review of Economic Studies 30 (June): 119–127.

MENSCH, G. O. (1982) "Innovation management in diversified corporations." Human Systems Management 3 (April): 10–20.

_____ (1981) "A bi-equilibrium model of bi-valued technical progress embedded in innovative industrial investments in U.S. industry between 1900 and 1934." Cleveland: Case Western Reserve University, Department of Economics, Working Paper no. 12.

_____ (1978) "Thesen zur Wirkungsweise des Wirtschaftswandels." Bonn: Report to the Ministry of Economic Affairs.

———— (1975/1979) Das technologische Patt: Innovationen überwinden die Depression. Frankfurt-am-Main: Umschau-Verlag. (Tr. in 1979 as Stalemate in Technology: Innovations Overcome the Depression. Cambridge, MA: Ballinger.)

———— (1972) "Basisinnovationen und Verbesserungsinnovationen." Zeitschrift für Betriebswirtschaft 42 (April): 291–297.

———— (1971) "Zur Dynamik des technischen Fortschritts." Zeitschrift für Betriebswirtschaft 41 (May): 295–314.

———— W. WEIDLICH, and G. HAAG (1985) The Schumpeter Clock. Cambridge, MA: Ballinger.

MENSCH, G. O., K. KAASCH, A. KLEINKNECHT, and R. SCHNOPP (1980) "Innovation trends, and switching between full- and underemployment equilibria, 1950–78." Berlin: Science Center Berlin, International Institute of Management, Working Paper no. 80-5.

President's Commission for a National Agenda for the Eighties (1980) The American Economy in the Eighties. Washington, DC: Government Printing Office.

ROETHLISBERGER, F. J. (1977) The Elusive Phenomena: An Autobiographical Account of My Work in the Field of Organizational Behavior at the Harvard Business School. Boston: Harvard University, Graduate School of Business Administration.

SCHUMPETER, J. A. (1942) Capitalism, Socialism, and Democracy. New York: Harper & Row.

SOLOW, R. M. (1961) "Note on Uzawa's two-sector model of economic growth." Review of Economic Studies 29 (October): 48–50.

———— (1956) "A contribution to the theory of economic growth." Quarterly Journal of Economics 70 (Feburary): 65–94.

UTTERBACK, J. M. and W. J. ABERNATHY (1975) "A dynamic model of process and product innovation." Omega, The International Journal of Management Science 3 (December): 639–656.

UZAWA, H. (1963) "On a two-sector model of economic growth II." Review of Economic Studies 30 (June): 105–118.

———— (1961) "On a two-sector model of economic growth." Review of Economic Studies 29 (October): 40–47.

CHAPTER 12

SOCIAL KNOW-HOW AND ITS ROLE IN INVENTION AND INNOVATION

M A N F R E D   K O C H E N

Boulding (1979) has pointed out that know-how is a major factor of production along with energy, space, and time rather than the assembly of land, labor, and capital postulated in traditional economics. Energy and nonrenewable raw materials, on which industry now depends, will almost certainly be our scarcest resources in the next few decades, and there is little we can do to prevent such things as oil and rubber from becoming increasingly scarce. Only know-how may enable us to find and use alternate sources of energy and substitute materials. The tasks that such know-how is expected to deal with are, however, increasingly complex. Moreover, their complexity and their number are rapidly increasing.

Is know-how growing fast enough to meet the world's need? Are we facing a future with relative scarcity of know-how as well? Fortunately, we may have some control over the growth of know-how. The resources of computer and communication technology, which are becoming more widely available, may greatly extend know-how. Planning for the growth and use of new know-how must take this trend into account.

Know-how comprises knowledge plus the information and data to support it. Know-how is not identical with the knowledge needed to achieve an end, nor is it the same as technology, even when technology is defined broadly as a "specifiable, reproducible, and communicable way of doing something" (Brooks, 1974). The conventional

AUTHOR'S NOTE: Thanks are due to Charles Barr for editorial assistance; to the WZB (Science Center Berlin), and particularly Karl W. Deutsch for support in the development of some of the ideas reported here; and to the NSF for partial support of the author under grant IST-8301505.

meaning of know-how is the faculty for a particular activity. That interpretation precludes using the term to refer to an ability to get something—anything—done rather than the knowledge needed to perform a specific activity.

The term is intended to denote a blend of expertise, management, and the faculty for generating and executing both general- and special-purpose programs of instructions or steps of action that will produce a specified result. Know-how is embodied, for example, in computer programs, in computers, and in a construction schedule plus blueprint. The programmer, engineer, or composer of instructions for a construction kit has know-how; his products do not. It is his creative ingenuity, his resourcefulness, and above all his orientation and perspective that enable him to set and attain goals. The hallmark of know-how is a way of thinking. It is the ability to represent the world and to shift such representations until clarity is attained about how to proceed.

We suggest that the essence of *social* know-how is in team formation. Newer forms of social organization may originate in at least two ways. The first depends on the efforts of charismatic individuals with the entrepreneurial and organizational know-how, dedication, energy, and leadership to mobilize and manage a team or masses. The future need for teams already exceeds the available supply of leaders with the needed strength and other qualities. We have little control over the flow of that supply. The second way is spontaneous team formation or mass movements. This is the natural response of social processes as they adapt to changing conditions. Understanding and facilitating conditions that favor team formation may be the essence of social know-how.

There is relatively little social know-how of this sort at the present time, but it will take precisely such know-how to plan for its own development. The production function for social know-how has social know-how as its key input variable. The purpose of this chapter is to shed some light on the possibility of the deliberate production of social know-how. It also discusses the role of computers and feedback in this process, as well as the role of know-how in transforming social inventions into social innovations. To this end I shall examine the institutional base for social innovations, propose a new conceptualization of the process for producing social know-how, argue for the proposition that "inquiring communities" are central to the process, and suggest experiments for involving such teams.

Institutional Loci for Innovation:
From Universities to Industrial Firms

Governmental institutions lie between industrial firms and universities in their ability to adapt to changing conditions by making changes in their organizational structure. Contrary to what one might expect, universities have very little social know-how. Firms in technology-intensive industries have far more. It may be instructive to analyze and compare the success and failure of these two institutions in using social know-how to produce social know-how and to generate and transform social inventions into innovations.

Innovations by an industrial firm can be easily recognized when they occur in the form of radically new products, such as nylon stockings or air conditioners. The following characteristics were agreed upon by authors of nine independent studies to be necessary for successful innovation (Rothwell, 1979):

(1) Top management fully supports the innovation, allocating sufficient resources to see it through its critical phases.

(2) Open-minded, progressive, middle-level managers of high quality and ability, often with formal technical qualifications, are involved with the innovation in a flat organizational structure that can adapt to change.

(3) There is a recognized need in an area as opposed to the recognition of technical potential.

(4) The new product or process is followed up with efficient technical service, spare parts, and user training.

(5) Innovators collaborate and communicate effectively with potential users from the earliest stage in the innovation process.

(6) Efficient research and development testing eliminate most of the bugs prior to marketing.

(7) A professional approach to planning and managing the innovation is used.

(8) "Key individuals," such as a product champion, technical innovator, or business innovator may be involved.

(9) Research and development, production, marketing, and other corporate functions are well coordinated.

Failure of innovations in firms, on the other hand, has been attributed to three kinds of factors related to markets, technologies, and management:

(1) Innovations failed when the firm

  (a) made no inquiries of users;

   (b) made inquiries, but too few or used poor instruments;

   (c) ignored the answers;

   (d) misinterpreted or misunderstood the answers;

   (e) committed itself inflexibly to a preconceived design;

   (f) made no on-the-spot investigations of potential users;

   (g) did no market research or ignored the results;

   (h) neglected publicity or underfunded marketing efforts;

   (i) failed to educate and train users; and/or

   (j) failed to anticipate changes in the market.

  (2) Innovations failed on technical grounds in firms that

   (a) did poor or insufficient development;

   (b) depended too much on outside expertise;

   (c) devoted insufficient resources to the project;

   (d) encountered superior competition that was unanticipated;

   (e) tolerated insufficient contact between research and development and production;

   (f) released products that were difficult to use or to maintain; and/or

   (g) tolerated engineering designs that were impractical.

  (3) Management contributed to innovation failures in firms when

   (a) the project was not taken seriously by top management;

   (b) it was not integrated into corporate strategy;

   (c) it received inadequate support or control;

   (d) there was failure to communicate with critically important outside interests;

   (e) innovators were too junior, weak, or inexperienced;

   (f) product champions were strong but wrong; and/or

   (g) internal communications were poor.

Similar factors operate to delay innovation. Considering the great opportunities for the failure or delay of industrial innovations, it is surprising that so many innovations have succeeded. The pace of scientific research might have greatly increased the rate of innovation if the conditions favoring success had been present more often while those favoring failure were absent.

Had that happened, however, it is possible that our social institutions might not have been able to absorb them. According to Fubini (1969), innovations can be classified along three lines:

(1) They enable us to do what we are now doing but cheaper, faster, better.

(2) They enable us to do things we could never do before.

(3) They change our lifestyles.

An increase in the pace of innovations would undoubtedly also increase the rate of stimuli that change our lifestyles, and this requires adaptation of social institutions. Too many major changes all at once— such as two-way cable TV, satellite communications, two-way radios, and so on—may impose too severe a load on regulatory agencies, for example, and the stress may induce breakdown. The Kemeny Report, for example, hinted strongly that the failure of nuclear reactors such as the one at Three-Mile Island is largely attributable to the "mindset" of people in regulatory agencies.

Large public universities appear to have evolved structures that make them impervious to processes of innovation affecting their main output: new knowledge and educated persons. This is an apparent paradox, because the advances in knowledge they generate are often the scientific basis for innovation. In order to preserve the highest standards of excellence, quality, and purity, the responsibility for evaluating who is qualified to teach, do research, or administer; what is to be taught; and who may study and obtain degrees resides exclusively with specialists segregated into departments. All knowledge and intellectual jurisdiction are compartmentalized and divided among them. Occasionally a center or institute that performs research or services can bridge some departments, but too often such centers become polarized by the structure of their environment and degenerate into disciplinary specialties as well. Pressures on individuals to have publications, grants, and titles associated with their names effectively discourage team formation even in response to situations that require team approaches. Competition is fostered even when cooperation would be a far more beneficial pattern to encourage, as in the production of know-how.

Many innovations in all aspects of university operations have been proposed and tried—from revisions of curriculum, faculty development, organizational structures, changes in the reward system, to novel means for extended, personalized education with the help of computers, communications, classrooms without walls, and so forth.

Yet the basic structure has endured with few fundamental changes since the Middle Ages. Few modern colleges or universities have gotten as close to the ideal of the collegium as Plato's Academy. One reason for the remarkable resistance to change is the lack of incentive for department chairmen, deans, and center directors to effect major changes, even if their successors or the rest of society may have to carry the burden passed on to them.

Tenured professors, like Supreme Court justices, are in a relatively secure position until they retire. Just as established scientists often become the main champions of a dying paradigm, stalwart department specialists uphold the sanctity and purity of their discipline to a fault. An innovation such as matrix management (Knight, 1977) may be viewed as a threat. Suppose, for example, that the columns of a matrix represented classical disciplines such as pure physics and chemistry. The rows correspond to mission-, task-, or project-oriented activities such as "Health Systems," "Fusion Reactors," or "Global Information Transfers." It is proposed that a junior faculty member in the department of some column spend some time on an important project corresponding to a row. But time spent toward the goal corresponding to the row may not lead to the quantity and quality of publications in what key members of the column regard as the mainstream of their specialty. If the latter are primarily responsible for deciding on his qualifications for tenure—assuming that is his highest value—then he would be wise to spend all his effort on the discipline corresponding to the column, whatever the benefits generated for society at large.

Time spent on the attainment of excellence, eminence, and perfection in the specialized discipline is time not spent in contributing toward important goals requiring the use of knowledge drawn from many specialties. If those who support or come to universities perceive the primary purpose of universities to be the furthering of those goals, at least indirectly, and if control over promotions and the like were to be in their hands, then a young faculty member would be wise to spend all his effort on goals corresponding to the rows. Insofar as this may mean expending too much effort in using knowledge with no effort spent in adding to it, there may soon be insufficient new knowledge to use. That is why academicians insist on maintaining control over the disciplinary tools for adding to knowledge.

But tools used only to make more tools, that are in turn used only for toolmaking, soon lose their utility even if they have great beauty. It is primarily through the interplay of rows and columns that valuable knowledge is both generated and used. New forms of teamwork are called for, new forms of social know-how. Yet the minimal amount of social know-how needed to produce this kind of social know-how is scarce in universities. Perhaps the pressure for revolutionary change in response to declining support and declining enrollment may evoke an adaptive response. This could happen if universities look to themselves for the causes of the distress they are likely to experience in the future. For many universities, the response may be even more maladaptive—more specialization and compartmentalization—until breakdown occurs.

As suggested at the beginning of this section, governmental institutions lie between industrial firms and universities in their abilities to adapt. The role of government in the innovation process has evolved in response to the failure of unconstrained market forces to generate technological strength and independence (U.S. Congress, 1978). One role is to compensate for underinvestment by the private sector in such fields as public health. Another role of government in innovation is to support as well as perform research requiring large capital expenditures, such as high-energy physics. A third role is regulation to correct market failures, as in pollution control, and to replace market allocation of resources by social decisions, such as transportation for the elderly or handicapped.

Japanese governmental institutions have adapted to modern conditions more successfully than those of the United Kingdom in the following ways: They emphasized technical education, while the British had no policy to prepare technical personnel for industry and for technological change. They stressed consumer technologies responsive to demand, rather than investing in basic science. They oriented their economy to exports, to competing with the most technologically advanced international firms. They protected infant industries and phased out technologically weak firms. They avoided monopolies by mandatory licensing to competitors. Finally, they supported industry through analysis of export markets and foreign technologies. There is much to be learned by governmental institutions in other countries in positions somewhat similar to Japan's in the last two decades, particularly from their adaptiveness and relations to both universities and industries.

Pattern Formation

What follows are some ideas for a model of invention that may lead to new social know-how. Matrix management is a good example of an invention in organization. Zero-based budgeting is one in man-

agement that has become new social know-how. The notion of "inquiring communities" (Kochen, 1979) may, under appropriate
conditions, become an important innovation in governmental policymaking. To discover those conditions, an understanding of the
process by which innovations in governmental policymaking come
into being is essential.

(1) The invention process begins with "latent ideas," which suggests an
    imprecisely perceived need and how to meet it. For example, the need
    for engineers to further their professional development or sharpen
    their disciplinary tools while at the same time using those tools in the
    development of products suggests the idea of matrix management.
    The latent idea corresponds to a "niche" in Boulding's terms (Bould-
    ing, 1978), or to a generalized lock to doors barring need-satisfaction,
    to use a more picturesque metaphor.

(2) The latent idea becomes actual. Thus, the above latent idea of matrix
    management is explicitly articulated, named, and presented in public
    in a form that can be replicated, communicated, and used. The ac-
    tualized idea corresponds to a pattern that tries to fit into the niche,
    a key that approximately fits the lock. Thus, the key is produced by
    the lock, with each part of the lock simultaneously forming a com-
    plementary part of the key, using whatever components are available
    at the location at which they are needed just then.

(3) Actualization of the latent idea also generates a latent community—
    an "invisible college" or group of people concerned with the idea and
    prepared to develop it further—and a latent trail of potential publi-
    cations in the form of proposals for further inquiry.

(4) The latent community develops into an actual community or team;
    the latent trails become actualized tracks; the idea is further devel-
    oped. If the key does not fit the lock, the community works backward
    to search for that part of the lock which, if modified, is likely to
    improve the fit. Tests are made and parts modified with a new view
    toward improving the fit. This alternation of analysis and synthesis is
    repeated according to the inquiry strategy (latent trails) until the key
    fits. During this convergent process, members of the community com-
    municate their findings to one another in (publishable) packets.

(5) This communication stimulates the generation of new latent ideas.
    Under certain conditions the group process will refine, screen, and
    improve them until they seem to be potentially fruitful inventions for
    furthering the group process. The lock changes more slowly than the
    key, so the key can fit the lock for a longer time than it took to get
    it to fit. The lock itself fits into a higher-order pattern, which changes
    even more slowly.

(6) The dynamics of the formation of ideas, communities, and trials are describable by a set of nonlinear difference equations that are specified by more slowly varying parameters. The system incorporates the analogs of replication, recombination, mutation, realization, and fitness testing. When some of the parameters change sufficiently (for example, when a < 4 in $X_{t+1} = aX_t[1-X_t]$), the solutions behave as if they were random. Solutions of the system at one level are parameters of a system at the next level. Random fluctuations in a parameter can produce qualitative changes in the nature of the equilibrium points. This, according to Prigogine (1976), is the origin of genuine novelty.

Policymaking as a Process of Social Innovation

A policy is an "expression of a stance in relation to a class of problem situations, formed by a set of actors with a legitimate concern in such situations" (Friend, 1977). It is intended to lead to a succession of decisions and a course of action, a procedure that is adopted and followed in the pursuit of a purpose or goal. A policy is a unit of social know-how. Public or governmental politics involve many persons with diverse interests, world-views, and values. A course of action cannot be followed if it is sabotaged by key people. Thus, policy formation is a political group process. It is a craft that requires political know-how. Perfection in the products of such group craftsmanship is not expected. Scientific predictions of the consequences of politics that affect complex systems in major ways may, in principle, be impossible because the policies shape and shift the very systems to be described. For instance, we may not be able to prove that a policy of installing rapid-transit facilities in a region will reduce the average number of cars per family in that region, but installing such a rapid transit system will change the character of the region.

We can often recognize the flaws in a policy, if not by foresight, then at least through hindsight. We may also be able to learn from such "mistakes" by transferring to a similar policy issue the know-how and wisdom necessary to do it better if given a chance to do it over. If the flawed policy is still in effect when we recognize the flaws, we may be able to transfer such learning to revisions of the policy, by "near-hindsight." Ideally, we would like to shorten the hindsight lag as much as possible, and use "side-sight." Indeed, we could decompose a policy into elemental policy steps or units. *Each step is both exploratory and effective in varying degrees.* Drake et al. (1983) have developed in some detail a similar principle, which they call "reflection in action," as applied to nutrition program implementation in developing countries.

A policy know-how network consists of a variety of stakeholders, each of whom has adopted a problem-solving orientation (Fisher and Ury, 1981) in a particular arena. They agree to avail themselves of all effective tools for genuine communication, such as computer conferencing, the use of shared databases, and knowledge bases coupled to inference systems. These resources and model bases support decision making, argumentation, the clarification of issues, and the justification of positions. They focus on interests and issues with a view toward resolving conflicts and attaining consensus. Above all, they learn by doing.

Issues are resolved when an action is chosen. Representations of an issue involve six aspects:

(1) the set of policy options that the group concerned with the issue has agreed to consider;

(2) the set of desiderata and constraints, affects, and values which the group has agreed to use in choosing an option;

(3) the collective memory of experiences, general knowledge about the background, and specific beliefs about the likely consequences of various policy options—including an expression of how familiar, or similar to issues previously encountered, the issue is;

(4) the urgency with which a resolution is needed;

(5) the know-how, including the capacity for analysis, computation, and the exercise of other tools required to reach a satisfactory resolution— including an estimate of the effort needed for resolvability; and

(6) the stakes for the various members of the group; this includes all expressions of affect and saliency of the issue.

All six aspects of the representation contribute to its complexity, especially (1) through (3). The greater the number of people involved in policymaking, the more difficult it is to attain agreement on the set of options, desiderata, and constraints, and on what knowledge to bring to bear; also, the larger the set of options, the more and more interdependent the desiderata and constraints, and the more vast, imprecise, and incompatible the collective memory. All these increase complexity.

Beliefs about the likely consequences of a policy should not only be "true," but justified as well. That is part of aspect (3). Social know-how must be mobilized and used. This includes the cajoling, wheeling and dealing, horsetrading, and the like that is part of most political group processes. It is important to recall that this must not only lead to a resolution of the issue in the form of a policy, but also to an adequate resolution, a good policy. We consider one policy better than another (side-sight) if the level of debate and communication about it is of higher quality. This means that the communications exchanged among the members of the policymaking team have as their primary goal the justification of beliefs, the clarification of the issue representation, the expression of know-how that brings to bear the needed analytic capacity, awareness of deadlines, mutual emotional support of participants (morale, consensus), awareness of diverse orientations, values, interests, and abilities.

Conclusion

This chapter has proposed two testable hypotheses: First, there is a way of organizing and managing policymaking groups that generates better policies than we now have. Second, there is a way to build into such improved policymaking teams a capacity for self-improvement of the group process.

The major feature of groups that produce better policies is the fact that they are composed of both policymakers and social scientists, as well as policy analysts. They also engage in a new mode for team operation characterized by "inquiry"—that is, by an absence of fear of making mistakes from which to learn—and by using newer modes of communication and collective memory. The process of policymaking is initiated when one potential teammate records his or her representation of an issue into a computer-communications network. This input is stored for possible forwarding, on demand, to designated others or those assigned by a computer program. They are alerted to the availability of the original input when (and where) they "sign on" or at the initiative of the system. The person's initial assessment of the urgency or saliency of the issue is elicited if he or she has not supplied it; additional assessments are requested from all others who respond to the input and one another's subsequent inputs. The initial representation of the issue is thus replicated.

A potential community becomes actual as indivduals with a similar stake in an issue begin to recognize one another. To avoid errors of omission and commission, every effort is made to contact potential stakeholders, opinion leaders, and resource persons named by persons contacted so far; a directed self-selection process will begin to screen a core group that is able and willing to raise the level of communication. Thus an "inquiring community" will form under certain conditions. It will develop and mature, perhaps grow to twenty or so teammates, select a specific end-product for the team to produce by some deadline—such as a well-reasoned legislative proposal—and disband when it has done what it can. Understanding what these conditions are and bringing them about are part of the social knowhow displayed by some facilitators, managers, and participants in the system.

Communication proceeds to change beliefs and the representation of an issue by processes analogous to recombination and mutation. Policies are formed and carried out, a step analogous to realization. It is important to insist that the team does not disband before it follows through. Actions corresponding to the adopted policy lead to new states, and these consequences are then compared with the beliefs in the issue representation. Even more important, the representation of the new state is evaluated to determine if policy revisions are required. If so, policy improvements are now sought not only by examining the level of communication, but also by the reality feedback that is now on hand.

Finally, there is a test to ascertain whether or not the policy improvement occurred fast enough. If it did not, the group looks at some of the original contributions to social know-how that helped establish this "inquiring community" in the first place. In other words, the group turns its attention to policies that will improve its own operation. The efficiency of its group process is at issue, and the very know-how that brought it to the present level of efficiency is used to generate additional know-how. Therein lies a potentially powerful method for social innovation.

REFERENCES

BOULDING, K.E. (1979) Lecture, Science Center Berlin.
——— (1978) Ecodynamics. Beverly Hills, CA: Sage.
BROOKS, H. (1974) Lecture, Harvard University (24 September).
DRAKE, W. D., R. I. MILLER, and D. A. SCHON (1983) "The study of community-level nutrition interventions: an argument for reflection-in-action." Human Systems Management 4 (Autumn): 82–97.
FISHER, R. and W. URY (1981) Getting to Yes: Negotiating Agreement Without Giving In. Boston: Houghton Mifflin.
FRIEND, J. K. (1977) "The dynamics of policy change." Long Range Planning 10 (February): 40–47.

FUBINI, E. (1969) "Electronically expanding the citizen's world." Presented at the IEEE international convention, highlight session.

KNIGHT, K. [ed.] (1977) Matrix Management. New York: Petrocelli.

KOCHEN, M. (1979) An Inquiring Community: Proposal for an Experiment in Scientific Policymaking. Berlin: Science Center Berlin, IIVG Report.

PRIGOGINE, I. (1976) "Order through fluctuation: self-organization and social system," pp. 93–126 in E. Jantsch and C. H. Waddington (eds.) Evolution and Consciousness: Human Systems in Transition. Reading, MA: Addison-Wesley.

ROTHWELL, R. (1979) "Successful and unsuccessful innovators." Planned Innovation 2 (April): 126–128.

U.S. Congress, Office of Technology Assessment (1978). Government Involvement in the Innovation Process. Washington, DC: Government Printing Office.

DISCUSSION ON THE CHAPTER BY KOCHEN

MANFRED KOCHEN

Karl Deutsch opened this workshop with a very stimulating and interesting discussion of theory. It may therefore be fitting for me, as his disciple, to close it with a complementary discussion of theory from a slightly different perspective. My focus is on information and feedback processes in the public sector and on two experiments dealing with innovation in that arena. Two hypotheses are to be tested. The first is that the level of debate on public policy issues can be raised by forming what I have called an "inquiring community," a mix of analysts, scientists, and policymakers who can communicate with one another by means of a computer conferencing system. The second is that conflict management can be improved by such a community.

People who are motivated to create an inquiring community will do so with or without the technology of computer conferencing. The technology itself won't bring them together. What it does do, however, is decrease greatly the cost of feedback and coupling; it also eliminates the need for synchrony. That is quite important. Policymakers are constrained by deadlines, by the need to make decisions and resolve issues immediately (or in a relatively short period of time). Social scientists, in contrast, delay judgment on the worthiness of a piece of work until it has been subjected to peer review and passed the test of scientific respectability.

I would like to sketch a model of the production process for an innovation and what it takes to facilitate the process. The key word in this model is "actualization," borrowed in a general sense from Abraham Maslow. We begin with a latent idea, corresponding to what Kenneth Boulding calls a "niche," somewhat analogous to a lock. In the second step, the latent idea is actualized: A conjecture becomes a theorem and is proved or disproved; a hypothesis is tested; an issue is resolved. In the analogy of the lock, the realization of a latent idea corresponds to the forming of a key. This process is described in the section entitled "pattern formation" in my chapter in this volume.

I believe that the experimental inquiring community I propose would raise the level of discussion, because people would justify the beliefs they express to a greater extent than they do now. Participants would ask more questions, approach issues from more diverse points of view, and consider more variables. Above all, they would have to admit their willingness to produce possibly mistaken but correctable, rather than error-free, products. Researchers and professors like ourselves, as well as policymakers, must give top priority to learning on their own and from other participants.

KARL DEUTSCH

Most people in either scholarship or practice operate under time pressures and overload. One would assume that they could devote about as much time to the community as they would otherwise give to research. Would the inquiring community make better use of their time?

MANFRED KOCHEN

Participants would have to find it more profitable and rewarding to participate in an inquiring community; it would have to make a difference in the nonacademic world.

KARL DEUTSCH

Teleconferencing technology would make it possible for people to allocate a limited sector of their working day to this kind of activity without taking them out of everything else. You could, to some extent, mitigate the constraints imposed by lack of stimulation, lack of solitude for serious thinking (too much brainstorming), and not being able to get work done because of these situations. It could buy you a great deal of time.

However, let us suppose that somebody is a section head of some public agency. He or she has a high degree of expertise. Should such a person learn how to deal with a computer or have an assistant who comes in and talks to the computer for him or her? Operating the computer may prove to be frustrating enough to discourage its use.

MANFRED KOCHEN

Some participants will want to enter their input by themselves, and many of the problems that deter others will be overcome by technological breakthroughs. Innovation requires follow-through by people at the right level.

I am proposing an experiment that I think will teach us something about the optimal mix of people, about how to clarify issues and how to spur innovation. If it works with a few salient issues, then perhaps it can become an effective process. Computer conferencing, applied to the notion of an inquiring community, may be a way to study innovation in and by the public sector.

RICHARD MERRITT

To what kinds of potential innovations in the public sector would this idea of the inquiring community apply?

MANFRED KOCHEN

Consider, for instance, the case of a legislator concerned with an issue that he or she feels may become clarified by interaction with scientists or policy analysts. The wintertime use of road salt to prevent icing is a concrete example. Legislative staffs in one state have been concerned about this and wish to communicate about it with legislative staffs in another state. Did the salt crack the pavements? Are there significant laboratory findings that may be brought into the discussion?

LAWRENCE MOHR

You're thinking, then, about situations where somebody thinks that input from different sources would be valuable—for example, when Alpena, Michigan, is considering whether or not to adopt a Dial-a-Ride system?

MANFRED KOCHEN

This is, in fact, the sort of problem that was actually discussed in a computer conference.

KARL DEUTSCH

How do you get people to participate? How do you get the right network together?

MANFRED KOCHEN

Some people will agree to participate only if certain others whom they consider valuable contributors are also participants. Other people will not be in it if certain persons *are*. We must honor all of these constraints. The conference will bog down if we don't. I don't really know how the optimal group, or even a compatible group, finds itself, but I believe it does.

KARL DEUTSCH

Probably someone who is a specialist on organizing teleconferences will start the process. Then you change the topic of inquiry according to the need. The participants will discuss who should be asked to join, and who might accept. People don't have to travel. At any hour of the day or night they can respond to questions put to them.

MANFRED KOCHEN

You might make an analogy to a yellow-pages directory—a biographic directory, with potential participants entering their personal profile.

HANS WEILER

What is it specifically that the computer adds?

MANFRED KOCHEN

It makes people less dependent on being together at one time and in one place. They can interact over a period of weeks from wherever they happen to be, and take time to think through their responses. I once presented a talk over a computer conference network, one paragraph at a time; everyone could react to each item as I finished it, and then react to each other's comments at the moment the ideas and questions occurred to them.

HANS WEILER

Couldn't that be handled through telephone conferencing?

KARL DEUTSCH

Then you would have to remember what everybody said. The computer provides the group with a collective memory.

LAWRENCE MOHR

How about writing letters?

MANFRED KOCHEN

In a crude way, sending letters with copies to everyone else is similar. But the time element is not unimportant. Sending letters introduces delays. The cost of mail is, or soon will be, greater than that of electronic transmission.

RICHARD MERRITT

My mind is boggled by the thought that, if you communicate your idea to ten people, you get ten reactions, which means that the next person has to react to nine, and so on.

MANFRED KOCHEN

The problem of overload and filtering for relevance and quality is serious. One must balance errors of omission with errors of commission, and minimize both. A receiver could automatically mask messages from certain people, of certain kinds or of certain lengths. The receiver could have programs that prescreen some of the things coming in, and could browse. There are many quality filters that can be tuned to personal preferences.

HELGA KÖRNIG

Individuals learn well, but it is much more difficult for businesses to learn. The German experience shows that you must work hard to get the right inquiring group together, and even harder to get the institution or organization to learn from their ideas. The problems raised are very often quite different from the practitioners' concerns. For this reason, we do not know if the problems get worse when we talk more seriously with each other, or whether such talk compounds the problem of the practitioners' concerns being so different from those of the theorists. An example of this is the present conference. We are speaking largely about things of no direct concern to the practical people, If we had used a computer, it wouldn't have been any better.

MANFRED KOCHEN

The difficulties might have been amplified, unless special precautions were taken to avoid them in the first place. How to bridge the gap between the concerns, attitudes, world-views, values, and so forth of practitioners and theorists/experimentalists is perhaps the most crucial issue here. I suggest two modest experiments to shed light on that issue. The crucial question is how to find the groups and facilitate their spontaneous formation. We cannot select people out of a list of 10,000. There are too many possible combinations. There wouldn't be enough time to examine them all. But I believe that the right 20 people, or at least an appropriate set of people, will recognize themselves. The spontaneous formation of an invisible college in science is an example. Usually a hundred people in a given specialty (according to Derek de Solla Price) somehow find and recognize themselves as communities because they communicate during the time that it's fruitful for them to do so. In certain fields, such as physics, theorists and practical people (experimenters) share concerns and find it essential to talk with one another. Perhaps an understanding of how such an invisible college forms could be transferred to the creation of an interface between practice and scholarship.

RONALD FRANCISCO

Columbus, Ohio, has a two-way interactive cable TV network. Many people vote on that system using dichotomous choice. There are a lot of people who vote on issues for liberal, philanthropic, or other reasons, and who are then appalled by the outcome of the vote. It might raise their taxes, and that isn't what they really wanted. Any time that someone cannot see the consequences in every stage of decision making, there is a face validity vote. Does that present a serious problem?

HANS WEILER

That problem exists even without computers. That's exactly what happened with Proposition 13 in California. People voted for one thing and got something entirely different.

LAWRENCE MOHR

One way to proceed in response to Helga Körnig's concern is that, whereas it might not be possible to apply this kind of procedure to all problems, we could look for some of the problems where it could be applied. Energy policy is such an area. As Everett Rogers has pointed out, many people believe that major decisions in the area of conservation must be made on a decentralized basis; the federal government, they say, cannot possibly tell Alpena, Detroit, Davis, and other cities how best to conserve energy in their communities, since a large part of the necessary information is in the hands of the communities. Congressman Phil Sharp of Indiana has introduced legislation that could make a fairly substantial amount of money available for an information exchange system among communities. This procedure might really have an interesting application.

ABSTRACTS/RÉSUMÉS

Innovation in the Public Sector: An Introduction
Richard L. Merritt

New, complex problems and recognition of their own limited capacities are forcing industrialized states to seek innovative strategies, to expand their learning capacity. This calls for research on innovation oriented to governmental practice, to adaptation rather than system transformation, and comparative across nations, policy areas, and system levels.

L'innovation dans le secteur public: une introduction

L'apparition de nouveaux problèmes et la reconnaissance de leurs propres capacités limitées sont en train de forcer les pays industrialisés à rechercher des stratégies innovatives pour étendre leur capacité d'apprentissage. Ceci demande des recherches dans le domaine de l'innovation orientées vers l'exercice du gouvernement, vers l'adaptation plutôt que vers la transformation de système, innovation qui puisse être comparable entre nations, domaines de politiques et niveaux de systèmes.

1

On Theory and Research in Innovation
Karl W. Deutsch

Social innovation, as Schumpeter taught, depends on the frequency of acts of individual learning. It thus depends on reinforcement at micro and macro levels offered to those who innovate or accept innovation, as well as on the learning capacity of the society, and, given its routine-prone bureaucracy, on the procedures adopted to make learning more probable (such as social-political thinktanks). Innovation theory requires more research on case studies, adoption curves (as well as public-private sector differences), and the distribution among groups of its benefits and costs, including the cost of *not* innovating. A generative model of the innovation process would help us to predict the direction and dimensions of future innovativeness and to model probable futures.

Théorie et recherche dans le domaine de l'innovation

L'innovation dans le domaine social, ainsi que Schumpeter le pensait, dépend de la fréquence des actes d'apprentissage individuel. Elle dépend donc des avantages offerts, aux niveaux micro et macro, aux innovateurs et aux personnes ouvertes à

291

l'innovation, de sa capacité d'apprentissage, et, étant donné sa bureaucratie à tendance routinière, des procédures adoptées pour rendre plus probable l'acquisition des connaissances (comme, par exemple, les "thinktanks"—groupes d'experts sociopolitiques). La théorie de l'innovation demande plus de recherches sur des cas particuliers, sur les courbes d'adoption (ainsi que les différences constatées entre le secteur public et le secteur privé) et la distribution entre les différents groupes des bénéfices et des coûts, y compris les dépenses entraînées par le *manque* d'innovation. Un modèle génératif du processus d'innovation nous aiderait à prévoir les directions et les dimensions d'innovations à venir et à constituer des modèles pour un avenir probable.

2

Individual Creativity and Political Leadership
Dean Keith Simonton

Since a creative society consists of creative individuals, historiometric study of individual and social conditions accounting for creativity may point to ways to enhance a society's creativity. Life in politically fragmented societies or times of turmoil (but not day-to-day instability) is linked to creativity, as is the presence of role-models for the young. Innovativeness and openness to it peak around forty years of age. Intelligence, high productivity, and cognitive complexity are important (but too much may hamper political leaders). Genius and conditions in a field both contribute to scientific creativity. Not all these variables are equally subject to governmental efforts to enhance or dampen them; effects of such steps are not likely to be felt for some fifty years.

La créativité individuelle et le leadership politique

Puisqu'une société créative est constituée d'individus créatifs, l'étude historiométrique des conditions, tant individuelles que sociales, à prendre en compte pour expliquer la créativité peut faire découvrir des procédures pour améliorer la créativité dans une société. La vie dans des sociétés politiquement fragmentées, ou en des temps troublés (mais nous ne parlons pas de l'instabilité de la vie de tous les jours), est liée à la créativité, de même que l'est la présence de modèles à suivre pour les jeunes. L'innovation et l'ouverture d'esprit à son égard atteint son sommet quand les individus atteignent l'âge de 40 ans. L'intelligence, une productivité élevée, une complexité cognitive sont des qualités importantes (mais en quantité trop élevée elles risqueraient de gêner les dirigeants politiques). Le génie aussi bien que les conditions rencontrées dans un domaine particulier contribuent à la créativité scientifique. Toutes ces variables ne sont pas également soumises aux efforts que fait le gouvernement pour les promouvoir ou pour les étouffer; il est peu probable que les effets de telles actions puissent se faire sentir avant un délai d'environ cinquante ans.

3

Groups and the Innovation Process
Joseph E. McGrath

Social psychological data suggest that groups are not good generators of ideas. The value of "brainstorming," the alleged tendency of decision-making groups to shift toward risky solutions, and the danger of "groupthink" find little research support. Groups are better at dividing up labor to perform tasks, legitimating decisions, and mobilizing members for action. Among the research-supported "rules" that can facilitate innovative decision making are: provide rewards for trying an innovation without making them contingent on its success; assign to an individual the task of generating new ideas but to a group the task of reviewing and evaluating them; and create a negotiation group if the task at hand involves conflict between two or more contending factions.

Les rapports des groupes avec le processus d'innovation

Des données sociopsychologiques suggèrent que des groupes ne sont pas de bons générateurs d'idées. La valeur du "brain-storming", avec la prétendue tendance des groupes décideurs à se diriger vers des solutions risquées, et le danger du "groupthink" (réflexion en groupe) ne trouvent que peu de soutien au travers des recherches. Les groupes sont mieux à même de diviser le travail pour assurer l'accomplissement de tâches, de légitimer des décisions, et de mobiliser leurs membres pour l'action. Parmi les "règles" supportées par la recherche et qui peuvent faciliter les prises de décision innovatrices, on trouve: récompenser des essais d'innovation, sans que ces récompenses soient liées à la réussite de ces innovations; assigner à un individu la tâche de générer de nouvelles idées, mais à un groupe la tâche de les revoir et de les évaluer; créer un groupe de négociation, si la tâche en cours de discussion amène un conflit entre deux ou plusieurs factions opposées.

4

Diffusion of Innovations in Public Organizations
Everett M. Rogers and Joung-Im Kim

The classic model of innovation focused on four elements: relative advantage of the innovation; effectiveness of channels for diffusion; time; and social system characteristics, such as structure and kinds of change agents. Early research focused on organizational innovativeness and especially individuals responsible for diffusion. It was highly structured, quantitative, and hypothesis-testing. Research since the 1970s has looked more at the innovation process. It consists of five stages: an initiation phase (agenda-setting and matching existing agendas with alternative solutions, that is, innovations); and an implementation phase (adapting the innovation to the relevant organization and problem, structuring the organization to accommodate it, and institutionalizing it).

La diffusion d'innovations dans les organisations publiques

Le modèle classique de l'innovation se concentre autours de quatre éléments: avantage relatif de l'innovation, efficacité de canaux de diffusion, époque, et caractéristiques du système social, tels la structure et le genre des agents amenant le changement. Les premières recherches étaient concentrées sur l'innovation organisationnelle et tout spécialement sur les individus responsables de la diffusion. Tout cela était hautement structuré, quantitatif, et reposait beaucoup sur la mise à l'essai d'hypothèses. Les recherches depuis les années 70 se sont plus préoccupées du processus innovatif. Celui-ci consiste en cinq niveaux: une phase d'initiation (mise en place des agendas et coordination des agendas existants avec des solutions de remplacement, c'est-à-dire l'innovation); et une phase d'éxécution (adaptation de l'innovation à l'organisation et au problème auquel elle s'applique, structuration de l'organisation pour l'accomoder, et son institutionnalisation).

5

Innovation in West Germany's Public Sector
Thomas Ellwein

The success of structural innovation in the Federal Republic, including changes in communal territories, civil service functions and status, and governmental procedures, varies inversely with the number of administrative layers and strength of the hierarchical relationship. Support by top-level administrators helps, but realizing structural innovation depends solely on internal conditions. Process innovations—for example, in the fields of information and data processing, coordination, planning and decision making, and the legislative process—have a better chance for success if they do not threaten the status of top-level administrators, and virtually no chance if they call for a realignment of the legal relationship among parliament, government, and high-level bureaucracy.

Innovation dans le secteur public de l´Allemagne de l'Ouest

L'innovation structurelle en R.F.A. comprend des changements dans les territoires communaux, dans le fonctions et les statuts de la fonction publique, et dans des procédures gouvernementales. Le succès de cette innovation varie en proportion inverse avec le nombre de couches administratives et avec la force des relations hiérarchiques. Le soutien apporté par des administrateurs de haut niveau vient en aide, mais la réalisation d'innovations structurelles dépend uniquement des conditions internes. Des innovations de processus—c'est-à-dire dans les domaines de l'information et du traitement de l'information, de la coordination, de la planification et de la prise de décisions, et dans le processus législatif—ont une meilleure chance de réussite si elles ne menacent pas le statut des administrateurs de haut niveau et n'ont virtuellement aucune chance si elles exigent un réalignement des relations légales entre le parlement, le gouvernement, et la haute bureaucratie.

6

Innovation in West Germany: Retrospect and Prospects
Herbert König

Encouraging innovations that can improve governmental effectiveness requires three changes in the Federal Republic's public policymaking process. First, appropriate guiding principles (for example, subsidiarity, targeted action, and the primacy of political over administrative considerations) are needed. Second, a problem-oriented approach must include joint discussions among various levels of government, action based on politically determined agendas, and enhanced governmental capacity to steer political programs. Third, a comparative framework is needed. But for idea-producing institutions to have any positive effects, they must have access to the political leadership, which may require involving the latter in the thought processes entailed in systematic innovation.

Innovation en Allemagne de l'Ouest: rétrospective et prospectives

Trois changements dans le processus de création des lignes d'action publique en R.F.A. sont nécessaires pour encourager les innovations qui peuvent améliorer l'efficacité du gouvernement. Tout d'abord on a besoin de principes directeurs appropriés (c'est-à-dire, la subsidarité, l'action ciblée, et la primauté de considérations politiques par rapport aux considérations administratives). Deuxièmement, une approche orientée vers le problème doit inclure des discussions en commun parmi les différents niveaux du gouvernement, une action basée sur des agendas déterminés politiquement, et une capacité accrue du gouvernement pour diriger des programmes politiques. Troisièmement, il faut un cadre d'analyse comparatif. Mais pour que des institutions productrices d'idées puissent avoir de quelconques effets positifs, il faut qu'elles aient accès à la direction politique. Ceci peut demander que cette dernière soit impliquée dans les processus de pensée occasionnés par l'innovation systématique.

Comment
Wolfgang Zeh

Innovations and innovativeness ebb and flow cyclically. Thus the role of the political leadership is critical –in changing the legal basis of administrative procedures through the legislative process, in the governmental communications system, and especially in generating ideas for political change. If only crises alert leaders to the need for innovation, and if crises themselves are cyclical, then crisis and innovation may be merely two sides of the same coin.

Commentaire

Les innovations et le caractère innovatif subissent des flux et reflux cycliques. Donc le rôle de la direction politique est primordial, notamment en changeant les bases légales des procédures administratives dans le système gouvernemental de communications, et tout spécialement en générant des idées pour un changement politique. Si l'attention des dirigeants est seulement éveillée en temps de crise, et si les crises elles-mêmes sont cycliques, alors crise et innovation pourraient bien être les deux facettes d'une même médaille.

7

Technology Policy in the Federal Republic of Germany
Frieder Naschold

The socially oriented technology policy of the 1970s expanded government's role in managing corporate investment and the role of the unions and work councils in developing and applying that policy, but without much changing social relations in the production process. The world economic crisis led the Social Democratic leadership to combine austerity at home with an aggressive modernization policy (including direct R&D support) for the export sector. As growth gave way to stagnation, and the lot of workers did not improve markedly, the unions received part of the blame. This encouraged those in the work force who favored confrontation over cooperation. The unions were more successful when taking a strong participatory stance while firmly avoiding governmental co-optation.

Politique de la technologie dans la République Fédérale d'Allemagne

La politique technologique orientée vers le social, développée dans les années 70, a fait s'étendre le rôle du gouvernement jusqu' à englober la gestion des investissements corporatifs. Elle a aussi fait s'étendre le rôle des syndicats et des comités d'entreprisse jusqu'à développer et appliquer cette politique. Mais elle n'a pas beaucoup changé les relations sociales au sein du processus de production. La crise économique mondiale a conduit la direction socio-démocrate à combiner l'austérité intérieure avec une politique de modernisation agressive (comprenant une aide directe en recherche et développement) dans le secteur des exportations. Quand la croissance fit place à la stagnation, et quand le sort des travailleurs ne s'améliora pas grandement, alors on reporta une partie du blâme sur les syndicats. Ceci encouragea ceux parmi les travailleurs qui préféraient la confrontation à la coopération. Les syndicats eurent plus de succès en prenant une position ferme de participation, tout en évitant nettement toute cooptation gouvernementale.

8

Politics of Educational Reform
Hans N. Weiler

Close examination suggests at best a tenuous relationship between research and innovative educational policy. Even when research leads to experimentation, its results are difficult to evaluate, because the programs were not designed for rigorous scientific evaluation; moreover, besides unintentionally creating new problems, experimentation is sometimes too ideologically burdened to gain political success. Studies of educational reform must examine the linkages of research to practice—its ties to such goals as democratization, equality, and ideological legitimation, as well as how conventional paradigms of educational planning have actually inhibited reform—and most particularly the role of educational innovation in legitimating the existing political and social structure.

Politiques de réforme de l'éducation

Un examen approfondi suggère au mieux une relation minime entre recherche et politique éducationnelle innovative. Même quand la recherche conduit à l'expérimentation, ses résultats sont difficiles à évaluer parce que les programmes n'ont pas été construits pour une évaluation scientifique rigoureuse; de plus, mis à part le fait qu'elle crée sans le vouloir de nouveaux problèmes, l'expérimentation est parfois trop chargée idéologiquement pour pouvoir obtenir un succès politique. Des études de réforme éducationnelle doivent examiner les relations entre recherche et pratique—leurs liens avec les buts tels que démocratisation, égalité et légitimation idéologique. Elles doivent aussi examiner comment les paradigmes conventionnels de la planification de l'éducation ont effectivement inhibé les réformes—et tout particulièrement le rôle que l'innovation éducationnelle a joué en légitimant la structure politique et sociale existante.

Discussion

Dietrich Goldschmidt, Karl W. Deutsch, Theodor Hanf, and Hans N. Weiler

Theodor Hanf, and Hans N. Weiler Goldschmidt pointed to several problems of functional equivalence in the social contexts of school systems and suggested that educational research generally proceeds too slowly either to help legitimate the social structure or to assist in making educational policy. Deutsch, in calling for more usefully operationalized concepts in research on educational processes and outcomes, stressed the importance of social mobility and the development of human capacities in any notion of "educational equality." Hanf lamented West Germany's reliance on "education brokers," whose narrow expertise contributes to a fragmentation of educational policymaking.

Commentaire

Goldschmidt a attiré l'attention sur plusieurs problèmes d'équivalence fonctionnelle dans les contextes sociaux des systèmes scolaires et a suggéré que la recherche dans le domaine de l'éducation avance généralement trop lentement, ceci soit pour aider à légitimer la structure sociale, soit pour aider à la création d'une politique de l'éducation. Deutsch réclame des concepts plus utilement opérationnels dans la recherche sur les processus et les résultats de l'éducation: ce faisant, il insiste sur l'importance, dans toute notion "d'égalité de l'éducation", de la mobilité sociale et du développement des capacités humaines. Hanf regrette la dépendance ouest-allemande vis-à-vis des "courtiers de l'éducation", dont l'expertise étroite contribue à une fragmentation dans la création de politiques dans le domaine de l'éducation.

9

Legal Culture and the Chances for Legal Innovation
Erhard Blankenburg

Innovative efforts in the United States, Britain, the Netherlands, and elsewhere in West Europe to help the common citizen obtain legal assistance reveal sharp differences in their legal culture (that is, legal institutions, norms, and patterns of behavior). Such responsiveness to new social problems—legal aid, public-interest law, and neighborhood law centers—is more likely in settings in which the law is initiated on a case-by-case basis, but procedures for recruiting and training lawyers and legal officials, as well as the degree to which patterns of law and legal behavior are institutionalized, also play a role. Advocacy leads to a legal market, whereas legalism in the sense of formulating binding codes of law leads to a centralization of legal authority.

Culture légale et possibilités d'innovation dans le domaine des lois

Les USA, l'Angleterre, les Pays-Bas, et d'autres pays d'Europe de l'Ouest font des efforts innovatifs pour aider le citoyen moyen à obtenir une assistance légale. Ces efforts révèlent des différences accentuées entre leurs cultures légales (c'est-à-dire institutions légales, normes, et types de comportement). Une telle réponse à de nouveaux problèmes sociaux—aide légale, lois intéressant le grand public, et cabinets d'assistance légale de quartiers—est plus vraisemblable dans des cadres dans lesquels la loi est mise en application sur une base ponctuelle; mais les procédures pour recruter et entraîner des juristes et des officiers judiciaires jouent aussi un rôle, ainsi que le degré d'institutionnalisation de ces types de loi et de comportement légal. Plaider entraîne l'existence d'un marché légal, tandis que légiférer, dans le sens de formuler des codes de loi contraignants, entraîne la centralisation de l'autorité légale.

10

Large-Scale Policy Innovation in East and West European Agriculture
Ronald A. Francisco

The European Community's Mansholt plan of 1968, which sought larger farms with a smaller, more innovatively oriented work force, ran afoul of individualistic perceptions that the need for major structural reform did not justify its cost and potential risk. A watered-down version adopted in 1971 contained little of the reform originally sought. In East Europe's CMEA, national decision making within a common framework secured greater coordination across farm units (horizontal integration), and between agriculture and the industrial and food-processing sectors (vertical integration). The gain, greater agricultural productivity, was considered worth the cost and risk and, through emulation rather than the European Community's collective decision making, spread throughout East Europe.

Innovation en politique sur une large échelle dans l'agriculture de l'Europe de l'Est et de l'Ouest

Le plan Mansholt pour la Communauté Européenne, entériné en 1968, qui cherchait à promouvoir l'existence d'exploitations agricoles plus grandes conduites par une main-d'oeuvre plus réduite et plus orientée vers l'innovation, s'est attiré le mécontentement des individus qui percevaient que le besoin d'une réforme structurelle majeure ne justifiait pas son coût ni ses risques potentiels. Dans la version affaiblie adoptée en 1971, on ne trouve plus qu'un petit nombre de réformes originellement recherchées. Au sein du Comecon de l'Europe de l'Est, la prise de décision au niveau national dans un cadre commun assurait une plus grande coordination entre chaque exploitation en tant qu'unité (intégration horizontale), et entre le secteur agricole et le secteur industriel et le secteur de transformation agro-alimentaire (intégration verticale). Le gain, une meilleure productivité agricole, avait été considéré comme justifiant les coûts et les risques et, à cause de l'émulation plus que d'une prise de décision collective de la Communauté Européenne, cette méthode s'est étendue à travers toute l'Europe de l'Est.

11

Trends and Perspectives in Innovation Policies
Gerhard O. Mensch

The socioeconomic dynamics of entrepreneurial innovation may be viewed in terms of the theory of economic motion. Basic-product innovation leads to improved products and manufacturing processes, and eventually to basic-process innovations. Before the last phase sets in, however, capital intensity in the consumer goods sector may fall behind that in the investment goods sector and, as the marketing of consumer goods slows down and intermediate products stack up, create a structural crisis. The solution is a shift from mostly basic-process innovations to mostly basic-product innovations. Meanwhile, effective governance requires internal reform in response to the contextual turbulence (and exogenous developments due to "irrational" foreign policy considerations).

Tendances et perspectives dans les politiques d'innovation

La dynamique socioéconomique de l'innovation entrepreneuriale peut être examinée en termes de la théorie du mouvement économique. L'innovation sur un produit de base conduit à l'amélioration des produits finis et des procédés de transformation, et finalement à des innovations dans le domaine des processus de base. Mais avant que la dernière phase ne devienne effective, le volume monétaire présent dans le secteur des biens de consommation peut se retrouver inférieur au volume présent dans le secteur des biens d'investissement, et comme la commercialisation des produits de consommation se ralentit et les produits intermédiaires s'accumulent, une crise structurelle se crée. Pour résoudre ce problème, il faut passer d'innovations principalement orientées vers des processus de base à des innovations principalement orientées vers des produits de base. En même temps, une gestion efficace réclame des réformes internes pour répondre aux turbulences contextuelles (et aux développements exogènes dus à des considérations "irrationnelles" de politique étrangère).

12

Social Know-How and Its Role in Invention and Innovation
Manfred Kochen

"Inquiring communities" can help to meet the need for social know-how to manage ever more complex societies. Such teams of social scientists, policy analysts, and policymakers would be structured both to take advantage of newer modes of comjmunication and collective memory (computer conferencing), and to reduce the fear of making mistakes from which may come learning. Members could inject into the network a policy concern or proposed solution which others interested or with expertise in the issue could pick up. They could then pursue it in their own thinking and research, all the while remaining in constant contact with each other via teleconferencing, exchanging data, testing out ideas on relevant populations, and, more generally, seeking solutions to the policy problem.

Le savoir-faire social et son rôle dans les domaines de l'invention et de l'innovation

Des "communautés curieuses de caractère" peuvent aider à répondre au besoin de savoir-faire social nécessaire pour pouvoir contrôler des sociétés encore plus complexes. De telles équipes de spécialistes des sciences humaines, d'analystes de lignes d'action, de dirigeants politiques devraient être structurées pour pouvoir à la fois profiter de nouveaux modes de communication et de stockage d'informations collectives (conférences par ordinateurs), et aussi pour réduire les craintes de faire des erreurs, ce qui pourrait augmenter le savoir. Les membres pourraient injecter dans le réseau leurs inquiétudes au sujet d'une politique d'action ou la solution qu'ils proposent. Alors, d'autres membres intéressés par le sujet ou encore des spécialistes dans le domaine, pourraient le reprendre et l'approfondir. Ils pourraient continuer en appliquant leurs propres recherches et leur propre réflexion, tout en restant en contact constant les uns avec les autres grâce à des téléconférences, en échangeant des données, en testant des idées sur des populations adéquates, et plus généralement, en cherchant des solutions à ces problèmes de politique d'action.

INDEX

ABOUT THE CONTRIBUTORS

ERHARD BLANKENBURG, formerly at the Science Center Berlin, is professor of law at the Free University of Amsterdam. After completing the doctorate at the University of Basel and his postdoctoral "Habilitation" at the University of Freiburg, he directed his research to issues of the police, public prosecutors, civil and labor courts, labor administration, legal aid, and legal insurance. He has coedited the *Jahrbuch für Rechtssoziologie und Rechtstheorie* and the *Zeitschrift für Rechtssoziologie.*

KARL W. DEUTSCH is Stanfield Professor Emeritus of International Peace at Harvard University and director of the International Institute of Comparative Social Research at the Science Center Berlin. He is a member of the National Academy of Sciences in the United States and has been president of the American and International Political Science Associations. His books include *Nerves of Government* (1963, 1966), *Politics and Government* (1970, 1974, 1980), *The Analysis of International Relations* (1968, 1978), and *Decentralization* (with Manfred Kochen, 1980).

THOMAS ELLWEIN, who received the degree of doctor of jurisprudence at the University of Frankfurt, has been professor of political science at the University of Constance since 1976. His numerous books and articles have focused on various aspects of politics and public administration in West Germany, and include *Regierung als politische Führung* (1970), *Politische Verhaltenslehre* (7th ed., 1972), *Regieren und Verwalten* (1976), and *Das Regierungssystem der Bundesrepublik Deutschland* (5th ed., 1983).

RONALD A. FRANCISCO is associate professor of political science at the University of Kansas. After completing his doctorate at the University of Illinois at Urbana-Champaign, he turned his attention to issues of comparative public policy, especially agricultural politics.

In 1980 he coedited *Agricultural Policies in the USSR and Eastern Europe.*

DIETRICH GOLDSCHMIDT is director of the Max Planck Institute for Educational Research in West Berlin. He has his doctorate in political science from the Free University of Berlin, where he is also honorary professor, and has written extensively on educational policy, including *Power in Academia* (1978), *Alternative Schulen?* (1979), and *Die Soziologie in Wechselwirkung mit Bildungssystem, Bildungspolitik und Erziehungswissenschaft* (1979).

THEODOR HANF directs the Social Science Division of the Institute for International Pedagogical Research, Frankfurt-am-Main, and is honorary professor of political science at the University of Freiburg (where he received the doctorate). His publications have dealt with education and politics in Lebanon, the Congo, Ruanda, the Republic of South Africa, and other countries.

JOUNG-IM KIM received her Ph.D. in communication research from Stanford University, and currently is assistant professor in the Department of Communication at the University of Hawaii at Manoa, Honolulu. She received a baccalaureate degree from Yonsei University in Seoul, Korea, and a master's degree from the University of Hawaii. Her special interest is in the role of social networks in the diffusion of innovations.

MANFRED KOCHEN, who received the doctorate in applied mathematics at Columbia University, is professor of information science and a research scientist at the Mental Health Research Institute, University of Michigan. His publications include *Principles of Information Retrieval* (1974), *Information for Action* (1975), "Models of Scientific Output" (1978), and, with Karl W. Deutsch, *Decentralization* (1980).

HERBERT KÖNIG was an active civil servant even before receiving the doctorate in economics at the University of Graz and has subsequently served in posts at the federal level (Ministerialdirigent in the Federal Ministry of Economics), as well as the OECD and Council of Europe. Since 1978 he has also been professor of public administration at the Bundeswehr College in Hamburg. He has authored or coauthored several books in public administration, including *Dynamische Verwaltung* (1977, 1979), *Anwendungsprobleme moderner*

Planungs- und Entscheidungstechniken (1978), *Ziel- und ergebnis-orientiertes Verwaltungshandeln* (1979), *Science et Action Administratives* (1980), and *Verwaltungsführung* (1982).

JOSEPH E. McGRATH is professor of psychology at the University of Illinois at Urbana-Champaign. He received his doctorate in social psychology from the University of Michigan. His past research has included studies of interaction processes and task performance of problem-solving and negotiation groups, social psychological factors in stress, and methodological issues in behavioral science.

GERHARD O. MENSCH is professor of management and economics at Case Western Reserve University, Cleveland, Ohio. After earning a doctorate from Bonn and working at Stanford and Tulane universities, for ten years he was senior researcher at the International Institute of Management and Administration, Science Center Berlin. His research has focused on new technology, entrepreneurship, and the socioeconomic conditions for innovation; included among his publications is *Stalemate in Technology* (1979). He received the Prognos Prize in 1983.

ANNA J. MERRITT is editor and staff associate at the Institute of Government and Public Affairs, University of Illinois at Urbana-Champaign. She has coauthored and edited several books on West German politics and on U.S. local issues, most recently *Legislative Oversight in Illinois* and *Redistricting* (both 1982).

RICHARD L. MERRITT is professor of political science and research professor in communications, University of Illinois at Urbana-Champaign. His research has examined international political communication and West German politics, and he is currently completing a book on integrative and disintegrative trends in postwar Berlin. He has been vice president of the International Political Science Association and the International Studies Association.

FRIEDER NASCHOLD was appointed professor of political science at the University of Constance in 1970 and rector in 1974. Since 1976 he has been director of the International Institute of Comparative Social Research at the Science Center Berlin. His research recently has investigated the social context of health, especially in the work place.

EVERETT M. ROGERS is Janet M. Peck Professor of International Communication at Stanford University. Some of the ideas in his chapter are drawn from *Diffusion of Innovations* (1983), the third revision of his volume on this topic. His recent *Silicon Valley Fever* (with Judith Larson, 1984) describes the nature of innovation in this high-technology complex located in northern California. He has been president of the International Communications Association.

DEAN KEITH SIMONTON received the doctorate in social psychology from Harvard University. He is now associate professor at the University of California, Davis. His research focuses on the application of multivariate statistics and quasi-experimental designs to historical and biographical data in order to study creativity and leadership. He is the author of *Genius, Creativity, and Leadership* (1984).

HANS N. WEILER has been on the faculty of Stanford University since 1965 and is now professor of education and political science. He has been director of the International Institute for Educational Planning (IIEP) in Paris. His research has dealt with various aspects of the relationship between education and politics in Africa and Western Europe. His publications include *Education and Politics in Nigeria* (1964), *Educational Planning and Social Change* (1980), and numerous articles and monographs.

WOLFGANG ZEH, who received his doctorate in jurisprudence after law studies at the Universities of Tübingen and Kiel, is Regierungsdirektor in the Advisory Services of the German Bundestag, Bonn. He has published widely in the fields of constitutional law, legislatures, federalism, and public administration.